VISUAL QUICKSTART GUIDE

GARAGEBAND 2

FOR MAC OS X

Victor Gavenda

◉ **Peachpit Press**

Visual QuickStart Guide
GarageBand 2 For Mac OS X
Victor Gavenda

Peachpit Press

1249 Eighth Street
Berkeley, CA 94710
510/524-2178
800/283-9444
510/524-2221 (fax)

Find us on the World Wide Web at: www.peachpit.com
To report errors, please send a note to errata@peachpit.com

Peachpit Press is a division of Pearson Education

Editor: Judy Ziajka
Project Editor: Becky Morgan
Production Editor: Myrna Vladic
Compositors: Rick Gordon, Debbie Roberti
Indexer: FireCrystal Communications
Cover design: The Visual Group
Cover Production: George Mattingly / GMD

Notice of Rights

Notice of Liability

Trademarks

ISBN 0-321-33544-9

9 8 7 6 5 4 3 2 1

Printed and bound in the United States of America

Dedication

To the entire staff of Peachpit Press, from
Alison to Zigi, in gratitude for all of their
support and affection over the years. A guy
couldn't ask for a better bunch of colleagues!

Acknowledgments

Special thanks to:

Nancy Aldrich-Ruenzel, Peachpit Press's intrepid publisher, for giving me the chance to do this book in the first place.

Nancy Davis, Cliff Colby, and Marjorie Baer, acquisitions editors at Peachpit, for supporting my original proposal for this book.

Becky Morgan, my Peachpit editor, for her wisdom and guidance.

Judy Ziajka, my development editor, for once again helping me to shape the book into a coherent entity and for patiently fixing my bad writing habits.

Myrna Vladic, my production editor, and Rick Gordon, our skilled compositor, for crafting the handsome volume you now hold in your hands.

Chris Breen, for letting me borrow his splendid MOTU 828mkII audio interface.

Andrei Pasternak and Helen Hampton, for lending me their electric guitars.

Steve Dampier, for creating the elegant line drawings in Chapter 5.

Reinel Adajar of Digidesign, for agreeing to supply the photo of the Mbox used in Chapter 5.

Jim Cooper of Mark of the Unicorn, Inc., for granting permission to use the photograph of the 828mkII, also used in Chapter 5.

Jeff Taylor Cross of Apple Computer, for clarifying some of the mysteries of Apple's audio software products.

And of course, to Linda and Emma, my wife and daughter, for cheering me on.

TABLE OF CONTENTS

PART 1: **GETTING MUSIC INTO GARAGEBAND**

Chapter 1: **GarageBand Overview**   **3**

What GarageBand Does 4
Launching GarageBand 6
Getting Help 7
The GarageBand Interface 8
Anatomy of the Timeline 12
Working in the Timeline 14
Using the Time Display 16
Zooming in the Timeline 19
About the Timeline Grid 20

Chapter 2: **Working with Songs**   **23**

About Songs 24
Opening a Song 25
Saving a Song 27
Saving a Song as an Archive 28
Playing a Song 30
Creating a New Song 31
About Tempo 33
About Time Signatures 34
About Keys 36
About Song Length 38
Undoing Your Work 39

Chapter 3: **Working with Tracks**   **41**

About Tracks 42
About the Track Header 43
Selecting Tracks 44
Muting a Track 45
Soloing a Track 46
About the Track Mixer 47
Real vs. Software Instrument Tracks 48
About Adding Tracks 51
Adding a Real Instrument Track 53
About Basic Tracks 56
Adding a Software Instrument Track 57
Duplicating a Track 59
Renaming a Track 60
Changing the Stacking Order of Tracks 61
Locking a Track 62
Deleting Tracks 64
About the Track Info Window 65
Changing a Track's Instrument 67

Chapter 4: Working with Loops   **71**

About Apple Loops 72
About the Loop Browser 73
Displaying the Loop Browser 74
About the Loop Browser Views 75
Using Button View to Find Loops 76
Customizing Button View 77
Using Column View to Find Loops 80
Finding Loops by Other Methods 82
Restricting the Loop Browser Display 83
Working with the Results List 85
Sorting the Results List 86
Marking Loops as Favorites 87
Auditioning Loops 89
Adding a Loop to Your Song 90
Adding More Loops to GarageBand 94
Creating Your Own Loops 97

Chapter 5: Hardware for Recording   **101**

About Hardware 102
Hardware for Recording Audio 103
Audio Sources 105
Audio Interfaces 108
Hardware for Recording Software Instruments 113
Hardware for Playback 119
Setting Audio Preferences 120

Chapter 6: Recording Real Instruments   **123**

About Recording in GarageBand 124
Using the Metronome 126
Monitoring 128
Using the Instrument Tuner 129
About Setting the Recording Level 131
Using the Track Level Meters 132
Setting Input Levels 133
Using the Track Mixer Volume Slider 134
Enabling a Track for Recording 135
Recording into Real Instrument Tracks 136
Re-recording a Section of a Song 138

Chapter 7: Recording Software Instruments   **141**

About Recording Software Instruments 142
Working with the Onscreen Music Keyboard 143
Configuring the Onscreen Keyboard 145
About Musical Typing 149
Adjusting Keyboard Sensitivity 153
Using the MIDI Status Light 154
Using the Metronome 155
Recording into a Software Instrument Track 157
Re-recording a Section of a Song 160

PART 2: POLISHING YOUR SONG

Chapter 8: Arranging Regions in the Timeline   165
About Regions 166
About Editing Regions 167
Selecting Regions 169
Basic Editing Functions 170
Moving Regions 172
Resizing Regions 173
Looping a Region 174
Splitting Regions 175
Joining Regions 176

Chapter 9: Advanced Editing with the Track Editor   177
About Editing Real Instrument Regions 178
About Editing Software Instrument Regions 179
About the Track Editor 180
Displaying the Track Editor 183
Unlocking the Timeline and Track Editor Playheads . . 185
Renaming Tracks and Regions 186
About Transposition 189
Transposing Regions 191
Enhancing Real Instrument Track Tuning or Timing . . 193
Fixing Software Instrument Region Rhythm 196

Chapter 10: Editing MIDI Data   199
Editing MIDI Data 200
Changing Note Velocity 201
Adding and Deleting Notes 202
Using Cut, Copy, and Paste 203
Working with MIDI Data in Notation View 204
Editing Notes Using Notation View 206
Changing Note Velocity in Notation View 209
About Pedal Markings 210
Editing MIDI Controller Information 212

Chapter 11: Applying Effects   217
About Effects 218
About the Master Track 219
The Track Info Window Effects Controls 220
Applying Effects 222
Choosing Which Presets Are Displayed 224
Saving Effects Presets 225
Saving Instrument Presets 227
Using the Echo Effect 230
Using the Reverb Effect 232
Using the Equalizer Effect 234
Using the Compressor Effect 236
Using the Gate Effect 237
About the Other GarageBand Effects 238
Editing Software Instruments 243
About Audio Units 246

Chapter 12: Mixing Your Song   **249**

Choosing a Volume Level for Each Track 250
Setting the Volume Level for a Track 252
Setting the Pan Position 253
About Track Automation 255
Using an Automation Curve 257
Creating a Basic Crossfade 261
Working with Master Track Automation Curves 263
Setting the Output Volume 266

Chapter 13: Exporting and Importing   **267**

GarageBand and Other Applications 268
Exporting a Song to iTunes 269
Using iTunes to Compress Your Song 272
Using GarageBand Songs in Other iLife Programs 275
Bringing Audio Files into GarageBand 279
Bringing MIDI Files into GarageBand 283

Appendix A: Improving Performance   **287**

General Performance Tips 288
Bouncing Tracks to Improve Performance 294

Appendix B: GarageBand Jam Packs   **297**

Index   **301**

Part 1: Getting Music into GarageBand

Chapter 1: GarageBand Overview 3

Chapter 2: Working with Songs 23

Chapter 3: Working with Tracks......................41

Chapter 4: Working with Loops 71

Chapter 5: Hardware for Recording..................101

Chapter 6: Recording Real Instruments..........123

Chapter 7: Recording Software Instruments 141

GarageBand
Overview

Though it had long been rumored that Apple had a music creation iApp in the works, the announcement of GarageBand at Macworld 2004 sent waves of delight through the Mac music community. Since it burst on the scene as part of the software package iLife '04, GarageBand has proved to be a major hit with amateur and professional musicians alike. GarageBand 2, introduced at Macworld 2005 as part of the newly revamped iLife '05, builds on the successes of its predecessor.

Every Macintosh computer, starting with that adorable little 128K model in 1984, has shipped with some kind of audio hardware built in (unlike many Wintel machines), and Mac users have been in the forefront of the computer music revolution. Yet not all has been smooth sailing. Getting external audio or MIDI hardware to work with your Mac has often been a titanic struggle between man (or woman) and machine, and recording and sequencing software can be so complex that the documentation resembles the pilot's manual for the space shuttle. For many ordinary folks, performing and recording music on their Macs has always seemed just out of reach.

But GarageBand (with a little help from Mac OS X)—with its streamlined interface (one window, and one window *only*) and seamless integration with your Mac's audio hardware— is finally: music software for the rest of us.

What GarageBand Does

There is nothing radically new or revolutionary in anything that GarageBand does. Instead, in typical Apple fashion, it combines the most commonly used functions from a host of music applications into one program. Then it sweetens the deal by packaging the whole thing in a straightforward, unintimidating interface.

GarageBand provides one-stop shopping for all of your musical needs. In this one program you can:

◆ Compose songs using loops.

◆ Record live performers through a microphone or by plugging electronic instruments such as an electric guitar or bass or a synthesizer into your Mac (what GarageBand calls *Real Instruments*).

◆ Record performances on MIDI instruments attached to the computer (called *Software Instruments* in GarageBand lingo).

◆ Import audio and MIDI files created in other programs.

◆ Edit MIDI data.

◆ Write songs that make use of all of the above.

GarageBand also provides extensive mixing and arranging tools. And when your magnum opus is complete, you can export it to your iTunes playlist so it's available for sharing with your friends or with the world.

But as the late-night infomercials say, "That's not all!"

Apple ships GarageBand with a treasure trove of musical goodies to help get you started:

◆ Over 1,000 Apple Loops.

◆ More than 100 high-quality Software Instruments (over 50 of them new to GarageBand 2), which use both synthesized sounds and sounds sampled from real-world instruments.

◆ Dozens of effects that you can apply to your recorded tracks, including hundreds of professional-level presets, many of them new to GarageBand 2.

And if all that isn't enough, for a bit of extra dough you can buy any or all of Apple's four GarageBand Jam Packs at $99 apiece. Each one is crammed with 2,000 more Apple Loops, plus dozens of new Software Instruments, audio effects presets, and special goodies like guitar amp settings and exotic drum kits (see Appendix B).

Enough talk. Let's take a look at this very cool sandbox Apple has made for us to play in.

Easy Does It

Throughout this book, I assume that you allowed the iLife '05 Installer program to perform an Easy Install operation. This option installs all of the iLife '05 programs in the Applications folder on your system disk. It also performs a few housekeeping chores, such as these:

◆ Adds an icon to the Dock for each iLife application.

◆ Places certain important files in the Library folder at the root level of your hard disk. This is where, for example, GarageBand expects to find its Apple Loops, Software Instruments, and other presets. Don't move them!

◆ Creates a folder called GarageBand in the Music folder within your Home folder. This is the default location for saving songs you create in GarageBand. In official Mac OS X jargon, the path to this folder is ~/Music/GarageBand, where the tilde (~) represents your Home folder, or /Users/[*your username*]/.

WHAT GARAGEBAND DOES

Launching GarageBand

Apple provides several ways to start GarageBand. As it launches, the program opens the song you were working on the last time it was running. The first time you start GarageBand, the process is a little different: GarageBand gives you several choices to get underway.

To launch GarageBand:

◆ *Do one of the following:*

▲ Open the Applications folder on your hard drive and double-click the GarageBand icon (**Figure 1.1**).

▲ Click the GarageBand icon in the Dock (**Figure 1.2**).

▲ Double-click the icon for a GarageBand project file in the Finder (**Figure 1.3**).

Don't worry if a window containing the word *Initializing* and a cycling progress bar appears for several moments (**Figure 1.4**). This is normal.

If you have opened GarageBand before, the main GarageBand window appears, showing the last song you worked on.

If this is your first time launching GarageBand, the Welcome to GarageBand dialog opens, giving you several buttons to choose from (**Figure 1.5**):

▲ Clicking Create a New Project starts a brand-new song file. We'll talk about creating new songs in Chapter 2.

▲ Clicking Open an Existing Project displays a standard Open dialog. Use it to navigate to the song file you wish to open.

▲ Clicking the button with the question mark (?) opens the GarageBand online Help file (see the next section, "Getting Help").

▲ Clicking Quit exits the program. Use this button if you decide that now's not the time for a GarageBand session.

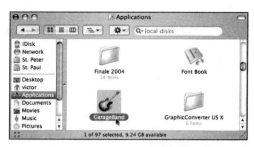

Figure 1.1 GarageBand at home, in the Applications folder.

Figure 1.2 GarageBand at large, hanging out in the Dock.

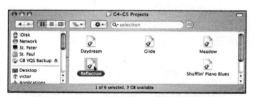

Figure 1.3 Double-clicking the icon for a GarageBand project file starts the program.

Figure 1.4 GarageBand usually displays this progress bar while starting.

Figure 1.5 This friendly dialog greets you the first time you start GarageBand.

Figure 1.6 The main page of the online Help file.

Figure 1.7 Tool tips provide convenient reminders of the functions of interface elements.

✔ Tips

■ According to the Help menu, Command-? is the keyboard shortcut for GarageBand Help. Unfortunately, it's easy to forget (well, at least I don't have any trouble forgetting it) that the question mark is produced by pressing Shift-/ (forward slash). Some programs are more forgiving of human frailty and will display the online Help file even if you merely press Command-/. Alas, GarageBand goes strictly by the book in this matter.

■ GarageBand also includes context-sensitive help in the form of tool tips. If you want to learn what a button or slider or some other part of the user interface does, simply allow the mouse pointer to rest over the item in question. A label bearing a brief description of the widget will appear (**Figure 1.7**).

Getting Help

GarageBand, alas, does not come with a printed manual. But, then, you already knew that, didn't you? That's why you're here, after all.

Apple does ship some fine online help with the program. The Help file even includes links to Apple's support Web site for answers to your more perplexing questions.

To use the online Help system:

1. Choose Help > GarageBand Help (Command-Shift-/).

   The Help Viewer application opens and displays the main page of the GarageBand Help file (**Figure 1.6**).

2. *Do one of the following:*

   ▲ Click the Contents link to view the list of topics covered in the file.

   ▲ Click the What's New in GarageBand link to read a description of the things that have changed in GarageBand 2.

   ▲ Follow the Learn About GarageBand link to find other documents in PDF format.

   ▲ Click the Solving Problems link to troubleshoot problems.

   ▲ Click the link under the "GarageBand Help" title to go to the main GarageBand Web page at Apple's Web site.

The GarageBand Interface

When you start GarageBand, a single large window gobbles up most of your screen (**Figure 1.8**). The window displays the contents of a single song; you can have only one song open at a time. Designwise, it owes much to its older sibling application, Soundtrack. The faux-walnut strips along each side are unique to GarageBand, however. Apparently, the designers meant to recall the look of 1960s audio hardware. Groovy!

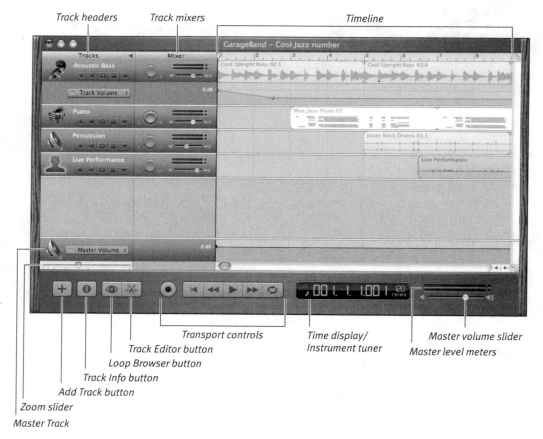

Figure 1.8 The GarageBand window in all its glory.

Figure 1.9 The loop browser, in button view.

Most of the window is laid out as a grid. Each horizontal row represents a single track in your song. The leftmost column contains the *track headers*, which identify each track by name and instrument icon. In the second column, you'll find the *track mixer* for each track. These contain controls for the track's volume and pan position (where the track seems to sit in the stereo field), as well as level meters that show changes in the track's volume as the track is played. At the bottom of the stack of individual tracks is a place reserved for the *master track*, which is hidden by default. Use the master track to control overall volume and pitch levels (a new feature in GarageBand 2) for the song as a whole. You'll learn more about the master track in Chapter 12.

The lion's share of the window is taken up with the *timeline*, which displays the actual data that makes up your song. It's complex enough that it rates its own section, right after this one.

Below the Track headers column, you'll find the *zoom slider*. Use this to display more or less detail in the timeline. (I'll describe how the zoom slider works later in this chapter.)

Various controls for working with the tracks in the timeline live along the timeline's bottom edge. (You'll learn how to use them in Chapter 3.) The button with the plus sign (+) is the *Add Track button*; click it to add a new track to the timeline. The button with the circled *i* opens the *Track Info window*, which you use to set parameters for each track.

Clicking either the *Loop Browser* or *Track Editor button* causes a new pane to grow up out of the lower edge of the GarageBand window. (Click either button again to close the pane.) The button bearing the eye icon opens the *loop browser*, which you use to search for loops for your song (**Figure 1.9**). I'll describe it in more detail in Chapter 4.

continues on next page

Click its neighbor, the button with the scissors icon, to open the *track editor* (**Figure 1.10**). The track editor takes different forms, depending on whether a Real Instrument track or a Software Instrument track is selected. A feature new to GarageBand 2 allows you to display the data in Software Instrument tracks as musical notation. Skip ahead to Chapters 9 and 10 to read more about the track editor.

Next comes a group of buttons that look just like controls you might see on a VCR or a CD player (**Figure 1.11**). These are the *transport controls*, and they allow you to move through the timeline and hear different parts of your song. The round *Record button* starts and stops recording. The next four buttons are self-explanatory: *Go to Beginning*, *Rewind*, *Play*, and *Fast Forward*. The last of the transport controls, the *Cycle button*, turns the cycle region on and off (see Chapters 6 and 7 to learn about the cycle region). The buttons turn a vivid blue when engaged (except for the Record button, which turns traffic-light red).

The numerical readout is the combination *time display* and *instrument tuner*. By default, the time display shows you where the playhead is in the timeline. You can choose whether time is displayed in absolute time (hours, minutes, seconds, and fractions) or as musical time (measures, beats, and ticks). The tempo of the song is also shown here. (If you need help with any of these musical terms, read the sections "About Tempo" and "About Time Signatures" in Chapter 2.) To learn more, see "Using the Time Display" later in this chapter.

Figure 1.10 The appearance of the track editor changes depending on the kind of track that is selected. Top: A Real Instrument track, displayed as a waveform. Middle: A Software Instrument track displayed as MIDI data. Bottom: The same Software Instrument track displayed as musical notation.

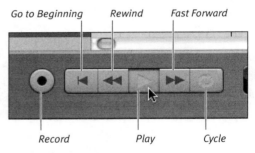

Figure 1.11 The transport controls work just like the buttons on your VCR.

The GarageBand Interface

Figure 1.12 Drag this corner of the window to resize the window.

Figure 1.13 Clicking the Zoom button snaps the GarageBand window to the edges of your screen.

The instrument tuner is another new GarageBand 2 feature. This clever gizmo guides you as you adjust the tuning of any Real Instrument attached to your computer before you start recording. The instrument tuner is discussed in more detail in Chapter 6.

At the lower right of the window, the horizontal line with the pearlescent slider is the *master volume slider*. The pair of colored bars above it are the *master level meters* for the song as a whole. While you mix and arrange your song, be sure to watch these meters and make sure they don't bump into the right end of the meter too often (recording engineers call it "going into the red"). If they do, you'll hear distortion, or *clipping*. This is not the good kind of distortion, like on a Rolling Stones record, but really horrendous-sounding digital distortion. For more about setting the song's final volume level, see Chapter 12.

✔ Tip

- While playing a song, don't use the master volume slider to adjust the volume purely for your listening pleasure. Use your computer's volume control instead.

To resize the GarageBand window:

- Drag the lower-right corner of the window up and to the left to shrink the window (**Figure 1.12**); drag down and to the right to enlarge it.

✔ Tip

- To enlarge the GarageBand window to fill your entire display in one quick stroke, click the green Zoom button in the window's upper-left corner (**Figure 1.13**). To snap the window back to its former size, click the button again.

Anatomy of the Timeline

The timeline is where the magic happens (**Figure 1.14**). Here's where you record Real and Software Instruments into individual tracks, add loops, and arrange regions. Right now, I'll just identify the pieces; in the next section, I'll show you how to operate the controls.

Running along the top of the timeline is the *beat ruler*, calibrated in measures and beats. The *playhead* (a vertical bar with a triangular top) moves along the ruler as the song is played, showing the point in the song being heard at any given moment. The playhead also indicates where cut and copied items will be pasted in the timeline. The *Timeline Grid button* lives at the right end of the ruler. Clicking this button displays a pop-up menu from which you can choose the units displayed on the ruler. (You'll learn more about the timeline grid later in this chapter).

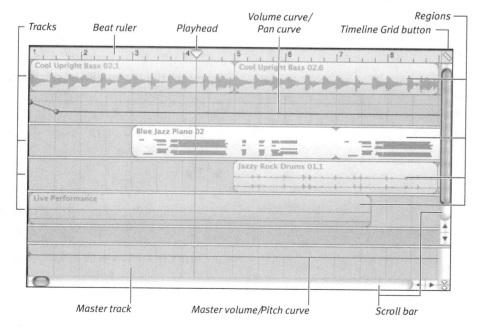

Figure 1.14 The timeline, where the pieces of your song come together.

Most of the timeline is taken up with *tracks*, which represent different layers of musical data in your song. When you add loops to your song or import audio or MIDI files, they're placed in tracks. Likewise, when you record Real or Software Instruments, the recordings appear here, in tracks. Finally, you fine-tune, or arrange, your song by adjusting loops and regions of tracks here. I describe tracks in Chapter 3.

Tracks may be empty, or they may contain colored, rounded rectangles, called *regions*. Each region represents a recorded passage (either Real or Software Instrument) or a loop that has been dragged to the timeline. To give your song its final shape, you work with these regions. You can cut, copy, or paste regions; move or resize them; and transpose them. Regions are discussed in Chapter 8.

Each track has a *volume curve*. By adding and adjusting control points along the curve, you can shape the dynamics of the track. New in GarageBand 2, each track can have a *pan curve*. As with a volume curve, by adjusting control points on a pan curve, you can make a track change its position in stereo space during the song.

Similarly, the song as a whole has a *master track*, which governs the dynamic level of the total of all the tracks. The master track also has a new feature: you can use a *pitch curve* to introduce key changes into the song. You can also use the master track to add special effects to your song. You'll learn more about volume, pan, and pitch curves and the master track in Chapter 12.

To move around in the timeline, drag the *scroll bars* at the bottom and right edges of the timeline. Dragging the bottom scroll bar moves you in time; the vertical scroll bar appears only if the song contains so many tracks that they can't all be displayed at once. Drag up and down on the vertical scroll bar to see the rest of your tracks.

ANATOMY OF THE TIMELINE

Working in the Timeline

The timeline is the part of the interface that holds all the parts of your song and keeps them in the proper order. Usually, your entire song won't fit onto the screen all at once; that's why GarageBand thoughtfully supplies many techniques for moving around in your song and for adjusting the amount of your song that you can see at once.

To work efficiently in GarageBand, you need to become proficient in using the timeline to zip from one part of your song to another. Doing this involves moving the playhead, which you can do in several ways. As you'll see, you can move the playhead directly, on the beat ruler, or you can use the transport controls. You can also use the time display. For the nimble-fingered, there are also keyboard shortcuts (**Table 1.1**).

✔ Tip

■ If you're using a PowerBook, you'll notice that the Home, Page Up, Page Down, and End commands are on the arrow keys. To get these commands to work, you have to hold down the Fn key (at the lower left of the keyboard) while pressing an arrow key. For example, to access the Home function, press Fn-left arrow.

To move the playhead directly using the beat ruler:

◆ *Do one of the following:*

▲ Drag the triangle at the top of the playhead to the desired spot on the beat ruler (**Figure 1.15**).

▲ Click a spot on the beat ruler to move the playhead to that position.

Figure 1.15 Drag the playhead to move it along the timeline.

Table 1.1

Keyboard Shortcuts for Moving the Playhead	
ACTION	KEY COMBINATION
Start/pause playback	Spacebar
Go to start of song	Home or Z
Go to end of song	End or Option-Z
Move backward one measure	Left arrow
Move forward one measure	Right arrow
Move backward a full screen	Page Up
Move forward a full screen	Page Down

To move the playhead using the transport controls:

◆ Review Figure 1.11; *do one of the following:*

▲ Click the Play button to start song playback. Click the button again to pause playback.

▲ Click the Go to Beginning button to jump the playhead to the start of the song.

▲ Click the Rewind or Fast Forward button to move the playhead backward or forward through the song one measure at a time.

▲ Hold down the mouse on the Rewind or Fast Forward button to move quickly backward or forward through the song.

WORKING IN THE TIMELINE

Using the Time Display

The time display provides a constant read-out of the position of the playhead. You can also use it to move the playhead to a precise moment in time. By default, time is displayed in musical units, but you can switch to an absolute time display if you wish.

▲ **Musical time (Figure 1.16):** Normally, the time display readout tells you where the playhead is in relation to the metric structure of the song. The numbers indicate the measure, beat, tick, and fractions of a tick. The tiny eighth note at the lower left of the display indicates that musical units are in use.

A *tick* is equivalent to a sixteenth note. Most songs use the quarter note as the beat, in which case there are 4 ticks to a beat. The three-digit number in the fractions field is a little more obscure. There are 240 of these fractions in a tick. Because 4 × 240 = 960, a fraction represents about one one-thousandth of a beat. Don't worry—it's not often that you'll need to locate the playhead with such precision!

▲ **Absolute time (Figure 1.17):** If the music you're composing is intended to be a part of a nonmusical project—if, for example, you're scoring a film—you'll find the absolute time display very handy. It greatly simplifies the process of fitting a piece of music to the length of a movie scene. Time is displayed in this format:

hours : minutes : seconds : thousandths of seconds.

You can tell that the display is recording absolute time because a miniature clock appears at the far left.

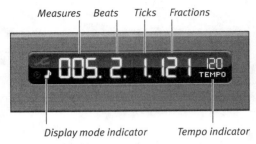

Measures   Beats   Ticks   Fractions

Display mode indicator   Tempo indicator

Figure 1.16 The time display, in musical time format.

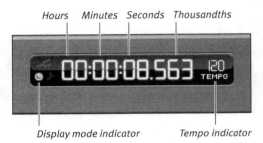

Hours   Minutes   Seconds   Thousandths

Display mode indicator   Tempo indicator

Figure 1.17 The time display, set to show absolute time.

Figure 1.18 Top: Click the almost-invisible eighth note to change the time display to show musical time. Bottom: Click the tiny clock icon to switch to absolute time display.

Figure 1.19 Click the tuning fork to access the built-in instrument tuner.

The time display also shows the tempo of the song. *Tempo* refers to the speed or pace of the song. It's measured in *beats per minute*, or *bpm*. The tempo readout doubles as a control for adjusting the song's tempo. For more about tempo, see Chapter 2.

To change the format of the time display:

◆ *Do one of the following:*

▲ If the display shows absolute time, click the eighth note, barely visible to the right of the clock, to switch to musical time (**Figure 1.18**).

▲ If the display shows musical time, click the faint clock icon, just to the left of the eighth note, to change to absolute time.

To move the playhead using the time display:

◆ *Do one of the following:*

▲ Drag up or down on any of the numbers in the time display to increase or decrease the value of the number.

▲ Double-click the number you want to change to select it. It will blink to show that it is selected. Type a new number and press Return or Enter.

✔ Tip

■ As of GarageBand 2, the time display also contains a nifty instrument tuner, which you activate by clicking the ghostly tuning fork (**Figure 1.19**). See Chapter 6 for a description of its use.

USING THE TIME DISPLAY

To adjust the tempo:

1. Place the mouse pointer over the tempo indicator and press the mouse button. The tempo slider appears (**Figure 1.20**).

2. Drag downward to lower the tempo and slow down the song (**Figure 1.21**), or drag upward to speed up the tempo. The available values range from 60 to 240 bpm.

✔ Tip

- You can also adjust the tempo using the Tempo slider in the Track Info window for the master track (see "About the Master Track" in Chapter 11).

- Be careful! Changing the tempo of your song will throw your imported Real Instrument tracks out of synch with the rest of your tracks. For more information, see "Change Your Song's Key, Tempo, or Time Signature" in Chapter 11.

Figure 1.20 Whoa—176 bpm is way too fast for the rock ballad we're writing. Let's dial things back a notch or two.

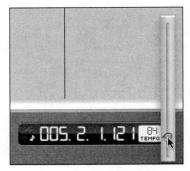

Figure 1.21 Ah! That's more like it. A nice, mellow 84 bpm suits the piece much better.

USING THE TIME DISPLAY

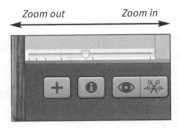

Zoom out   Zoom in

Figure 1.22 The zoom slider.

Figure 1.23 Top: The timeline set to a moderate level of zoom. Bottom: With the zoom slider dragged far to the right, much more detail is visible in the tracks.

Zooming in the Timeline

From time to time, you'll want to change the level of detail at which you view your song. Sometimes, a broad overview is just what you need; sometimes, you need to get in close. The zoom slider (**Figure 1.22**) is just the tool for the job.

To zoom into the timeline:

◆ Drag the zoom slider to the right (or press Control-right arrow) to magnify your view of the timeline (**Figure 1.23**).

To zoom out from the timeline:

◆ Drag the zoom slider left (or press Control-left arrow) to zoom out for a bird's-eye view of your song.

✔ Tip

■ Instead of dragging the slider, you can jump to a zoom level by clicking a spot on the slider scale.

About the Timeline Grid

As you build your song, you'll stack loops and recorded music on top of each other, to create a rich texture. Normally, you'll want to make sure that events in different tracks are aligned in time. GarageBand provides a timeline grid to help you maintain this alignment. There's a timeline grid in the track editor, but we'll save that subject for Chapter 9.

When the timeline grid is turned on, these operations snap to the nearest grid location in the timeline:

◆ Moving the playhead.

◆ Moving the cycle region.

◆ Placing loops into the timeline.

◆ Moving regions.

◆ Resizing regions.

◆ Moving the control points on volume and controller curves in the track editor.

The grid is visible in the tracks and the beat ruler. In the beat ruler, the grid takes the form of faint gray tick marks between the beat markers. Gridlines extend across the full width of tracks devoid of music data. If you choose an extremely small grid value, however, only the beat ruler will show all of the divisions. Only the larger divisions will be displayed in the tracks, to avoid cluttering the interface (**Figure 1.24**). The grid display also depends on the current zoom level. At higher zoom levels, more of the grid's detail is displayed.

You'll usually want to keep the grid in force, but if you crave more creative freedom, you can turn it off. The command is a simple toggle; to turn the grid back on, just repeat the action.

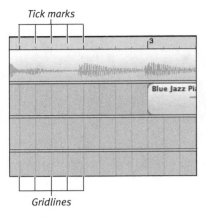

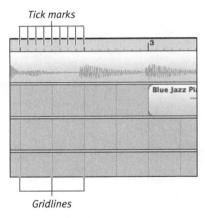

Figure 1.24 Top: The grid setting is $1/16$ notes. Both the beat ruler and track gridlines show four divisions per beat. Bottom: The grid setting is $1/32$ notes. Now the beat ruler shows eight divisions per beat, but the gridline display has been streamlined to show only two divisions per beat.

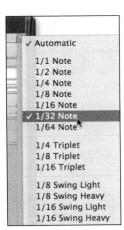

Figure 1.25 The timeline grid menu.

To disable or enable the timeline grid:

◆ *Do one of the following:*
   ▲ Choose Control > Snap to Grid to uncheck (or recheck) the command and turn the grid off (or on).
   ▲ Press Command-G.

Choosing a value for the timeline grid

You can set the grid to any of these note values:

◆ $^1/_1$ notes (whole notes), $^1/_2$ notes, $^1/_4$ notes, $^1/_8$ notes, $^1/_{16}$ notes, $^1/_{32}$ notes, $^1/_{64}$ notes.

◆ $^1/_4$-note triplets, $^1/_8$-note triplets, $^1/_{16}$-note triplets.

◆ $^1/_8$-note swing light, $^1/_8$-note swing heavy, $^1/_{16}$-note swing light, $^1/_{16}$-note swing heavy.

The smaller the note value, the finer the grid. The triplet settings push the subdivisions of the beat away from an even split toward an uneven split, with a ratio of 3:2. This lends a gentle swing to the rhythm. The swing settings do the same thing, but more noticeably, with the heavy settings having the strongest effect.

By default, GarageBand uses the Automatic setting, which resizes the grid according to the current zoom level. As you zoom into or out from the timeline, the grid setting adjusts to smaller and larger values, respectively.

To choose a value for the timeline grid:

1. Click the Timeline Grid button at the upper right of the timeline.

   The timeline grid menu appears (**Figure 1.25**).

2. Choose one of the settings from the menu.

ABOUT THE TIMELINE GRID

WORKING WITH SONGS

The *song* is the unit of creation in GarageBand. Whether you've expended hours of blood, sweat, and tears giving voice to your singular inspiration, or whether you're just noodling around with no specific goal in mind, a song is your finished product. Whenever GarageBand is running, there is one song open: no more, no less. This helps to keep things simple.

This chapter covers the basics of dealing with songs, including:

◆ Opening, saving, and playing songs.

◆ Starting a new song from scratch and choosing its tempo, time signature, and key.

◆ Setting a song's length.

◆ Undoing your work when you realize you've made a mistake.

About Songs

You build your song in the timeline, creating *tracks* to contain the various chunks of audio data that go into your song. (The GarageBand interface uses the word *project* from time to time rather than *song*, but it means the same thing.) You add Apple Loops (that use either Real or Software Instruments) and import MIDI and audio files to your song by dragging them to tracks. You record Real Instruments and Software Instruments into tracks. See Chapter 3 for more about tracks.

Each item that you've added to your song, whether it's a loop or 30 seconds of recorded sound, is called a *region* in GarageBand-speak. You refine the overall shape of your creation by *arranging* these regions (which I'll discuss in Chapter 8). Regions can be lengthened or shortened; looped, split, or joined; and moved around within a track or moved from one track to another.

The track editor, a more advanced feature of GarageBand, allows you to edit the fundamental characteristics of regions (more about this in Chapters 9 and 10). Using the track editor, you can transpose a region to another key (except for Real Instrument regions that consist of audio you imported from the Finder). You can tweak the tuning or timing of Real Instrument regions. You can even edit the individual notes of Software Instrument regions.

Finally, you refine your song's *mix*, setting each track's volume and stereo position and adding effects (see Chapter 11) and adjusting the overall volume level of the song (see Chapter 12). Then you're ready to share your magnum opus with the world. Use the Export to iTunes command (see Chapter 13) to consolidate all of your tracks into a single audio file, which is output to your iTunes library. From there, you can burn your song to a CD, post it to a Web site, or copy it to your iPod.

ABOUT SONGS

Figure 2.1 This dialog gives you one last chance to save changes to your song before you open another.

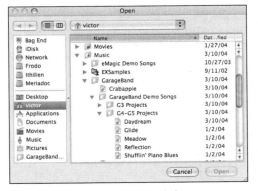

Figure 2.2 The ever-popular Open dialog.

Figure 2.3 A song open in GarageBand.

Opening a Song

GarageBand allows you to have only one song open at a time, so opening a song requires you to close the song that's already open.

To open a song:

1. Choose File > Open (Command-O).

   If you have made changes to the song that is currently open since the last time you saved it, you'll get a warning (**Figure 2.1**). Click Don't Save (Command-D) to discard the changes, or Cancel (Esc) to abort the Open command and continue working in the same song, or Save to save the changes you've made.

   The Open dialog appears (**Figure 2.2**).

2. Navigate to the folder containing your GarageBand songs. By default, this is ~/Music/GarageBand.

3. Select the desired song and click Open.

   The song and its tracks appear in the GarageBand window (**Figure 2.3**).

   continues on next page

✔ Tips

- GarageBand automatically keeps track of the last few songs you've opened. To reopen a song you were just working on, choose File > Open Recent and select a song from the submenu (**Figure 2.4**). If you're tired of seeing the same old song titles, choose Clear Menu from the same submenu to wipe the slate clean and start afresh.

- GarageBand 2 no longer quits if you close the current song, as did GarageBand 1, but that doesn't mean it's perfectly content to hang around with no song open. If you close the main window (Command-W) or start to open a song but change your mind and click the Cancel button, you'll be presented with the same dialog you saw when you started the program for the first time (Figure 1.5). Open or create a song, or just click Quit and call it a day. Or you can click the Close button to dismiss the dialog—no harm, no foul.

Figure 2.4 Use the Open Recent command to reopen a song you worked on before.

Looking for Inspiration?

GarageBand comes with some prebuilt songs that illustrate the program's capabilities and may give you some ideas for your own magnum opus. But the iLife '05 Installer no longer places them in the Music folder, as did iLife '04 (the complete path was ~/Music/GarageBand/GarageBand Demo Songs).

The new location is in your shared files folder, so they are available to all users of your Mac: /Users/Shared/GarageBand Demo Songs.

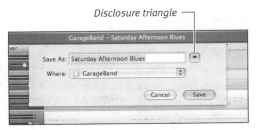

Disclosure triangle

Figure 2.5 The minimal Save As dialog.

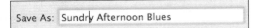

Figure 2.6 Rename your song by typing here.

Figure 2.7 When you click the disclosure triangle, the Save As dialog expands to reveal more features.

✔ Tip

■ The list of folders in the Where pop-up menu is pretty limited. If you want to be able to navigate to any folder on your hard disk, click the disclosure triangle to the right of the Save As field. The expanded version of the Save As dialog appears (**Figure 2.7**). This allows you to navigate to any folder on your computer. Click the disclosure triangle again to shrink the dialog back to its minimal form.

Saving a Song

If you have any experience with computers, you don't need reminding of this simple truth: Your computer, yes, even your lovely Macintosh, will crash when it is most inconvenient. Or GarageBand will suddenly vanish from the screen and leave you with nothing but one of those maddening "Unexpectedly Quit" messages.

So remember to save your work often. GarageBand's Save command gathers up copies of all the audio and MIDI data you've recorded in your song and packages it into one neat bundle. The bundle also includes pointers to any loops you may have used, without copying the loops themselves.

To save a song to disk:

◆ Choose File > Save (Command-S).

To save your song with a different name:

1. Choose File > Save As (Command-Shift-S). The Save As dialog (in its minimal form) drops down from the GarageBand window's title bar (**Figure 2.5**).

2. In the Save As field, type a new name for the song (**Figure 2.6**).

3. The program always assumes that you want to save the song in the default GarageBand folder in your Music folder. If you want to save a song elsewhere, choose one of the locations in the Where pop-up menu (Figure 2.5).

4. Click Save or press Return.

Saving a Song as an Archive

Suppose you're a loop fiend. You've bought all four of the GarageBand Jam Packs, and you download every free loop you can get your hands on. Your Apple Loops library threatens to overwhelm your hard disk, and your GarageBand compositions exploit the depth and richness of the collection. Unfortunately, if you save your songs using the ordinary Save command and try to open them on another Mac that has only the standard GarageBand loop library, you'll be bombarded with "File not found" error messages.

GarageBand 2 includes a new feature that helps you avoid this problem. The Save as Archive command copies every bit of audio or MIDI data your song uses into a single file: not just the Real and Software Instrument tracks you record, but also all the loops you may have used. That way, your song will sound just as you created it when played back on any Mac with GarageBand 2.

The Save as Archive command works just like the Save As command.

To save a song as an archive:

1. Choose File > Save as Archive (**Figure 2.8**). The minimal form of the Save As dialog unrolls from the GarageBand main window's title bar (Figure 2.5).

2. In the Save As field, type a name for the song archive (Figure 2.6).

3. Use one of these methods to choose a location for the file:
   ▲ Open the Where pop-up menu and choose a folder.
   ▲ Click the dialog's disclosure triangle to access the expanded Save As dialog and choose any folder on your hard drive (Figure 2.7).

Figure 2.8 The Save as Archive command consolidates all of the material for your song into a single file.

✔ Tip

■ The best way to ensure that your GarageBand creations will play properly on machines other than your own is to use the File > Export to iTunes command. This converts your GarageBand song to a standard audio file that just about any music software on any platform can recognize. For more about this option, see Chapter 13, "Exporting and Importing."

SAVING A SONG AS AN ARCHIVE

About Filename Extensions

One feature that distinguishes Mac OS X from earlier Mac operating systems is its greater reliance on filename suffixes, or *extensions*, to associate documents with the applications that created them. GarageBand, for example, will open only files whose filenames end in the extension *.band*.

Fortunately, you don't have to worry about this detail. GarageBand automatically appends the extension to every song you create or save. Furthermore, both GarageBand and Mac OS X are designed to protect you from inadvertently damaging your files by keeping their extensions hidden.

GarageBand does offer a peek behind the curtain. You can uncheck the Hide Extension box in the Save As dialog (**Figure 2.9**), but that shows you the extension only for the filename currently occupying the Save As field.

If you're curious about extensions, you can configure the Finder so it displays all of your files with their extensions exposed to the elements. In the Finder, choose Finder > Preferences (Command-,) and click the Advanced button. Then check the Show All File Extensions box (**Figure 2.10**).

But remember: look—don't touch!

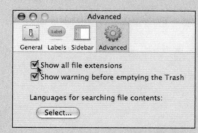

Figure 2.9 Uncheck the Hide Extension box to reveal the *.band* extension on your song's name.

Figure 2.10 Use the Advanced pane of the Finder Preferences dialog to turn on the display of all filename extensions.

SAVING A SONG AS AN ARCHIVE

Playing a Song

What's the use of having a fancy music program if you can't listen to the tunes you create? Don't worry—it's easy to play a song in GarageBand.

Figure 2.11 Click this button to play a song.

To play a song:

◆ Make sure the song you want to hear is open. *Then do one of the following:*

▲ Click the Play button under the timeline (**Figure 2.11**).

▲ Press the spacebar.

To pause playback, click the Play button or press the spacebar again.

Use the other transport controls (described in Chapter 1) to navigate through your song.

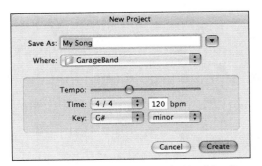

Figure 2.12 The New Project dialog (minimal form).

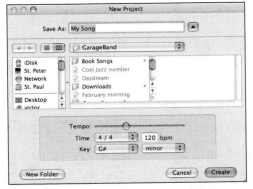

Figure 2.13 The expanded form of the New Project dialog.

Creating a New Song

When you start a new song in GarageBand, you're asked to set some basic parameters that will apply to the song as a whole. As you'll learn in Chapter 12, in the section "About the Master Track," it's possible to change these settings later, after you've worked on the song for a while. Doing this can have unpredictable results, however, so it's best to set up the song the way you want it from the beginning.

To create a new song:

1. Choose File > New (Command-N).

   If you've made changes to the song you're working on but haven't saved the document recently, you'll be asked if you want to save first (Figure 2.1). Click Save.

   The New Project dialog appears (**Figure 2.12**).

2. In the Save As field, type a name for your song.

3. Choose a location for the song *by doing one of the following:*

   ▲ Open the Where pop-up menu and make a selection.

   ▲ Click the disclosure triangle to display the expanded form of the New Project dialog (**Figure 2.13**). Now you're free to save your song anywhere you like.

4. Choose a tempo, time signature, and key for your song, according to the criteria described in the next sections.

   continues on next page

5. Click Create.

The New Project dialog closes, and a new GarageBand window opens, showing a song containing a single empty Grand Piano Software Instrument track (**Figure 2.14**).

✔ Tip

■ The vast majority of GarageBand songs that have been posted to Web sites since the appearance of the program use the default tempo, time signature, and key settings for a new song. The simplest thing you can do to demonstrate your creativity and individuality is to promise yourself *never* to use this combination of settings. Future generations will thank you.

Figure 2.14 A freshly minted song file: a blank slate ready to record your musical thoughts.

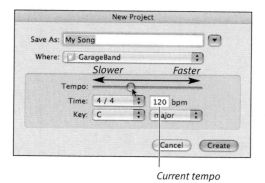

Current tempo

Figure 2.15 The Tempo slider and the current tempo readout, showing beats per minute.

About Tempo

Chapter 1 touched briefly on the subject of tempo. The word *tempo*, like many bits of musical jargon, comes from Italian. Translated literally, it means *time*. In music, it refers to the speed, or pace, of a piece of music. Tempo can be described in terms of how a piece feels: blues ballads have a slow tempo; punk rock songs have a fast, driving tempo. But tempo can also be described in numerical terms. Tempo is measured in beats per minute (bpm), where a *beat* is the background rhythmic pulse of a song. In GarageBand, you can choose any tempo between 60 and 240 bpm.

Your choice of tempo has a profound effect on the emotional content of your song. A fast tempo (also called an up-tempo beat) gets the blood pumping and is a feature of dance and rock 'n' roll music. Slower tempos set a mellower mood and are often found in hip-hop songs and ballads from any genre.

Each GarageBand song can have only one tempo, which remains in force through the entire song. The tempo you set affects mainly loops and Software Instrument recordings. It has no effect on Real Instrument recordings you add to your song.

To set the song's tempo:

◆ Working in the New Project dialog, *do one of the following*:

  ▲ Drag the Tempo slider left to choose a slower tempo; drag to the right to choose a faster one (**Figure 2.15**). (Watch the bpm field below the slider.)

  ▲ Type the desired tempo directly in the bpm field.

About Time Signatures

In addition to setting the tempo to define the rhythmic character of your piece, you need to set the time signature. The tempo describes the speed at which the beats go by, but the time signature defines the grouping of those beats.

Beats are grouped together into *measures*. The beat is the rhythmic pulse of the song, and the measure organizes these beats into repeating patterns of accented (or strong) beats. Measures begin with a strong beat, which is called the *downbeat*. The time signature determines the number of beats in a measure and the kind of notes that represent those beats. Time signatures look like fractions in GarageBand: two numbers with a slash between them. The number on the left is the number of beats in a measure. The number on the right indicates what kind of note gets the beat.

For example, the most common time signature in pop music (and the default for a GarageBand song) is 4/4. This means that there are four beats in a measure, and that each beat is represented by a quarter note.

These are the time signatures available in GarageBand:

- 2/2

- 2/4, 3/4, 4/4, 5/4, 7/4

- 6/8, 7/8, 9/8, 12/8

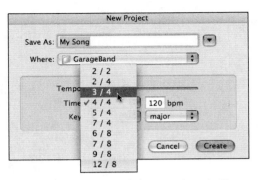

Figure 2.16 Choosing a time signature from the Time pop-up menu.

Some of these are not very common in pop music. Three-quarter time—3/4—is used most famously for waltzes. Marches tend to be in 2/4 time. The time signature 6/8 is distinctive to folk music from the British Isles when used at a brisk tempo (think Irish jig); taken at a slow tempo, you'll find 6/8 blues and jazz songs. The rest are rather obscure; you might encounter 7/8 or 7/4 time in some Eastern European folk music, and the others are used primarily by classical composers.

Just as with tempo, the time signature you choose remains in effect for the entire song. The time signature you set provides merely a metric framework for the song. There's nothing to stop you from adding to your song a Real Instrument or Software Instrument performance that uses a different time signature, although your song will remain in the original time signature.

To set the time signature:

◆ Working in the New Project dialog, choose the desired time signature from the Time pop-up menu (**Figure 2.16**).

ABOUT TIME SIGNATURES

About Keys

Tempo and time signature together define the rhythmic structure of your song. Now we need to talk about another characteristic of music: pitch. For each song, you need to choose a *key*. A key consists of a main note (called the *tonic*) and a scale that begins on that note. A song in a particular key will, in general, begin on the tonic and end on that note. The chords that accompany the song will be made up mostly of notes in the scale that starts on the tonic.

For example, if you choose the key of C, most of the notes in the song will come from the scale: C D E F G A B C—the white keys on the piano.

The choice of key depends on many factors. Sometimes you choose a key to fit an individual singer's voice. For instrumental pieces, you might choose a key that's easy to play on that instrument (guitarists tend to like G and D, whereas pianists often feel comfortable in keys with lots of sharps, like D-flat or E).

GarageBand lets you pick a key based on any note, and GarageBand 2 includes a new pop-up menu that allows you to choose either a major or minor mode, or scale. (Major keys generally sound happy, positive, upbeat, while minor keys sound melancholy, tragic, or pensive.) You can choose a key that starts on one of the black keys of the piano, though GarageBand names them differently depending on whether you've chosen the major or minor scale.

Whichever key you choose remains in effect for the entire song. Like the time signature, the "official" key of the song has no effect on music you record; however, the Apple Loops that come with GarageBand are smart enough to adapt to the key you have chosen

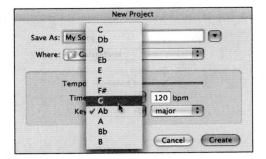

Figure 2.17 Choose the major or minor scale from this pop-up menu.

Figure 2.18 Choosing the key of G from the Key pop-up menu. Top: If you chose the major scale, you will see these note names. The notes that correspond to the black keys on the piano are written mostly as flats. Bottom: If you chose the minor scale, sharps predominate.

for your song. The loops won't, however, change to match the scale (major or minor) you've chosen. The only practical result of your scale choice can be seen in the Software Instrument track editor (see Chapter 10). If you display the track in notation view, the pitches will be notated slightly differently depending on the scale you picked.

To set the key and scale (or mode):

1. Working in the New Project dialog, from the pop-up menu to the right of the Key menu, choose the major or minor scale (**Figure 2.17**).

2. From the Key pop-up menu, choose the desired key (**Figure 2.18**).

   The names of the notes on the menu will differ, depending on which scale you chose.

About Song Length

When you create a new song using the default 4/4 time signature, its length is automatically (and arbitrarily) set to 90 measures (down from 200 in GarageBand 1). But if you set the time signature of your new song to 3/4, it will be 120 measures long. So, in truth, the default length of a new GarageBand song is 360 beats (90 measures × 4 beats per measure, or 120 measures × 3 beats per measure). If you record regions that extend beyond this limit, more measures are automatically added to accommodate the new material. When you export your song to iTunes, GarageBand includes only the measures up to the end of the final region in the song. In other words, if your last region ends at measure 64 but the song ends at 90, GarageBand trims the 26 empty measures from the end of the song. (More about this in Chapter 13.) You can also adjust the length of the song manually.

To change the length of a song:

1. Scroll to the end of your song and find the end-of-song marker. It's a purple triangle (**Figure 2.19**).

2. Drag the marker to the left to shorten the song (**Figure 2.20**), or drag to the right to lengthen it.

✔ Tip

■ When dragging the end-of-song marker, be very careful to place your mouse pointer exactly on the triangle. If you miss by even a little bit and click the beat ruler instead, the playhead will suddenly jump to that position. The playhead then covers up most of the end-of-song marker, making your task even harder (**Figure 2.21**).

Figure 2.19 The end-of-song marker.

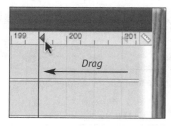

Figure 2.20 Dragging the marker left to trim some measures from the song.

Figure 2.21 Oops. Indiscriminate clicking can sometimes get you into trouble.

All Good Things Come to an End

There is an absolute limit to the length of a GarageBand song: 998 measures. You can drag the end-of-song marker out to the downbeat of measure 999, but no farther (**Figure 2.22**). Unlike the default length, this value doesn't seem to be related to a specific number of beats. If your end-of-song marker is at 999 and you change the time signature so it has fewer beats in a measure, the beat ruler will suddenly show numbers higher than a thousand. But the second you try to move the end-of-song marker into the four-digit realm, it snaps back to 999, and the higher numbers vanish like Brigadoon.

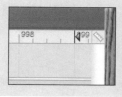

Figure 2.22 The end of the line. You can't drag the end-of-song marker past measure 999.

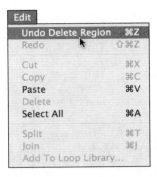

Figure 2.23 The Undo command.

Figure 2.24 Choosing the Revert to Saved command causes this warning to appear.

Undoing Your Work

Even the brightest and best among us make mistakes; that's why the Undo command exists. It lets you try out an adjustment to your song. If you don't like the result, you can return the song to its previous state. And because sometimes Undo is itself a mistake, you can use the Redo command to undo the Undo.

Then there are times when you suddenly realize that everything you've done to a song since you opened it has been a disaster, and you wish you could erase everything that's happened and go back to the saved version. That's what the Revert command is for.

To undo an action:

◆ Choose Edit > Undo [*name of the last action*] or press Command-Z (**Figure 2.23**).

To redo an action:

◆ Choose Edit > Redo [*name of the action that was undone*] or press Command-Shift-Z.

To go back to the last saved version of a song:

1. Choose File > Revert to Saved.

   An Alert dialog slides down from the GarageBand window's title bar (**Figure 2.24**).

2. Click Revert (or press Return) to undo all of the changes you have made to the song since you last saved it.

   If you decide to keep your changes intact after all, click Cancel (or press Command-. or Esc).

Multiple Undos

It's not mentioned in the documentation, but GarageBand supports multiple Undos. This means that, after using the Undo command, you can continue to issue further Undo commands and step backward through the history of your work in GarageBand.

Because the feature is undocumented, I don't know for sure how far you can retrace your steps. Another publisher's GarageBand book says that you can undo 10 steps, but on one occasion I was able to step back through 36 steps. But sometimes I can undo only 6 steps. Most likely, the number of possible undos is determined by the amount of RAM in your machine and the type of operations you are undoing. If you perform a series of steps that don't tax your machine's resources very much, then you can probably undo a good number of steps. If, on the other hand, you have performed some RAM-intensive operations, you will probably be able to undo fewer steps.

UNDOING YOUR WORK

WORKING WITH TRACKS

Most songs combine voices and instruments to create a layered texture. A typical song might include:

◆ A solo instrument or vocal line that carries the main melody.

◆ A bass instrument providing a solid foundation for the harmony.

◆ Percussion supplying a pervasive background beat.

◆ A body of other instruments that fill out the harmony and add color to the sound.

In GarageBand, you use tracks to organize these layers of sound. Each track has certain settings that remain constant for the length of the song and that keep the character of the track consistent. GarageBand 2 provides several new features that make working with tracks easier.

About Tracks

GarageBand associates each track with an "instrument." In GarageBand, this word really means "a source of musical data." Every track is either a Real Instrument track or a Software Instrument track. You can't record a Real Instrument into a Software Instrument track and vice versa. When you add a track, you first have to decide whether it will be a Real Instrument track or a Software Instrument track. And once you've chosen, you can't switch a track to the other flavor. Here's how to choose:

◆ Choose a Real Instrument track if you plan to use the track for audio recording.

◆ Choose a Software Instrument track if you plan to record from a MIDI device, such as a keyboard.

◆ Both kinds of tracks will accept loops, but you can drag Real Instrument loops only to a Real Instrument track. You can drag Software Instrument loops to either kind of track, but Software Instrument loops dragged to Real Instrument tracks are converted to Real Instrument regions. A new preference setting in GarageBand 2 causes all Software Instrument loops to be turned into Real Instrument loops when they are dragged into the blank part of the timeline (that is, when you create a new track). I'll talk more about this feature in the next chapter.

Color Coding

Tracks and regions are color-coded in GarageBand to remind you of their type.

◆ Green tracks and regions use Software Instruments, both recordings and loops.

◆ Blue tracks use Real Instruments and can contain:
  ▲ Blue regions (Real Instrument loops).
  ▲ Purple regions (Real Instrument regions that consist of audio recordings you create).
  ▲ Orange regions (imported audio recordings).

The orange coding of imported audio regions is new with GarageBand 2, and the feature still has some kinks to be worked out. The program tends to color just about every non-loop Real Instrument region orange, unless it witnessed you personally recording the region using GarageBand 2. Every GarageBand 1 song that I've opened in GarageBand 2 is a sea of orange—even regions that I know were recorded and not imported. Let's hope Apple straightens this out with an update soon!

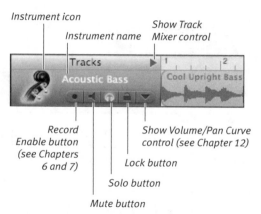

Instrument icon

Instrument name

Show Track Mixer control

Record Enable button (see Chapters 6 and 7)

Show Volume/Pan Curve control (see Chapter 12)

Lock button

Solo button

Mute button

Figure 3.1 Track header.

About the Track Header

Each track is identified by its *track header*, found in the Tracks column of the GarageBand window (**Figure 3.1**).

The header's principal features are the track's instrument name and icon.

The header also contains controls that govern the playback of individual tracks. The *Mute button* silences the track, and the *Solo button* allows the track to be heard alone.

Two new controls appear in the track header as of GarageBand 2. The *Record Enable button* allows you to specify which tracks will receive recorded audio or MIDI data (and is discussed in more detail in Chapters 6 and 7).

The *Lock button* performs two functions: it prevents the track from being changed, and it causes a rendered version of the track to be saved with your song file. Locking tracks can improve playback performance if your computer has a slow processor or if your song uses many Software Instruments or complex effects. I'll talk more about the Lock button later in this chapter.

Two of the controls in the track header reveal hidden interface elements that give access to more features of tracks. Clicking the triangle to the right of the word *Tracks* displays the *track mixer* (visible by default), which has controls for the volume level and pan position of individual tracks (see "About the Track Mixer" later in this chapter). The triangle to the right of the Lock button reveals the track's volume or pan curve, which I'll describe in Chapter 12.

ABOUT THE TRACK HEADER

Selecting Tracks

Some operations involving tracks require that you first select the track in question. Selecting a track is a simple procedure. Only one track can be selected at a time.

To select a track:

◆ *Do one of the following:*

▲ Click the track header (**Figure 3.2**).

▲ Click any region within the track (**Figure 3.3**).

The header of the selected track acquires a color cast (green for Software Instruments, blue for Real Instruments), and the instrument icon starts to glow in the same color (**Figure 3.4**).

✔ Tip

■ When selecting a track, don't click within the empty, gray area of the track. That selects nothing.

To select an adjacent track using the keyboard:

◆ Starting from a selected track, *do one of the following:*

▲ To select the next higher track, press the up arrow key.

▲ To select the next lower track, press the down arrow key.

Figure 3.2 Click the header of the track you wish to select.

Figure 3.3 Click a region in the desired track.

Figure 3.4 The header of a selected track.

Figure 3.5 The mouse pointer poised over the Mute button.

Figure 3.6 The Mute button is on.

Muting a Track

If you have one track that tends to overpower the rest, it can be helpful to silence it temporarily, while you work on the rest of the composition. Or if you want to refine the balance of your backup vocals, making the melody go away for a while can ease the process.

For these situations and others, the ability to mute a track comes in handy. You can mute more than one track at a time.

To mute a track:

◆ *Do one of the following:*

▲ Click the Mute button on the header of the track you wish to silence (**Figure 3.5**).

▲ Select the track you want to mute and press the M key.

The Mute button lights up and the track's regions turn gray in the timeline, indicating that muting is in effect (**Figure 3.6**).

To unmute a muted track:

◆ *Do one of the following:*

▲ Click the track's Mute button.

▲ Select the muted track and press the M key.

The Mute button darkens and the regions in the track regain their former color, showing that the track is no longer muted.

MUTING A TRACK

Soloing a Track

You'll occasionally find it handy to isolate a single voice (or several voices) in your composition. This is called *soloing a track*. It's especially useful when recording a new track in a song whose texture is getting rather busy. You can set the drum track or the bass track to solo to provide a simple accompaniment while you record the new track.

You can set more than one track to solo at a time.

To solo a track:

◆ *Do one of the following:*

▲ Click the Solo button in the track's header (**Figure 3.7**).

▲ Select the track you want to hear as a solo and press the S key.

The Solo button lights up bright yellow (it looks like a tiny pair of headphones) and the regions in the other tracks turn gray, indicating that soloing is in effect (**Figure 3.8**).

To turn off soloing for a track:

◆ *Do one of the following:*

▲ Click the track's Solo button.

▲ Select the solo track and press the S key.

The Solo button darkens and the regions in the other tracks are no longer dimmed, showing that the track is no longer set to solo.

Figure 3.7 Clicking the Solo button.

Figure 3.8 The Solo button is on.

Pan position control   *Level meters*

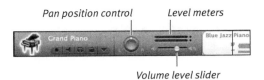

Volume level slider

Figure 3.9 The track mixer.

Figure 3.10 Click this triangle to show the track mixer.

Figure 3.11 The track mixer slides out from behind the track header.

About the Track Mixer

Also associated with each track is another control panel, the track mixer (**Figure 3.9**). The track mixer may be hidden; if so, you'll need to reveal it so it can be used. Use the controls on the track mixer to set the pan position (where the track seems to come from in the stereo field) and volume for individual tracks. The volume level meters show the track's output volume. I'll discuss these controls in more detail when we talk about recording Real Instruments in Chapter 6 and mixing in Chapter 12.

To reveal the track mixer:

◆ If the track mixer is hidden, *do one of the following:*

▲ Click the right-pointing triangle at the top-right corner of the Tracks column (**Figure 3.10**).

▲ Press Command-Y.

The track mixer slides out from behind the track header (**Figure 3.11**).

To hide the track mixer:

◆ If the track mixer is visible, *do one of the following:*

▲ Click the left-pointing triangle at the top-right corner of the Tracks column.

▲ Press Command-Y.

The track mixer disappears.

Real vs. Software Instrument Tracks

The two types of tracks used in GarageBand correspond to the two methods of recording musical information:

◆ Real Instrument tracks use recorded audio.

◆ Software Instrument tracks use MIDI (Musical Instrument Digital Interface) data.

Each of these track types has its advantages and disadvantages, and each one is derived from different source material.

Audio data consists of recordings of actual instruments or voices, captured with a microphone or a guitar pickup or similar electronic pickup. Such a recording stores a replica of the original sound in your GarageBand song, so when you play it back, you hear something that sounds just like the original. Because the original sound is reproduced with a high degree of precision, audio files tend to be very large.

MIDI data, on the other hand, records the details of an instrumental performance digitally. When you play your MIDI keyboard to create a Software Instrument track in GarageBand, the program records data about each keypress, including the note's name, duration, and velocity (how hard you struck the note). But your Mac plays (or *renders*) the sound of the music using the specific Software Instrument you've assigned to that track.

For example, if you create a Software Instrument track using the Live Pop Horns preset, the music you record on that track will sound like horns. But you can change the track's instrument to something totally different, like Hollywood Strings, and the same notes you recorded will now sound like a string section.

The sounds for Software Instrument tracks are produced by taking a sound source, called a *generator*, and applying effects to it. In fact, you can design your own instruments by varying the preset effects settings for a generator (you'll learn about tweaking effects settings in Chapter 11). There are two classes of generators: sampled and synthesized.

Sampled sounds are based on samples, or recordings, taken from actual musical instruments. A set of samples usually includes recordings of many individual notes played on the instrument at different volumes and with a range of articulations. In general, the Software Instruments that are named after normal acoustic instruments use sampled generators.

Synthesized sounds are completely computer generated and tend to sound artificial. These types of Software Instruments are based on synthesized generators: synthesizers, electric pianos, organs, and clavinets.

Software Instruments put a much greater strain on your computer than do Real Instruments, because GarageBand is creating the sound of each Software Instrument on the fly, in real time. To play a Real Instrument track, all the program has to do is read the recorded data from the hard disk and perhaps perform some effects processing. As a rule, the maximum number of Software Instrument tracks your Mac can handle in a GarageBand song is about half the number of Real Instrument tracks it can tolerate (see the sidebar "How Many Tracks Can I Use in My Song?" later in this chapter).

continues on next page

REAL VS. SOFTWARE INSTRUMENT TRACKS

Because MIDI files do not model the actual sound of a performance, they are smaller than audio files. They are also easily editable, because each note is recorded as a distinct unit of data. Compare **Figure 3.12** and **Figure 3.13**, which show, respectively, a Real Instrument track and a Software Instrument track as displayed in the track editor. Note the complexity of the audio file as depicted in Figure 3.12. It's difficult to make out individual notes or find a pattern of beats. The MIDI file in Figure 3.13, however, is clarity itself. Each little rectangle represents a single note. The color of the rectangle shows the volume of the note, and the horizontal size of the rectangle shows the duration of the note. You can change any of these parameters in the track editor. You can even correct mistakes you made while playing! (You'll learn the details of working in the track editor in Chapters 9 and 10.)

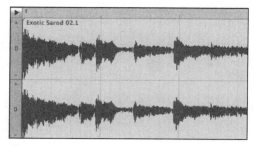

Figure 3.12 A region from a Real Instrument track, displayed in the track editor.

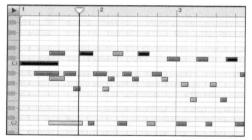

Figure 3.13 A region from a Software Instrument track, displayed in the track editor.

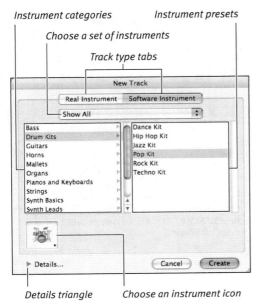

Instrument categories   Instrument presets

Choose a set of instruments

Track type tabs

Details triangle   Choose an instrument icon

Figure 3.14 The New Track dialog.

About Adding Tracks

You can add new tracks to your song at any time; the maximum number of tracks your song can contain is governed by several factors, including the processing power of your Mac (see the sidebar later in this chapter, "How Many Tracks Can I Use in My Song?").

When creating a track, you first choose whether it will be a Real Instrument track or a Software Instrument track. Once a track is created, you can't change its type from one to the other. You also choose an *instrument preset* for the track. That preset governs the sound of the track for the entire length of the song—a track can't start as one instrument and then change to a different instrument in the middle of the song. You can, however, change the instrument for the entire track at any time after it has been created, using the Track Info dialog (see "About the Track Info Window" later in this chapter).

You use the New Track dialog (**Figure 3.14**) to set up each newly created track. The dialog looks slightly different depending on whether you choose to add a Real Instrument track or a Software Instrument track. The features common to both versions of the dialog are shown in Figure 3.14.

continues on next page

Two new items have been added to the New Track dialog in GarageBand 2. The first is a pop-up menu at the top of the dialog that lets you narrow the list of instruments to a subset of all the instrument presets installed on your computer. This comes in handy if you've installed a GarageBand Jam Pack or two and the complete list of your instrument presets runs into the hundreds. The second is the Details triangle (taken over from the Track Info window), which, when clicked, opens the Details pane. This pane contains a wide array of controls for adjusting the effects that are part of the instrument's sound. We'll save discussion of the Details pane of the dialog for Chapter 11.

Figure 3.15 Use this menu to narrow your search of instrument presets.

To choose the instrument subset shown in the New Track dialog:

◆ From the pop-up menu at the top of the New Track dialog (**Figure 3.15**), *do one of the following:*

▲ To display all of the instruments installed on your computer, choose Show All (this is the default setting).

▲ To display only those instrument presets you yourself have created and saved, choose My Settings.

▲ To display only those instruments that are supplied with GarageBand itself, Choose GarageBand.

▲ To display only those instruments installed with a particular Jam Pack, choose a Jam Pack.

▲ To display third-party instrument presets you have installed, choose a folder listed under Other.

Note that your menu will likely look different from Figure 3.15, depending on the number and types of instrument presets installed on your machine.

Figure 3.16 The Add Track button.

Figure 3.17 Click the Real Instrument tab to choose an instrument preset for a Real Instrument track.

Figure 3.18 Choose a preset from the right column.

Adding a Real Instrument Track

When you create a Real Instrument track, the program asks you to choose an instrument for the track. This is more of a convenience than a necessity. GarageBand's Real Instruments are actually presets that include settings for effects, such as echo, reverb, and compression, that Apple's engineers think would enhance the instrument you're about to record. When you choose an instrument, you also get a lovely icon that helps to identify your track. You can always change any of these settings later, using the Track Info window (see "About the Track Info Window" later in this chapter).

To add a Real Instrument track:

1. *Do one of the following:*
   ▲ Choose Track > New Track (Command-Option-N).
   ▲ Click the Add Track button (**Figure 3.16**).
   The New Track dialog appears (Figure 3.14).

2. Click the Real Instrument tab, if it's not already selected (**Figure 3.17**).

3. *Optional:* Choose a collection of instrument presets from the pop-up menu above the instrument category list (Figure 3.15).

4. Select an instrument category in the left column; then, in the right column, select the specific instrument preset you want to use (**Figure 3.18**).

continues on next page

5. Choose an input channel and format by *doing one of the following:*

▲ If you've connected your instrument with a single mono cable (this is likely the case if you are recording an electric guitar, for example), or if you're recording through a single monaural microphone, choose one of the mono channels from the Input pop-up menu (**Figure 3.19**). The number of channels listed on the menu will depend on your audio hardware (see Chapter 5 for more details on the hardware you need for recording Real Instruments).

▲ If you're recording through a pair of stereo mikes (or some other stereo source), choose a pair of stereo channels from the Input pop-up menu (**Figure 3.20**).

Note that if your audio interface supports more than two input channels, your Input menu will have more choices (**Figure 3.21**).

6. Drag the Volume slider to set the input volume level for the track (**Figure 3.22**).

Note that this setting regulates the strength of the signal that comes from the audio source and is saved on your computer's hard disk. It is separate from the level set in the track mixer's Volume slider. That sets the level of the track's *output*; in other words, it controls how much of the sound stored in the track contributes to the overall mix of the song (see Chapter 12).

Figure 3.19 Select the input channel.

Figure 3.20 Choose a pair of stereo input channels.

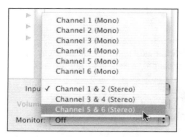
Figure 3.21 A multichannel audio interface gives you more than two input channels.

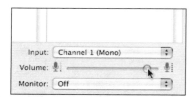
Figure 3.22 Use the Volume slider to set the input level for the track.

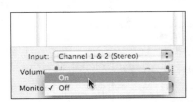

Figure 3.23 Choose On from the Monitor menu to listen to your track as you record it.

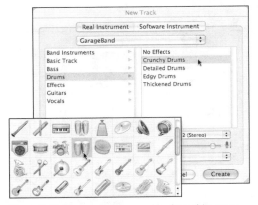

Figure 3.24 Choose an icon you like from this menu.

Figure 3.25 A new track appears in the timeline.

7. To listen to your audio as it is being recorded, choose On from the Monitor pop-up menu (**Figure 3.23**).

This menu is set to Off by default, which prevents your audio from being played back through your Mac's speakers during recording.

8. If you don't like the default icon for the instrument you've chosen, click the icon button and choose a new icon from the menu (**Figure 3.24**). (See "To change a track's instrument icon" later in this chapter.)

9. Click Create or press Return.

A new track is added to the timeline, below the other tracks (**Figure 3.25**).

✔ Tips

■ A new Real Instrument track is also created any time you drag a Real Instrument loop into the timeline (see Chapter 4). You can also have GarageBand create a new Real Instrument track whenever a Software Instrument loop is dragged to a blank part of the timeline. This is accomplished by way of a Preference setting, new in GarageBand 2, and it will be described in more detail in the next chapter. Likewise, if you drag an audio file into GarageBand from the Finder (see Chapter 13), it, too, is placed in a new Real Instrument track.

■ The Volume slider in the New Track dialog is connected to the software that controls your audio hardware, so it sets the level of all sound coming into your machine through the selected channels. For example, if you use your Mac's built-in audio hardware, the setting you choose for the Volume slider will be echoed in the Sound pane of System Preferences.

ADDING A REAL INSTRUMENT TRACK

About Basic Tracks

If you don't feel that you need GarageBand's assistance in setting up a track for recording a Real Instrument, you can skip the presets and fancy icons and start with a blank slate. To do this, you add a *basic* track to your song. This is a track with no effects applied (Echo and Reverb are enabled, but set to 0). You can adjust effects settings to your own liking and add an icon of your choice later, using the Track Info window (see "To change a track's instrument icon" later in this chapter; to adjust effects settings, see Chapter 11).

To add a basic track:

◆ *Do one of the following:*

▲ Choose Track > New Basic Track (**Figure 3.26**).

▲ Click the Add Track button or press Command-Option-N. The New Track dialog appears. Click the Real Instrument tab; then choose Basic Track in the left column and No Effects in the right column (**Figure 3.27**). Click Create or press Return.

A new Real Instrument track appears below the other tracks in the timeline, bearing a generic icon and the name "No Effects" (**Figure 3.28**).

Figure 3.26 The New Basic Track command.

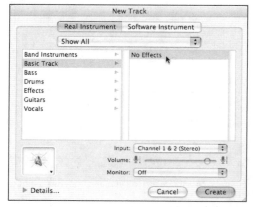

Figure 3.27 Choosing the preset for a new basic track.

Figure 3.28 The basic track takes its place in the timeline.

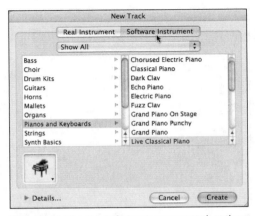

Figure 3.29 Click the Software Instrument tab at the top of the New Track dialog.

Figure 3.30 Use this menu to display a subset of your instrument preset library.

Adding a Software Instrument Track

The procedure for adding a Software Instrument track is very similar to that for adding a Real Instrument track. As with Real Instrument tracks, you are asked to assign an instrument to the track. Here, though, the two procedures diverge. Whereas you can decline to choose an instrument for a Real Instrument track and opt for a basic track with no effects applied, you have no such option with Software Instrument tracks. A Software Instrument track without an instrument would be silent! The instrument you choose for your new track defines the sound of the entire track.

Another difference is that you don't have to worry about telling the program what channels to use for input. Mac OS X handles the MIDI setup automatically, in the background.

To add a Software Instrument track:

1. *Do one of the following:*
   - ▲ Choose Track > New Track (Command-Option-N).
   - ▲ Click the Add Track button (Figure 3.16).

   The New Track dialog appears (Figure 3.14).

2. Click the Software Instrument tab, if it's not already selected (**Figure 3.29**).

3. *Optional:* Choose a collection of instrument presets from the pop-up menu above the instrument category list (**Figure 3.30**).

   continues on next page

ADDING A SOFTWARE INSTRUMENT TRACK

4. Select an instrument category in the left column; then, in the right column, select the specific instrument preset you want to use (**Figure 3.31**).

5. If you don't like the default icon for the instrument you've chosen, click the icon button and choose a new icon from the menu (**Figure 3.32**). (See "To change a track's instrument icon" later in this chapter.)

6. Click Create or press Return.

A new track is added to the timeline, below the other tracks (**Figure 3.33**).

✔ Tip

■ A new Software Instrument track is also created any time you drag a Software Instrument loop into the blank part of the timeline (unless you set your Preferences so that Software Instrument loops are always converted to Real Instrument loops; see Chapter 4).

Figure 3.31 Choose a preset for the new track.

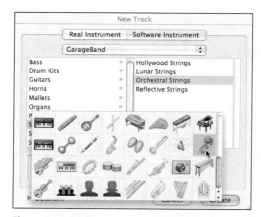

Figure 3.32 Choose a new icon for the track, if you like.

Figure 3.33 A brand-new Software Instrument track appears in the timeline.

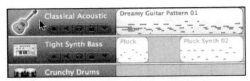

Figure 3.34 The Classical Acoustic track is selected.

Figure 3.35 The Duplicate Track command.

Figure 3.36 And now there are two.

Duplicating a Track

One way of beefing up one part, or voice, in a song is to double it with a copy of itself. It was not easy to make this happen in GarageBand 1.0—but happily, Apple's engineers smoothed the way in GarageBand 1.1 by providing a new command: Duplicate Track.

When you duplicate a track, you create a new track with all of the same instrument and effects settings as the original. None of the musical content of the original track is duplicated, however—but it's easy enough to copy the original track's regions into the new track.

To duplicate a track:

1. Select the track you wish to duplicate (**Figure 3.34**).

2. Choose Track > Duplicate Track (Command-D) (**Figure 3.35**).

   Voilà! A new empty track appears, bearing the same name and settings as the original, but containing no regions (**Figure 3.36**).

✔ Tip

- If you want the new track to contain the same music as the original, you can use ordinary Copy and Paste commands or Option-drag the regions you want to duplicate. See "To copy and paste a region" and "To duplicate a region by dragging" in Chapter 8.

Renaming a Track

When a track is created, it takes the name of the instrument preset you originally chose in the New Track dialog. But it often happens that a song will have several tracks using the same preset, and if that's the case it's nice to have some way of distinguishing among them.

In the original version of GarageBand, the only way to rename a track was to use the track editor (see "Renaming Tracks and Regions" in Chapter 9). But that method is pretty inconvenient if you don't already have the track editor open and ready to go. Fortunately, GarageBand 2 also employs a much simpler method (introduced in GarageBand 1.1) for giving a track a new moniker.

To rename a track:

1. Select the track whose name you wish to change.

2. Click the track's name once (**Figure 3.37**). The track's name becomes highlighted to indicate that the field is now editable (**Figure 3.38**).

3. Type a new name for the track (**Figure 3.39**) and press Return to confirm the change (**Figure 3.40**).

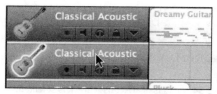

Figure 3.37 Let's select this track so we can give it a new name.

Figure 3.38 Clicking the name directly prepares it for editing.

Figure 3.39 We've typed the new name.

Figure 3.40 The track has a new identity.

Figure 3.41 Dragging the Detailed Drums track to a higher position the stack.

Figure 3.42 The track has been dropped into its new home.

Figure 3.43 The tracks are arranged by instrument types, and all's right with the world.

Changing the Stacking Order of Tracks

As you add tracks to your song, each new one takes its place at the bottom of the stack. In GarageBand 1.0, you were stuck with this vertical sequence of tracks, and if you were the sort of person who liked to have the tracks organized, you had to plan ahead very carefully.

But the Martha Stewarts of the music world may rejoice! GarageBand 2 uses a simple method for reordering your tracks (originally introduced in the GarageBand 1.1 update), so you can have your tracks grouped by family of instrument (all the strings together and all the basses together, for example) or by function (all the instruments on the melody line together).

And that's a good thing!

To change the vertical position of a track:

◆ Drag the header of the track you wish to move (**Figure 3.41**). The other tracks will adjust to make room for it. Release the mouse button when the track is over the new spot you have picked for it (**Figure 3.42**).

Repeat for other tracks until you achieve the degree of organization you desire (**Figure 3.43**).

✔ Tip

■ The order in which the tracks are stacked has absolutely no effect on the sound of your song. Its sole purpose is to satisfy your own need for visual organization.

Locking a Track

As mentioned earlier, GarageBand 2 now lets you *lock* tracks, which performs two beneficial functions. The more obvious benefit of locking a track is that the track (including both its regions and effects settings) is protected from accidental changes—say from a careless mouse click or a stray tap on the Delete key.

But using the track lock feature can also enhance the performance of GarageBand during playback. If your song contains many Software Instrument tracks or uses lots of effects, you may overload your computer's processing power, in which case playback will come to a halt, and you'll be presented with a delightful message (**Figure 3.44**).

Appendix A explains in more detail why this happens, but for now suffice it to say that while Real Instrument tracks (which are just audio files) can be played back from your computer's hard disk with no problem, Software Instruments and effects have to be *rendered*, that is, calculated, in real time. All that calculating can bring your poor Mac to its knees.

Here's how locking a track helps: When you lock a track, the next time the song is played, GarageBand makes an audio recording of the output of the track, capturing a rendered version of the track to disk. The upshot of all this is that from then on, when you play the song, GarageBand uses the prerendered versions of the locked tracks, requiring much less calculation by the computer.

Once the track is locked, you can no longer edit its contents. If you open the track's Track Info window, all of the controls are dimmed to prevent you from changing any effects. The track mixer controls are likewise disabled. If you try to select a region or click the Record Enable button, an alert will appear asking if you want to unlock the track (**Figure 3.45**). Click Unlock or press Return to unlock the

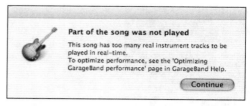

Figure 3.44 Oops—your computer is choking on your composition!

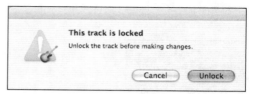

Figure 3.45 Before you can edit a locked track, you have to unlock it.

LOCKING A TRACK

Figure 3.46 Click the padlock to protect the track from changes.

Figure 3.47 The lock icon lights up to show that locking it is active.

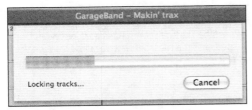

Figure 3.48 This window gives you something to watch while the locking process goes forward.

track, or click Cancel (Escape or Command-.) to leave the track as it is.

To lock a track:

1. Click the Lock button (which looks like a tiny padlock) on the track you wish to lock (**Figure 3.46**).

   The Lock button turns bright green to show that the track is locked (**Figure 3.47**).

2. Play the song.

   The playhead jumps from its current position to the beginning of the song, the entire song is played through once, and the newly locked tracks are rendered to disk. While the song is playing, the Locking Tracks progress bar drops down from the GarageBand window title bar (**Figure 3.48**). Click the Cancel button to stop the process if you change your mind about locking the track.

To unlock a track:

◆ Click the Lock button of a locked track (Figure 3.47).

   The track is now editable once again.

✔ Tips

■ While a track is locked, you can't change its contents, but you can use the Mute and Solo buttons, and you can make adjustments to the track's volume and pan curves. That's because these controls don't change any of the track's inherent characteristics. Rather, they affect only the track's output: that is, how the track fits into the overall mix of the song (see Chapter 12).

■ Locking a track in GarageBand 2 is exactly the same thing as *freezing* a track in Logic Express or Logic Pro.

Deleting Tracks

Sometimes you need to thin out the texture of your song by getting rid of a track or two. Fortunately, track deletion is undoable.

To delete a track:

1. Select the track you wish to delete (**Figure 3.49**).

2. Choose Track > Delete Track or press Command-Delete.

   The track is removed from the timeline (**Figure 3.50**).

✔ Tips

- If you press the Delete key by itself, all regions will be deleted from the track, but the track itself will stay put. This operation is also undoable.

- If you delete a track from the middle of the stack, the tracks below it move up to fill the gap.

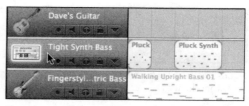

Figure 3.49 The Tight Synth Bass track is marked for oblivion.

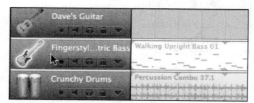

Figure 3.50 The Tight Synth Bass track has been deleted, and the track below it has moved up to take its place.

Figure 3.51 The Track Info window for a Real Instrument track.

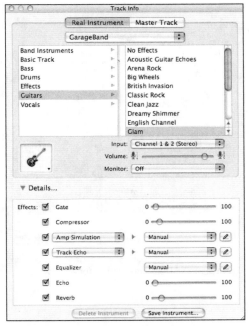

Figure 3.52 A Real Instrument Track Info window, showing the Details pane.

About the Track Info Window

If you want to change the basic characteristics of a track after you've created it, the Track Info window is the place to do it (**Figure 3.51**). It's almost identical to the New Track dialog, with a few significant differences. Also, there are separate versions of the Track Info window for Real and Software Instruments, so you can't convert a Real Instrument track to a Software Instrument track, or vice versa.

The Track Info window is used primarily for changing the instrument (or the instrument icon) assigned to a track. You can also change the recording settings for Real Instrument tracks; the Track Info window includes the same Input, Volume, and Monitor recording controls as the New Track dialog, and they work identically (see "To add a Real Instrument track" earlier in this chapter).

Both flavors of the Track Info window include an extra widget in the lower-left corner: the Details triangle. Clicking this triangle opens a new pane, which displays the effects settings for the selected track (**Figure 3.52**). I'll save the discussion of effects for Chapter 11.

You also use the Track Info window to alter the basic parameters of the song as a whole, by means of the song's master track, but that subject belongs to Chapter 11.

To view the Track Info window for a track:

◆ *Do one of the following:*

▲ Select the track header and click the Track Info button (**Figure 3.53**) or press Command-I.

▲ Double-click the track header.

The Track Info window opens (**Figure 3.54**).

✔ Tip

■ Note that the main part of the Track Info window for Real Instruments (Figure 3.51) is almost identical to that for Software Instruments (Figure 3.54). The only difference is the absence of recording options in the Software Instrument window.

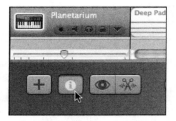

Figure 3.53 Click the Track Info button with a track selected. The track in this example is a Software Instrument track.

Figure 3.54 The Track Info window for a Software Instrument track.

Figure 3.55 After opening the Track Info window.

Figure 3.56 Choosing a new category and instrument preset.

Changing a Track's Instrument

Changing the instrument assigned to a track has very different consequences for Real and Software Instruments. As discussed earlier, a Real Instrument is just a collection of effects settings. Say that you create a Real Instrument track using the Solo Sax instrument and record a performance of a live saxophone player into it. If you switch the track's instrument to Pop Vocals, the basic instrumental sound of the track won't change. The effects that are part of the Pop Vocals preset will be applied to your recording, so its acoustical aura will change, but it will still sound like a saxophone.

Not so with Software Instruments. If you create a Software Instrument track using the Muted Electric Bass instrument and then change the track to something very different, like Synth Basics/Star Sweeper, the sound of the music recorded into the track will change completely. The notes will be the same, the dynamics and articulation will be the same, but the electric bass instrumental timbre will be gone and the synthesized sound will have taken its place.

To change a track's instrument:

1. Select the track whose instrument you want to change.

2. Open the Track Info window as described in "To view the Track Info window for a track" earlier in this chapter (**Figure 3.55**).

3. Select an instrument category in the left column; then, in the right column, select the specific instrument preset you want to use (**Figure 3.56**).

   You can leave the window open and try other instrument presets.

continues on next page

CHANGING A TRACK'S INSTRUMENT

✔ Tip

■ If, before choosing a new instrument, you opened the Details pane of the Track Info window and made any changes (or so much as opened a single pop-up menu), you will see an alert dialog (**Figure 3.57**). If you don't want to save any changes to the current instrument, click Discard. The consequences of clicking Save are rather complex, so I will refer you to the sidebar "The Confusing 'You Have Made Changes' Dialog" in Chapter 11.

To change a track's instrument icon:

1. Select the track to which you wish to give a new icon.

2. Open the Track Info window.

3. Click the icon button.

   The icon menu appears (**Figure 3.58**).

4. Click the desired replacement icon to select it. Use the scroll bar, if necessary, to view the entire collection of icons.

✔ Tips

■ The icon menu can be tricky to work with. Click the icon button and then release the mouse button. The menu will stay open, and you can scroll through the whole set. If you change your mind and decide that you don't want to pick a new icon, just move the mouse away from the menu and click. The menu will close with no changes made.

■ Don't continue to press the mouse button after clicking the icon button. Pressing the mouse button makes it easier to select a random icon inadvertently and prevents you from using the scroll bar.

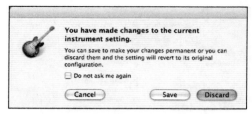

Figure 3.57 This dialog gives you an opportunity to save any changes you made to an instrument preset.

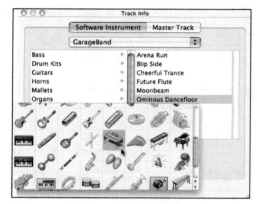

Figure 3.58 The instrument icon menu.

How Many Tracks Can I Use in My Song?

Each track you add to your song consumes a sizeable portion of your Mac's RAM, so try not to add unnecessary tracks. By default, GarageBand automatically limits the number of tracks available to you, taking into account the properties of your machine and the type of tracks you include in your song. The only way to find out what the limit is on your particular hardware is to bump into it by trying to add too many tracks. When you do, you'll get an alert (**Figure 3.59**), and GarageBand will refuse to carry out your last New Track command. On my 1 GHz G4 PowerBook, for example, with 1 GB of RAM, GarageBand maxes out at 16 Software Instrument tracks and 32 Real Instrument tracks.

GarageBand has your best interests at heart, of course, and is trying to help you keep the complexity of your songs to a level that your computer can handle. If you want to live dangerously and circumvent GarageBand's limits, you can change the Maximum Number of Tracks settings in GarageBand's Preferences.

1. Choose GarageBand > Preferences (Command-,).
   The Preferences dialog opens.

2. Click the Advanced button to display the Advanced pane (**Figure 3.60**).
   By default, the Maximum Number of Tracks is set to Automatic for both kinds of tracks.

3. Choose a new setting from the Real Instrument Tracks and/or Software Instrument Tracks pop-up menu (**Figure 3.61**).

4. Close the dialog.

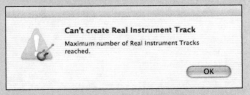

Figure 3.59 You've reached the maximum allowable Real Instrument tracks. The alert you see when you hit the limit of Software Instrument tracks is similar.

Figure 3.60 The Advanced pane of the GarageBand Preferences dialog.

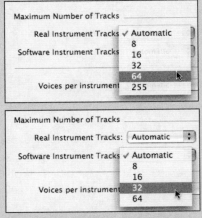

Figure 3.61 Setting the maximum number of Real Instrument tracks (top) and Software Instrument tracks (bottom).

CHANGING A TRACK'S INSTRUMENT

WORKING WITH LOOPS

Loops are short snippets of recorded music that are designed to fit together seamlessly. GarageBand ships with a large library of loops, so you can get started making music immediately, without the need for any special hardware other than your Mac.

In this chapter, you'll learn:

- What Apple Loops are and why they're so great.

- Several techniques for finding the perfect loop for your song among the thousand or so loops that are installed with GarageBand.

- How to audition loops before using them in your song.

- How to add Real Instrument and Software Instrument loops to your composition.

- How to add more loops to your library.

- How to create your own loops.

About Apple Loops

In general, loops are short, prerecorded pieces of music that are made so they fit smoothly together in sequence or so they can be repeated to create longer pieces of music.

What sets the Apple Loops that come with GarageBand apart from garden-variety loops is *metadata*. Metadata, here, is textual information that has been inserted into the file headers of Apple Loops. Without this metadata, a loop file would look like just an ordinary sound file to your computer. The metadata, however, includes loads of useful information about the sound file, such as the type of instruments recorded in the file, the style of the music in the file, and the music's key, tempo, and time signature. GarageBand maintains an elaborate index of the metadata for all the loops in its library. When you add a loop to the library, GarageBand adds its metadata to the index.

This metadata adds enormously to the usefulness of Apple Loops. It means that if you decide you want a loop with a techno beat in A that lasts eight bars, you don't have to test every single loop in the program to find one. Instead, you can use powerful search features built into GarageBand to turn up just the right loop in seconds.

Another cool feature of Apple Loops is that they have markers attached to each beat. This means that you can add a loop to your song even if it was recorded at a different tempo. Its beat structure will adjust to your song's tempo without gaps or distortion.

GarageBand includes Apple Loops of both Real Instrument and Software Instrument types. You can add Real Instrument loops to Real Instrument tracks, and Software Instrument loops to tracks of either type. Once added to your song, both types of loops behave just like Real Instrument and Software Instrument material you recorded yourself.

About the Loop Browser

Sifting through the thousands of loops that come with GarageBand to find just the right one for your song can be an intimidating task. Fortunately, the program provides a nifty tool for the job: the loop browser (**Figure 4.1**).

The loop browser allows you to sort your loops using the keywords embedded in the Apple Loops installed with the program. You progressively narrow your search for specific loops based on three criteria:

◆ Genre (or style)

◆ Instrument

◆ Mood

If you've bought one or more of the GarageBand Jam Packs, or if you've downloaded any of the myriad loops available online, your loop library may be so vast that searching for a specific loop seems like a hopeless task. Good news! GarageBand 2 lets you limit your search to a part of your collection.

The left part of the loop browser is taken up with the search interface, and the results of your search are displayed on the right, in a list that shows each loop's name and its type, tempo, key, and number of beats. You can also use the search results listing to mark frequently used loops as favorites for quick access. And the loop browser lets you preview, or audition, loops so you can try them out with your song.

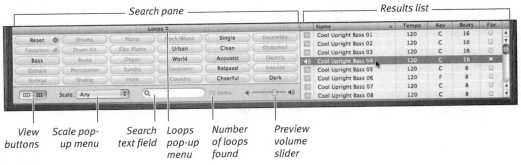

Figure 4.1 The loop browser.

Displaying the Loop Browser

When you first start GarageBand, the loop browser is hidden to allow more room for tracks in the timeline, but it's easy to display.

To display the loop browser:

◆ If the loop browser is hidden, *do one of the following:*

   ▲ Click the Loop Browser button, near the bottom of the GarageBand window (**Figure 4.2**).

   ▲ Press Command-L.

The Loop Browser button glows blue, and the loop browser itself slides into view (**Figure 4.3**).

To hide the loop browser:

◆ Click the Loop Browser button or press Command-L.

The loop browser goes back into hiding.

Figure 4.2 The Loop Browser button.

Figure 4.3 The loop browser appears.

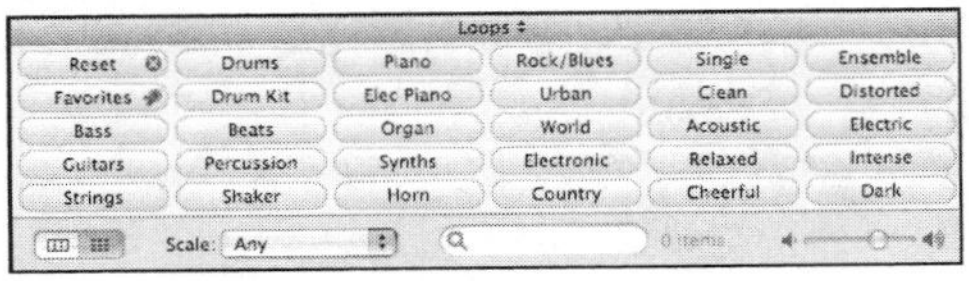

Figure 4.4 The loop browser in button view.

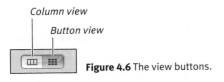

Figure 4.5 The loop browser in column view.

Column view

Button view

Figure 4.6 The view buttons.

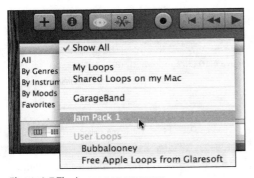

Figure 4.7 The Loops pop-up menu.

About the Loop Browser Views

The search pane (left side) of the loop browser has two viewing modes:

◆ Button view displays an array of buttons, each bearing a keyword (**Figure 4.4**).

◆ Column view sorts keywords using a three-column format resembling the Finder's column view (**Figure 4.5**).

Use the view buttons in the lower-left corner of the browser to choose a view (**Figure 4.6**).

✔ Tip

■ If you have installed libraries of loops produced by Apple or acquired from third-party developers, you may wish to simplify your search by limiting it to loops contained within one of those libraries. GarageBand 2 provides a simple means for accomplishing this: the Loops pop-up menu at the top of the loop browser's search pane (**Figure 4.7**). I'll explain the organization of this menu in more detail later in the chapter, after we've talked about adding more loops to GarageBand (see "Choosing the Loops the Loop Browser Displays").

Using Button View to Find Loops

In button view, you click keyword buttons to narrow the list of available loops. The first button you click brings up a long list of loops in the results list. Each succeeding button you click reduces the number of loops displayed. You can start with any button and click other buttons in any order, so button view encourages free-form searching. Note that as you click buttons, others become dimmed. This means there are no loops that share those two characteristics—there are no loops that share the keywords *Country* and *Strings*, for example.

To find loops using button view:

1. *Optional:* Open the Loops menu and choose a loop collection (Figure 4.7).

2. Click the button to switch to button view (Figure 4.6).

3. Click a keyword button that character-izes the kind of loop you're looking for (**Figure 4.8**).

   The button you clicked glows blue, and buttons with incompatible keywords are dimmed. A list of loops appears in the results pane of the loop browser (**Figure 4.9**). The number of loops in the list appears beneath the buttons.

4. You can choose a loop at any time from the results list, or you can continue to click buttons with keywords that describe your desired loop to narrow the search (**Figure 4.10**).

   Notice that the number of loops found shrinks with each button click.

5. Once the list of results produces the loop you want, add the loop to your song (see "Adding a Loop to Your Song" later in this chapter).

Figure 4.8 Preparing to click a keyword button.

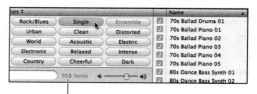

Number of loops found

Figure 4.9 After clicking, the button is selected, and the results list shows loops described by the keyword.

Figure 4.10 Click more buttons to narrow your search.

Figure 4.11 Click the Reset button to start searching from scratch.

✔ Tips

■ To deactivate a button you have clicked, click it again. It returns to its original state.

■ To start a fresh search, click the Reset button to deselect all of the buttons you clicked in the course of the previous search (**Figure 4.11**).

Figure 4.12 The keyword contextual menu.

Figure 4.13 Navigate through the menu hierarchy and choose a new keyword.

Figure 4.14
The button, now graced with a different keyword.

Figure 4.15
Starting to drag the button to move it.

Figure 4.16
Poised over the new position.

Figure 4.17
The keywords swap places.

Customizing Button View

GarageBand's collection of Apple Loops contains more keywords than there are buttons in the loop browser. Indeed, to save space, the loop browser doesn't even ordinarily display all of its buttons at once, but you can expand the loop browser to see more buttons (see the sidebar "Expanding the Loop Browser to See More Buttons" later in this chapter). You can reassign keywords to buttons to make sure that the keywords you use most often are available. You can also arrange keywords in the order that works best for you. And if you make a mess of things, you can use GarageBand's Preferences dialog to put the keywords back in their original places.

To change the keyword on a button:

1. Control-click the button whose keyword you wish to replace.

   A contextual menu appears, showing the types of keywords available (**Figure 4.12**).

2. Choose the type of keyword you want to assign to the button and then choose a new keyword from the submenu (**Figure 4.13**).

   The new keyword is assigned to the button (**Figure 4.14**).

To move a keyword to another button:

1. Drag the button whose keyword you wish to move over another button (**Figure 4.15**).

   The target button will darken when the button you're dragging is in the right position (**Figure 4.16**).

2. Release the mouse button.

   The two keywords exchange places (**Figure 4.17**).

To restore keywords to their original locations:

1. Choose GarageBand > Preferences (Command-,) to open the Preferences dialog (**Figure 4.18**). If the General pane is not visible, click the General button.

2. Click the Keyword Layout: Reset button.

   A warning dialog appears, asking whether you're sure that you want to continue (**Figure 4.19**).

3. *Do one of the following:*

   ▲ Click Yes to continue. The keywords will be reset to their original configuration.

   ▲ Click No to cancel the operation. The keywords will be left as they are.

4. Click the Close button (Command-W) in the Preferences dialog to close it.

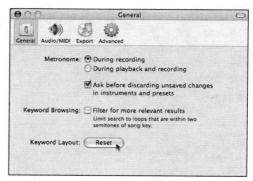

Figure 4.18 The GarageBand Preferences dialog, showing the General pane.

Figure 4.19 One last chance to make up your mind.

Expanding the Loop Browser to See More Buttons

Not only does the loop browser have fewer buttons than keywords, it doesn't even display all of the buttons it has when you first open it. By default, 30 buttons are shown (including the Reset and Favorites buttons), but the complete loop browser holds 66 buttons. That's 12 more than GarageBand 1 gave you! Plus the assortment of buttons now includes some blank ones for keywords that Apple didn't think of.

Here's how to see them all:

1. Move the mouse pointer to the area that divides the timeline from the loop browser. Stay to the left of the Record button or to the right of the time display. The pointer changes into a hand (**Figure 4.20**).

2. Drag upward to reveal more rows of buttons. You can display up to nine rows (**Figure 4.21**).

   If you stop dragging while a row is partially visible, the browser will snap to the next complete row.

Figure 4.20 Position the mouse pointer above the loop browser.

Figure 4.21 When you drag upward, more buttons are revealed.

Using Column View to Find Loops

Column view provides a more guided approach to searching for loops. The first column shows the three general keyword types (plus All and Favorites). The columns at the right narrow down the list of keywords, and clicking an item in the rightmost column results in a list of loops.

To find loops using column view:

1. *Optional:* Open the Loops menu and choose a collection of loops (Figure 4.7).

2. Click the button to switch to column view (Figure 4.6).

3. Click a keyword type in the left column to select it (**Figure 4.22**).

   The type you selected in the left column becomes the heading of the middle column, which displays the categories available within that type (**Figure 4.23**).

4. Click one of the categories in the middle column to select it.

   The item you selected becomes the heading for the third column, which lists the keywords available within that category (**Figure 4.24**).

5. Click one of the keywords in the third column to see a list of loops that satisfy the criteria you selected in the second and third columns. The number in parentheses indicates the number of loops that will be listed (**Figure 4.25**).

   The loops that have made it through the sorting process appear in the results list.

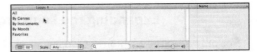

Figure 4.22 Click one of the types in the left column.

Figure 4.23 The categories within that keyword type appear in the second column.

Figure 4.24 Select a category to see a list of keywords.

Figure 4.25 Finally, click a keyword to generate a list of matching loops.

✔ Tip

- To see a broader range of loops in the results list, you can select multiple keywords in the third column. Shift-click two keywords in the list to select a range of keywords, or Command-click to select noncontiguous keywords. Apple's documentation says that you can also select multiple categories in the second column, but that doesn't seem to work in the shipping software.

Having Trouble Finding Loops?

When you open the loop browser, you sometimes may find many of the buttons dimmed even before you start sorting. Or in column view, when you click a category in the second column, nothing may show up in the third column.

There are two possible causes:

◆ GarageBand may be hiding loops whose original keys are far removed from the key of your song. Although the program can transpose any loop to your song's key, not all such key shifts are desirable. For example, if your song is in D and you add a trumpet loop that was originally in A, the loop has to be transposed downward seven semitones. The loop will not only change pitch, but will also change substantially in color. It may not even sound much like a trumpet any more!

By default, GarageBand is set to show you only loops whose original keys are within two semitones (a whole step) of the song's key. If you want to turn off this protective behavior, you need to visit GarageBand > Preferences (Command-,) and click the General button. Uncheck the box next to Keyword Browsing: Filter for More Relevant Results (**Figure 4.26**). Now GarageBand won't restrict your loop browsing based on key.

◆ If your song uses a time signature other than 4/4, very few loops will show up in the loop browser. Indeed, if you choose one of the more exotic time signatures, like 5/4 or even 2/2, you may see no loops at all. The situation improves somewhat if you purchase and install one or more of the supplemental GarageBand Jam Packs. Among the thousands of loops each one adds to your library, a few are in these unusual time signatures, but for now, if you plan to do a lot of composition with loops in GarageBand, stick to 4/4.

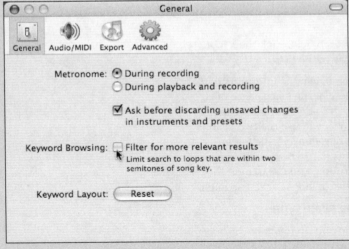

Figure 4.26 Uncheck the Keyword Browsing box to get a wider choice of loops.

Finding Loops by Other Methods

GarageBand allows you to augment your search for the perfect loop with a few auxiliary techniques. You can search for loops with specific text in the name or path (the categories and keywords GarageBand uses to classify loops). Or you can look for loops that are compatible with certain types of scales (major, minor, neither, or both) to narrow the list to loops that are more compatible with the scale your song uses.

You can use either of these methods instead of the button and column search methods or to further refine the results you get from those techniques.

To find loops by using a text search:

◆ In the search field (identified by the magnifying glass icon) at the bottom of the loop browser, type the text you are looking for and press Return (**Figure 4.27**).

Loops whose name or path includes the search text will appear in the results list (**Figure 4.28**).

✔ Tips

■ To clear the search field, click the *x* icon at the right side of the field.

■ The GarageBand Help file interprets *path* as it is used here in the usual sense of "the hierarchy of folders containing a file" and says that you can use the text search to find all the files in a specific folder. Alas, this seems not to be true. In my testing, performing a text search on the name of a folder of loops turned up zilch.

To find loops by scale type:

◆ From the Scale pop-up menu at the bottom of the loop browser, choose the type of scale you prefer (**Figure 4.29**).

Loops that do not match the selected scale type will be removed from the results list.

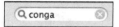

Figure 4.27 Type search text in this field.

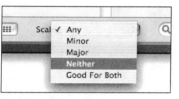

Click here to clear the search text field

Figure 4.28 Matching loops appear in the list.

Figure 4.29 The Scale pop-up menu.

Figure 4.30 Use the Loops menu to limit your searches to a part of your loop library.

Restricting the Loop Browser Display

GarageBand ships with well over a thousand Apple Loops. If you purchase and install any of the Jam Packs, each one adds more than 2000 loops to the library. Furthermore, there are many music sites on the Web that offer loops as free downloads or sell collections at reasonable prices.

As you can see, it's not difficult to amass a sizeable library of loops, and the more loops you have, the harder it is to find just the right one for your song. But never fear— GarageBand 2 introduces a loop-management tool that is sheer genius in its simplicity: the Loops pop-up menu (**Figure 4.30**), accessed from the top of the loop browser's search pane. When searching for loops, you use the Loops menu to restrict your search to a specific collection of loops within your loops library.

The contents of the Loops menu will vary, depending on the sorts of loops you have installed. The specific items on the menu may also differ according to the My Apple Loops preference setting that was active when you installed the loops (see "To set access permissions for user-installed loops" later in this chapter).

The following items won't change, no matter how your permissions are set for the loops library:

Show All (the default): Every loop installed in your loops library is fair game.

GarageBand: Only those loops originally installed with the program will appear in your search.

Jam Pack 1, 2, 3, or 4: Choosing any of these limits your search to loops contained in that collection.

continues on next page

Other loops you installed while your preferences were set to Share with All Users on This Mac will show up in these portions of the menu:

Shared Loops on My Mac: Single loops added to your loop browser and stored in /Library/Audio/Apple Loops/User Loops/Single Files.

User Loops: Whole folders added to the loop library at once; their storage location is /Library/Audio/Apple Loops/User Loops.

Other: Aliases to folders of loops on the same partition as GarageBand.

Loops you installed while your preferences were set to Available to [*user name*] Only can be accessed by means of these menu items:

My Loops: Loops added individually to the loop browser and stored in: ~/Library/Audio/Apple Loops/User Loops/Single Files.

Other: Folders (and aliases to folders) of loops in ~/Library/Audio/Apple Loops/User Loops.

To choose which loops are displayed in the loop browser:

1. Open the Loops pop-up menu (**Figure 4.31**).

2. Choose the collection of loops you wish to search (**Figure 4.32**).

   The Loops menu displays the name of the collection you have chosen (**Figure 4.33**). The loop browser now includes only loops from that collection.

Figure 4.31 The Loops pop-up menu is perched atop the loop browser.

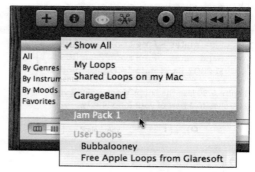

Figure 4.32 Choose the collection you want to search.

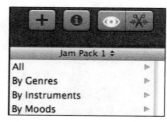

Figure 4.33 The menu displays the name of the collection of loops you chose.

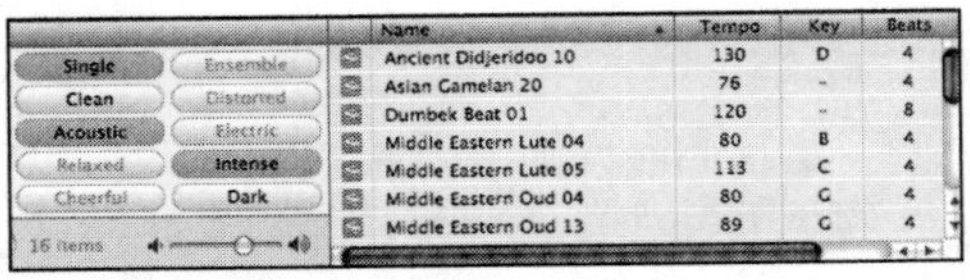

Figure 4.34 The results list.

Working with the Results List

Whether you use the button view or the column view to sort GarageBand's loops, the loops that make it through the winnowing process are listed in the results list, at the right side of the loop browser (**Figure 4.34**). The number of loops in the list is shown to the right of the text search field.

By default, the loops found are listed alphabetically by name. Other columns show the original tempo and key and the length, measured in beats, of each loop. There's also a check box that allows you to designate loops you like as "favorites." Each listing includes an icon that distinguishes Real Instrument loops (a blue waveform) from Software Instrument loops (a green eighth note). You can re-sort this list using any of the columns and invert any column's sorting order.

If you want to listen to a loop before plopping it into your song, click its name in the list. And when you're ready to add a loop to your composition, you drag it from this list into the timeline.

Sorting the Results List

By default, the loops in the results list are sorted by name, but you can also sort the list on any of the other columns as well:

◆ Software or Real Instrument

◆ Tempo

◆ Key

◆ Beats (length)

◆ Fav (whether the loop has been marked as a favorite)

You can also change the sort order for any column. The sort order is indicated by a tiny triangle at the right side of the header of the active column. If the triangle points upward, the column will sort in ascending order. If the triangle points downward, the column will sort in descending order.

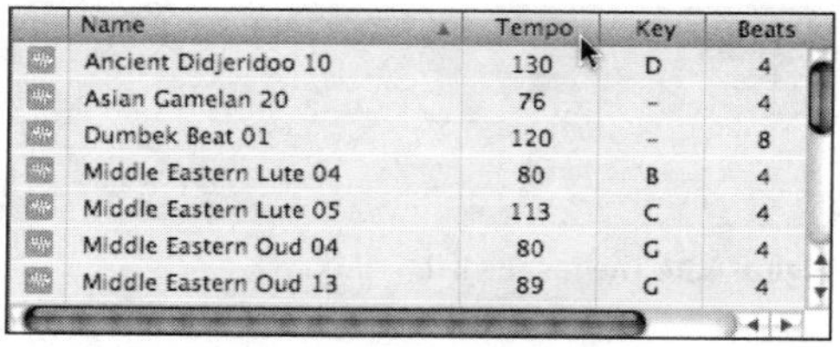

To sort the results list:

◆ Click the heading of the column on which you want to sort the list (**Figure 4.35**).

GarageBand re-sorts the list (**Figure 4.36**).

To change the sort order of a column:

◆ Click the header of the currently active column (Figure 4.36).

The column's sort order is inverted (**Figure 4.37**).

Figure 4.35 Clicking the Tempo column header to re-sort the list based on tempo.

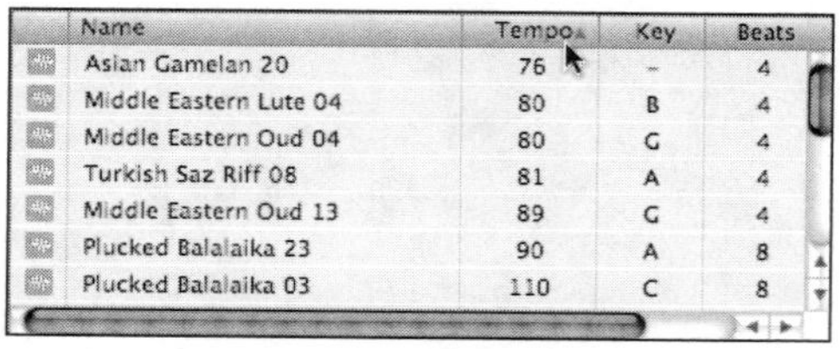

Figure 4.36 The list is now sorted by tempo, in ascending order.

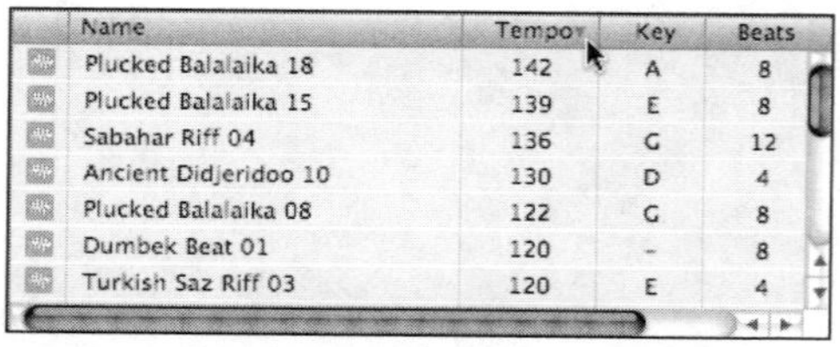

Figure 4.37 After you click the Tempo header again, the list is sorted in descending order.

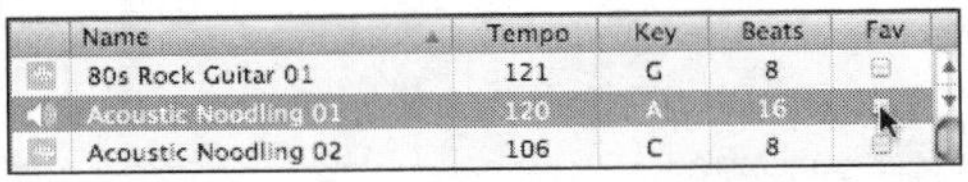

Name		Tempo	Key	Beats	Fav
	80s Rock Guitar 01	121	G	8	
	Acoustic Noodling 01	120	A	16	
	Acoustic Noodling 02	106	C	8	

Figure 4.38 Click the Fav box to mark the loop as a favorite.

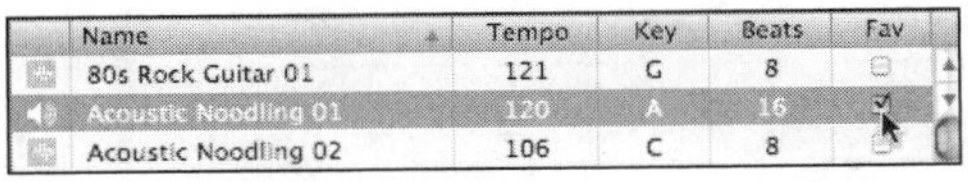

Name		Tempo	Key	Beats	Fav
	80s Rock Guitar 01	121	G	8	
	Acoustic Noodling 01	120	A	16	✓
	Acoustic Noodling 02	106	C	8	

Figure 4.39 Now the loop will appear in the Favorites category.

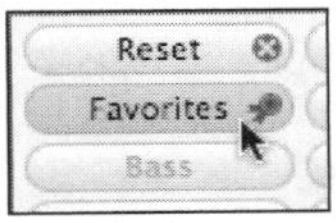

Figure 4.40 The Favorites button.

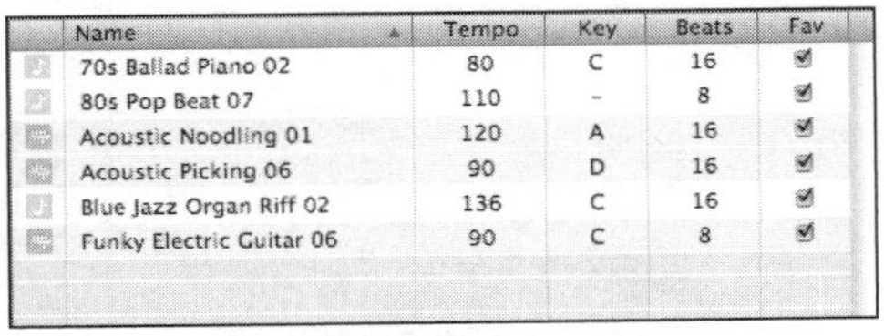

Name		Tempo	Key	Beats	Fav
	70s Ballad Piano 02	80	C	16	✓
	80s Pop Beat 07	110	–	8	✓
	Acoustic Noodling 01	120	A	16	✓
	Acoustic Picking 06	90	D	16	✓
	Blue Jazz Organ Riff 02	136	C	16	✓
	Funky Electric Guitar 06	90	C	8	✓

Figure 4.41 Your favorite loops are listed.

Marking Loops as Favorites

If you find yourself using certain loops over and over again, you can save yourself the trouble of searching for them each time by declaring them as *favorites*. Each favorite loop has its own keyword that brings the loop to the surface quickly when you're browsing in either button view or column view. These favorites are not song specific—they'll show up as favorites in every song you work on in GarageBand.

To mark a loop as a favorite:

◆ Find the loop in the loop browser and make sure it is visible in the results list. Click the loop's check box in the Fav column (**Figure 4.38**).

A check appears in the Fav box, denoting it as a favorite (**Figure 4.39**).

To find favorite loops in button view:

◆ Make sure button view is active; then click the Favorites button (**Figure 4.40**).

The loops you have marked as favorites appear in the results list (**Figure 4.41**).

✔ Tip

■ The Favorites button is available in the loop browser only if you have marked some loops as favorites. Otherwise, it's dimmed.

To find favorite loops in column view:

1. Make sure the loop browser is displayed in column view; then click Favorites in the Loops column.

   A list of the keyword categories that include favorite loops appears in the second column (**Figure 4.42**).

2. Click a category in the Favorites column.

   A list of the keywords associated with favorite loops appears in the third column (**Figure 4.43**).

3. Click a keyword in the third column.

   The favorite loops associated with that keyword appear in the results list (**Figure 4.44**).

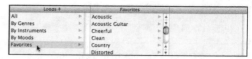

Figure 4.42 Clicking Favorites in the first column displays categories that contain favorite loops.

Figure 4.43 Clicking one of these categories generates a list of keywords.

Figure 4.44 Click a keyword to see a list of favorite loops categorized under that keyword.

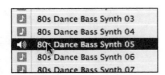

Figure 4.45 Click a loop in the results list to listen to it.

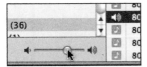

Figure 4.46 Drag the slider to adjust playback volume.

Auditioning Loops

As The Bard said, "What's in a name?" You can't tell if a loop is right for you just from its name; you need to listen to it. Once loops appear in the results list, you can click them to hear how they sound. Apple calls this *previewing* a loop, but that seems an odd word to use for a nonvisual activity; *audition* seems like a more appropriate word.

You can audition a loop by itself or try it with the song playing in the background. No matter what tempo and key are given for a loop in the results list, they will always match the tempo and key of the song when you audition it.

To audition a loop in the loop browser:

1. Click the loop's name in the results list (**Figure 4.45**).

   The loop will start to play, and its icon will change to a loudspeaker. The loop's tempo and key will be synchronized with those of the song.

2. To adjust the playback volume of the loop, drag the volume slider in the loop browser (**Figure 4.46**).

3. To stop playback, click the loop's listing again.

✔ Tip

■ If you change a loop's volume while auditioning it and then drag the loop to a new track in the timeline, that track inherits the loop's volume setting. If you drag the loop to an existing track, the loop uses the volume setting of the existing track.

AUDITIONING LOOPS

Adding a Loop to Your Song

Once you've found a loop you like, you can add it to your song's timeline by dragging it from the list produced by your search. The left edge of the loop snaps to the nearest downbeat (the first beat of a measure). Alternatively, you can drag a loop to the track header, and GarageBand will place the loop at the beginning of the song.

You can drag the loop to a pre-existing track of the appropriate kind, or you can create a new track. Adding a loop to the timeline creates a region from the loop. Any changes you make to the region do not affect the original loop (see Chapter 8 to learn about editing regions). The tempo and key of this new region automatically adapt to the tempo and key of the song.

Real Instrument loops can be placed only in Real Instrument tracks. Software Instrument loops, on the other hand, can be placed in tracks of either type; however, if you drag a Software Instrument loop to a Real Instrument track, GarageBand converts it to a Real Instrument region. You can also have GarageBand convert any Software Instrument loop to a Real Instrument region. This is desirable because (as we've discussed before) Software Instruments put quite a strain on your Mac's processor. Converting them to Real Instruments gives GarageBand some breathing room.

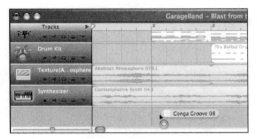

Figure 4.47 Dragging a loop to the timeline.

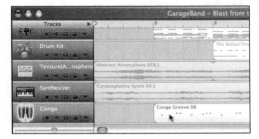

Figure 4.48 A new track is added to the song.

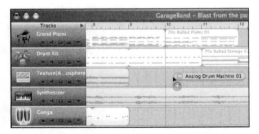

Figure 4.49 The green plus icon and gray vertical bar show you that you're in the right place.

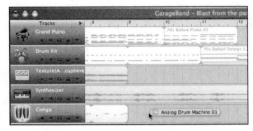

Figure 4.50 If the plus icon and gray bar are missing, you're in the wrong neighborhood.

To add a loop to your song while creating a new track:

1. Drag a loop of either type (Real or Software Instrument) to the blank area of the timeline (**Figure 4.47**).

   As your pointer enters the timeline, a gray vertical bar appears, indicating the downbeat where the start of the loop will be placed.

2. Release the mouse button when you find the right spot.

   A new track is created below the pre-existing tracks (**Figure 4.48**). By default, the new track is of the same type (Real or Software Instrument) as the loop, and it takes its instrument, icon, effect, and input settings from the loop as well.

To add a loop to a pre-existing track:

1. *Do one of the following:*

   ▲ Drag a Real Instrument loop to a Real Instrument track.

   ▲ Drag a Software Instrument loop to a track of either type.

   If you are dragging the loop over the correct type of track, the pointer will have a green plus (+) icon attached (**Figure 4.49**), and a gray vertical bar will appear, indicating the downbeat where the start of the loop will be placed. If these items are missing, you're over the wrong kind of track (**Figure 4.50**).

2. When you find the right location for the loop, release the mouse button to add the loop to the track.

   The loop will snap to the location of the vertical gray bar.

Let's Get Real!

To convert a Software Instrument loop to a Real Instrument loop on the fly, hold down the Option key while dragging the loop to the empty part of the timeline (this feature was added in GarageBand 1.1). A new Real Instrument track will be created, containing the loop you dragged from the loop browser.

If you want this to happen every time you create a new track by dragging a Software Instrument loop to your song, there's a Preferences setting designed just for you. Choose GarageBand > Preferences (Command-,) and click the Advanced tab. Check the Adding Loops to Timeline: Convert to Real Instrument box and close the Preferences dialog (**Figure 4.51**). To reverse this setting temporarily, hold down the Option key while dragging a Software Instrument loop to the timeline.

Figure 4.51 With the Convert to Real Instrument box checked, dragging a Software Instrument loop into the empty part of the timeline will always create a new Real Instrument track.

Region Names

When you drag a Real Instrument loop to the timeline and drop it into place, a new region is created. Each new region is named after the loop that it's derived from, with a numerical suffix appended.

The first time you drag Blip Synth 01 into your song, for example, the region added to the target track is named Blip Synth 01.1. If you add the same loop to your song again, the resulting region will be Blip Synth 01.2. Names of additional instances of the same loop will continue to be incremented by 0.1 (**Figure 4.52**). The same thing happens if you copy a region and paste it into a song: the name of the pasted region will be incremented by 0.1.

Software Instrument loops that are dragged into Real Instrument tracks receive the same treatment; they are, after all, turned into Real Instrument regions by the action (**Figure 4.53**). This is not true for Software Instruments added to Software Instrument tracks, however; all instances of Software Instrument regions have the same name (**Figure 4.54**).

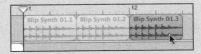

Figure 4.52 Each time the same loop is added to a Real Instrument track, the name of the resulting region is incremented by 0.1.

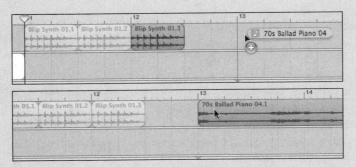

Figure 4.53 Software Instrument loops become Real Instrument regions and are named like other Real Instrument regions.

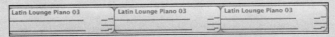

Figure 4.54 All instances of Software Instrument regions have the same name.

Adding More Loops to GarageBand

In large part due to the popularity of GarageBand, the supply of Apple Loops is growing rapidly. GarageBand can also use any loops made for Soundtrack (which also uses the Apple Loop format). You can add individual loop files to GarageBand or a whole folder full at once. A new Preference setting in GarageBand 2 allows you to choose whether newly added loops are available to all users of your machine or only to the user who added them.

To set access permissions for user-installed loops:

1. Choose GarageBand > Preferences (Command-,) and click the Export tab (**Figure 4.55**).

2. In the My Apple Loops area of the dialog, *choose one of the following:*

   ▲ Available to [*user name*] Only.

   This option stores user-installed loops in ~/Library/Audio/Apple Loops/User Loops. These loops will be available only to the user who was logged into the Mac at the time the loops were installed. This is GarageBand's default setting.

   ▲ Share with All Users on This Mac.

   If this option is selected, user-installed loops will be placed in /Library/Audio/Apple Loops/User Loops. This collection of loops will be available to any user of your Macintosh.

Figure 4.55 Use this dialog to specify who gets to use your loops.

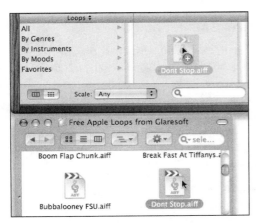

Figure 4.56 Drag the loop file's icon into the loop browser.

Figure 4.57 If adding loops from GarageBand's partition, choose whether to move the loops or keep them where they are.

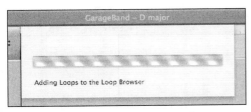

Figure 4.58 If adding loops from another partition, choose whether to copy the loops into the library or keep them in their current location.

Figure 4.59 GarageBand may take several minutes to finish the process of copying and indexing the added loops.

To add Apple Loops to GarageBand:

1. Make sure that the Finder icon for the loop file (or folder of loops) is visible.

2. Drag the file (or folder) icon into the loop browser (**Figure 4.56**).

   Depending on the location of your loops, one of two dialogs will open.

3. *Do one of the following:*

   ▲ If your loops are already stored on the partition where GarageBand is installed, the Adding Loops to the Loop Browser dialog will appear (**Figure 4.57**); choose Move to Loops Folder (or press Return) to move the files into GarageBand's loop library, choose Current Location to leave the loop files where they are but place an alias to them in the loop library, or choose Cancel to do nothing.

   ▲ If your loops are on a different partition from GarageBand, the Adding Loops from Another Disk or Partition dialog will appear (**Figure 4.58**); choose Copy to Loops Folder to make copies of the loops in the loop library but leave the originals where they are, choose Current Location to leave the loop files where they are but place an alias to them in the loop library, or choose Cancel to do nothing.

   Depending on your choice in the preceding dialog, GarageBand will add the loops to the Apple Loops library and incorporate the information about the loops in the index (**Figure 4.59**).

Using Non-Apple Loops in GarageBand

Apple's marketing materials and the GarageBand 2 documentation both insist that the program now accepts loops in ACID format. This is the granddaddy of loop formats, originally devised for a Windows-only loop-composition program: ACID Pro (now owned by Sony). Like Apple Loops, ACID loops support extensive metadata, so they can easily be categorized by key, tempo, mood, instrument, and so on.

However, I have not yet been able to import an ACID loop into GarageBand and have it appear in the loop browser. This seems to be a feature that is not quite ready for prime time. While we wait for Apple to fix this problem, there is a workaround:

1. Drag the ACID loop from the Finder to the GarageBand timeline (either to a Real Instrument track or to a trackless part of the timeline) and release the mouse button (this is the standard procedure for importing an audio file into a GarageBand song, which will be described in Chapter 13).

   The ACID loop will become an ordinary Real Instrument region.

2. With the newly imported region still selected, choose Edit > Add to Loop Library and follow the procedure outlined in "To create an Apple Loop" later in this chapter.

You'll have better luck with this process if you set the song to the same tempo as the ACID loop before choosing the Add to Loop Library command. Many times, the filename of a loop contains its original tempo (in beats per minute). If you don't know the original tempo of the loop, adjust the tempo of your song until the imported loop takes up exactly an integral number of measures—that is, it starts on the downbeat of a measure and ends precisely at the downbeat of another measure.

Another method for converting ACID loops to Apple Loops is to use the Soundtrack Loop Utility (see the sidebar "Industrial-Strength Loop Creation" later in this chapter).

Figure 4.60 This region will be turned into a loop.

Figure 4.61 Dragging a Real Instrument region to the loop browser.

Figure 4.62 The Add Loop dialog.

Creating Your Own Loops

The original version of GarageBand didn't include any facility for creating loops. If you weren't satisfied with the loops provided, you were pretty much left to the mercy of third-party vendors. You did have the option of cooking up some loops of your own, but only if you were willing to struggle with the complexities of the Soundtrack Loop Utility (see the sidebar "Industrial-Strength Loop Creation" later in this chapter).

Happily, GarageBand 2 provides a basic tool for converting just about any recording to an Apple Loop: the Add to Loop Library command.

To create an Apple Loop:

1. Select the region in your song that you wish to convert to a loop (**Figure 4.60**).

2. *Do one of the following:*
   ▲ Choose Edit > Add to Loop Library.
   ▲ Drag the region to the loop browser and release the mouse button (**Figure 4.61**).
   The Add Loop dialog slides down from the main window's title bar (**Figure 4.62**).

3. In the Name field, type a name for the loop. By default the loop takes the name of the region from which it was made.

continues on next page

CREATING YOUR OWN LOOPS

4. Choose a type for the loop:

▲ Choose Loop to create an Apple Loop whose speed will expand and contract along with the song's tempo.

▲ Choose One-shot for sounds that don't need to match a song's tempo, like sound effects.

Note that if the selected region is not an integral number of measures long, these choices will be dimmed, and One-shot will be selected automatically.

5. From the Scale pop-up menu, choose Major or Minor if the loop clearly uses one of those scales. Otherwise, choose one of the other options (**Figure 4.63**).

6. From the Genre pop-up menu, choose the term that best describes the style of the loop (**Figure 4.64**).

7. In the Instrument Descriptors area, choose a category from the list on the left; then choose a specific instrument from the list on the right (**Figure 4.65**).

The information from the original region is selected by default.

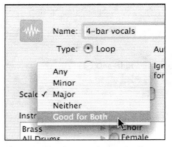

Figure 4.63 Choose the scale that most closely matches the loop.

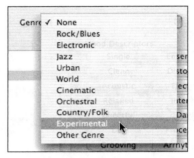

Figure 4.64 Choose the genre that fits the loop best.

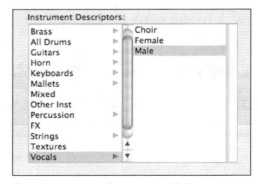

Figure 4.65 Match an instrument to the loop.

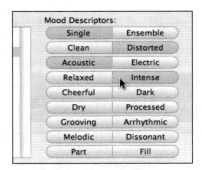

Figure 4.66 Characterize the overall feeling of the loop by assigning mood descriptors.

8. In the Mood Descriptors area, click one or more buttons that describe the emotional character of the loop (**Figure 4.66**).

These buttons are equivalent to the keywords used to sort loops in the loop browser.

Note that you can click only one button of each pair. If you click Single, for example, and then click Ensemble, the Single button will be deselected.

9. Click Create or press Return.

10. If you happen to give your new loop the same name as an existing loop, you'll be presented with the Loop Name Already Exists dialog (**Figure 4.67**). *Do one of the following:*

▲ Click Do Not Add This Loop to cancel the loop creation.

▲ Click Add Loop Using a New Name to add the loop to your library. A numeral will be added to the end of the loop's name to distinguish it from the original loop with the same name.

▲ Click Replace Original with New Loop (or press Return) to delete the pre-existing loop with the same name and save the new loop to your library.

Depending on your selection, the loop is added to your loop library.

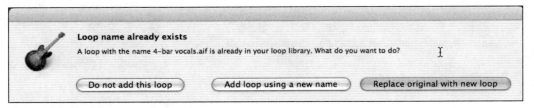

Figure 4.67 The Loop Name Already Exists dialog.

Industrial-Strength Loop Creation

If you've tried GarageBand's built-in loop-creation tool, but you feel like you need more control over the process, you can use the same program the big kids use: Apple's Soundtrack Loop Utility (SLU) (**Figure 4.68**). This application will convert any AIFF or WAV file to an Apple Loop. The SLU is bundled with the Soundtrack application, but if you don't own that program, you can get the SLU from Apple free of charge. Download the Apple Loops SDK from ftp://ftp.apple.com/developer/Development_Kits/.

Run the installer contained in the downloaded file, and it will put the Soundtrack Loop Utility in your /Applications/Utilities folder. The installer will also place some thorough documentation in /Developer/Apple Loops SDK.

The SLU has loads more bells and whistles than the Add Loop dialog in GarageBand—meaning that learning to use it will require a correspondingly greater investment of time and energy. You'll find an excellent tutorial on using the Soundtrack Loop Utility at maczealots.com/tutorials/loops/.

Figure 4.68 The main interface for Apple's Soundtrack Loop Utility.

HARDWARE FOR RECORDING

If you want to go beyond composing with Apple Loops and include original material in your songs, sooner or later you'll have to deal with hardware. It's certainly possible to sink a lot of money into creating a first-class recording studio, but it's not necessary. You can have a lot of fun creating music with GarageBand and produce fine-sounding results with a modest outlay of your hard-earned cash.

This chapter doesn't attempt to cover the universe of music hardware in encyclopedic fashion. I describe the general types of equipment available and then zero in on specific features that are of use to GarageBand artists. In the course of the chapter, you'll learn about:

◆ Hardware for recording audio.

◆ The different types of microphones.

◆ What to look for in a computer audio interface.

◆ Hardware for recording MIDI data.

◆ MIDI controllers.

◆ What to look for in a MIDI keyboard.

◆ What to look for in a MIDI interface.

About Hardware

Audio recording (for Real Instrument tracks) is completely different, technically speaking, from recording MIDI data (for Software Instruments), and in the past, you needed separate equipment for each. Nowadays, with the continuing advances in the miniaturization of electronic circuitry, you can find some components that can be used for both tasks.

Hardware for Recording Audio

The hardware requirements for computer-based audio recording can be boiled down to two fundamental items:

◆ An audio source.

◆ An audio interface.

The audio source can take any of a number of forms; it can be an electric guitar (or any guitar with a pickup), or a microphone in front of a singer, or an electronic keyboard. The audio source takes the sound produced by the singer or instrument and converts it to an electronic signal. The signal is still in analog form, however, and for the computer to be able to record the sound, the signal has to be translated into digital information that the computer can understand. That's where the audio interface comes in. It's a piece of hardware that converts the original analog sound wave into digits. This component can be either inside your Mac or in a box connected to your Mac via a USB or FireWire cable.

Most modern Macintoshes come with some kind of hardware for digitizing analog audio built in as standard equipment. If you have one of these machines, you can use a $1/4$-inch-to-miniplug adapter cable (available for a few dollars at any electronics store) to plug your electric guitar directly into your Mac's audio-in port. That's about the simplest recording setup imaginable. Likewise, you can buy a basic stereo microphone for under $100 to record acoustic instruments or small ensembles (just make sure it's self-powered and puts out a line-level signal). But if you don't have an electric guitar, or if you want to record input from more than two sources at once, there are many other options available to you.

continues on next page

In the first edition of this book, it was a relatively simple task to talk about audio hardware, because the original version of GarageBand was limited to very basic two-track recording. Multitrack audio interfaces were of no use, and thus an extravagance.

One of the earth-shaking innovations in GarageBand 2, however, is the ability to record on more than two tracks at once—up to eight audio tracks and one MIDI track, in fact. Equipment that will allow you to indulge in this luxury, however, is significantly more expensive than two-track equipment, and I suspect that most people using a $79 piece of music software will hesitate before making a huge investment in music hardware. But I'll lay out the options for you anyway.

HARDWARE FOR RECORDING AUDIO

Audio Sources

Audio sources fall into two general categories:

◆ Performer and microphone.

◆ Instrument with electronic audio output.

Microphones

For recording musical instruments that don't have an audio-out port (such as acoustic guitars, saxophones, percussion instruments, and human beings), a microphone is indispensable. A really good microphone will make a significant difference in the quality of your recording. Even if you're assembling the rest of your studio on a shoestring, buy the best mike you can possibly afford.

Keep in mind that a microphone puts out a tiny signal, much smaller than that produced by electronic instruments like guitars and synthesizers. You need to plug the mike into another component called a *pre-amplifier*, or *pre-amp* for short. This boosts the microphone's output to the same level as the output from a guitar or synthesizer, which is called a *line-level* signal. Pre-amps are often separate units, but some mixers and audio interfaces have pre-amps integrated into them.

There is great variety among microphones, not only in terms of quality and fidelity of music reproduction, but also in terms of suitability to task. For example, some mikes are great for voices in live performance, and some work better for recording voices in the studio. Some are good for capturing the nuances of acoustic guitar sound, but are overwhelmed by the violent attack of a drumstick on a cymbal.

continues on net page

AUDIO SOURCES

Microphones use an extremely thin membrane called a *diaphragm* (usually made of plastic or Mylar) to pick up sound waves in the air. The resulting vibrations of the diaphragm are converted to electrical impulses by a mechanism called a *transducer*. Microphones are commonly classified according to the type of transducer they incorporate. The two most common types of transducer in use today are *dynamic* and *condenser*.

◆ **Dynamic:** In dynamic microphones, the diaphragm is attached to an object that conducts electricity, such as a coil of wire. This coil is suspended between two magnets, so that when the diaphragm (with its attached coil) vibrates in response to a sound wave, an electric current flows through the coil.

Dynamic mikes are resilient and are good at handling high sound-pressure levels (SPLs). You'll often find them onstage in rock concerts, because they can handle loud percussion attacks, hard-driven guitar amps, and equally hard-driving vocalists. They also stand up to physical abuse well.

As you might guess from the preceding description, dynamic mikes aren't terribly subtle in terms of sonic reproduction. They produce a sound that is sometimes called "gritty" rather than warm and nuanced.

◆ **Condenser:** A condenser microphone's diaphragm is suspended in front of a metal plate, and a constant voltage is applied across the gap, creating an electric field. Sound waves cause the diaphragm to vibrate, producing ripples in the field, which, in turn, cause a current to flow.

Figure 5.1 A condenser microphone.

The diaphragms in condenser mikes have less mass than those in dynamic mikes and so are more easily moved by sound waves. As a result, condenser mikes are better at picking up the fine details of a sound and are more sensitive to high frequencies. Because condenser microphones more faithfully reproduce the original sounds, they tend to be popular in recording studios (**Figure 5.1**).

On the other hand, their greater sensitivity can make them tricky to work with, because they're not only sensitive to the subtleties of music, but also to stray noises that may afflict your recording session. They're also more fragile than dynamic mikes—you don't want your performers bumping into them.

One last point: condenser mikes need a constant source of juice to maintain that electrical field. Most mikes can be battery powered, but batteries always run out just when you need them most. Many mikes will also run on *phantom power*, which is supplied through the microphone cable by some pre-amps, mixers, and audio interfaces.

Other audio sources

By "other audio sources," I mean electronic instruments that have audio-out ports.

Digital pianos and other keyboard synthesizers (or samplers) fit into this category. You can also buy electric pickups for violins, cellos, mandolins, and other stringed instruments. But the most common electronic instrument is the electric guitar or bass. To record an electric guitar in GarageBand, simply unplug the guitar from its amp and then plug that same cable into an audio interface. GarageBand's Real Instruments include effects settings that reproduce several types of guitar amp, so you have a wider range of sound available than if you used just your physical amp.

Audio Interfaces

An audio interface performs one basic function: it converts the analog signal from your audio source to a digital signal that your computer can understand. The audio interface receives the analog signal either from your pre-amp or by direct input from an electronic instrument such as an electric guitar or synthesizer.

Choosing an audio interface

At the core of any audio interface is the *analog-digital converter*, or *ADC*. This is the circuitry that does the heavy lifting of sampling the audio waveform many times per millisecond and converting the results to numbers. The more often it samples the wave, the more accurately the numbers it comes up with describe the original sound. The number of times the ADC samples the wave each second is referred to as the *sampling rate* and is expressed as a frequency, in kilohertz (thousands of samples per second), abbreviated kHz.

It's also important to know the ADC's maximum *resolution*. This value tells you how precisely the ADC measures the sound wave while taking each sample. Resolution is described in terms of the number of binary digits, or *bits*, in the resulting measurement; 24-bit resolution, for example, is more precise than 16-bit resolution.

Which Macs Have Audio-In Ports?

In April 2002, after a long period of absence, audio-in ports began to reappear on Apple's professional computers (and the eMac). The first iMacs included them in February 2003, and by September all iMac models had audio-in ports. Alas, iBooks have always been free of audio-in hardware.

Recent models with audio-digitizing hardware include the following:

PowerBooks

◆ All PowerBooks with G4 processors, except for the very first 400/500 MHz titanium models introduced in January 2001

Desktop Macs

◆ Power Macintosh G4 (mirrored drive doors)

◆ Power Macintosh G4 (FireWire 800)

◆ Power Macintosh G5 (all models)

iMacs

◆ iMac (early 2003) (1 GHz model only)

◆ iMac (USB 2.0)

◆ iMac G5

All eMac models

AUDIO INTERFACES

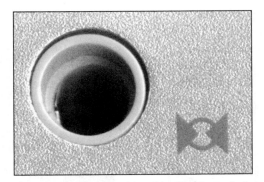

Figure 5.2 The icon shown here identifies the audio-in port on your Macintosh.

Built-in audio

As mentioned earlier, most recent Macs have audio digitizing capability built in (**Figure 5.2**). This built-in audio hardware is certainly convenient, but it has its limitations.

First, the ADCs built into current Macintosh systems max out at 16-bit resolution. This is adequate for basic recording purposes—for instance, to digitize an old LP or cassette that you plan to burn to CD or convert to MP3 and store in iTunes. It's also just barely adequate for GarageBand, because GarageBand supports only 16-bit recording. But this hardware doesn't leave you any headroom, nor will it be able to grow with you when your needs change in the future.

Second, the audio connector on these Macs accepts a line-level connection, meaning that you can't hook up a really high-quality microphone directly to your computer. You need to connect it to a pre-amp or mixer first. There are self-powered microphones (like the Sony ECM-MS907) that output a line-level signal, but they're not recommended for serious studio recording.

Third, the audio-in ports on these Macs use $\frac{1}{8}$-inch connectors, called *mini-jacks*, which do not provide top quality. Tiny connectors like these, which may be fine for Walkman headphones, are inadequate for truly high-quality signal transmission. Most of the components used for audio recording employ somewhat more substantial connectors and cables, which impede current flow less and provide more shielding from outside sources of interference. To connect your instrument, mixer, or pre-amp to one of these mini-jacks, you need an adapter, and adapters degrade signal quality as well.

And finally, and of most significance to GarageBand 2, the audio-in ports built into

continues on next page

AUDIO INTERFACES

Macs are limited to two channels. They won't do you any good if you plan to take advantage of GarageBand's new multitrack recording powers.

When choosing a third-party audio interface, the first decision is: internal or external?

Internal interfaces

Internal interfaces (also called *soundcards*) are installed either in a PCI slot in desktop machines (**Figure 5.3**) or, less commonly, in the PC Card/CardBus slot of a laptop. An internal interface saves you some space on your desk (and in your laptop bag), but has some disadvantages. The inside of your computer is a noisy place, electronically speaking, and internal audio interfaces are subject to interference from the other components inside the machine. Also, soundcards communicate with the outside world only through a narrow slot in the back (or side) of your Mac, which doesn't leave room for large, high-quality audio connectors.

Further, it's hard to share a soundcard among multiple computers. If you like to do some of your recording on a desktop Mac at home, but you also like to use your PowerBook as the hub of a portable studio while you're on the road, an external audio interface is probably what you're looking for.

External interfaces

An external audio interface is basically a box containing the same circuitry as an internal audio interface. Confusingly, you will find that many people use the term *soundcard* for this piece of equipment, just because the legacy of internal audio hardware is so strong. Because an external enclosure has more elbow room than a PCI slot, external audio interfaces often sport more rugged connectors (and more of them) than do soundcards (**Figure 5.4**).

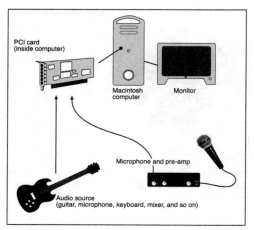

Figure 5.3 A typical desktop-based studio, using a PCI-slot audio interface.

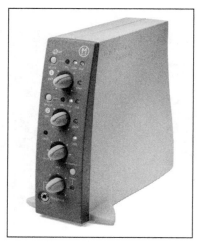

Figure 5.4 The Digidesign Mbox, a bus-powered USB audio interface with two analog inputs, two microphone pre-amps, phantom power, two analog outputs, 24-bit resolution, and more. (Photo courtesy of Digidesign.)

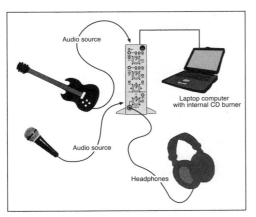

Figure 5.5 A typical two-track laptop-based recording studio, using a USB-connected audio interface incorporating microphone pre-amps.

Figure 5.6 The Mark of the Unicorn 828mkII, a FireWire audio interface with eight analog inputs and MIDI ports.

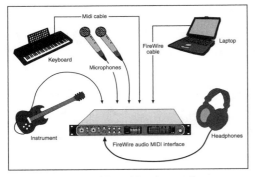

Figure 5.7 One possible multitrack recording setup, designed around a FireWire interface.

Once upon a time, external audio interfaces required that you install an accompanying proprietary card in your computer to mediate between the two devices. Nowadays, external audio interfaces connect to your Mac by means of either USB or FireWire.

◆ **USB:** The USB (or Universal Serial Bus) standard was originally designed for connecting computers to humdrum peripherals like keyboards (of the QWERTY variety) and mice and as a consequence supports only a relatively low data rate. But it turns out that that data rate is just sufficient to carry one or two tracks of digitized audio—perfect for recording two mono inputs or a single stereo pair of microphones (**Figure 5.5**).

◆ **FireWire:** Apple originally developed the FireWire bus standard (also known as IEEE 1394b) to provide a high-bandwidth data path for connecting hard drives to computers. With a throughput about 40 or 50 times the rate of USB, audio interfaces that connect via FireWire can easily handle multiple tracks of recorded data simultaneously (**Figure 5.6**). If you want to take advantage of the multitrack recording capabilities of GarageBand 2, you'll need a FireWire interface, which, alas, costs quite a bit more than a USB interface (**Figure 5.7**).

Features to look for in audio recording equipment

Audio equipment marketing materials emphasize long lists of features. Here are a few features that you'll actually find to be useful in either internal or external interfaces:

◆ **24-bit/96 KHz:** An ADC that digitizes audio with a sampling rate of 44.1 kHz at 16-bit resolution will do just fine for compact discs and GarageBand, but that

continues on next page

leaves you very little headroom for processing. The newly emerging standard for digital audio uses 24-bit resolution and a 96-kHz sampling rate for greater fidelity, dynamic range (the difference between the loudest and softest sounds), and signal-to-noise ratio. If you're serious enough about recording to buy a new audio interface, get one with a 24-bit/96Khz ADC, so whenever you're ready to graduate to more sophisticated software, your equipment won't hold you back.

◆ **Microphone pre-amps:** If your audio interface incorporates microphone pre-amps, that will save you having to buy, store, and schlep around a separate box. And as long as you're looking for an interface with pre-amps, check to see whether it has phantom power, too, to keep your condenser mikes running happily without batteries. Because of space constraints, it's rare to find pre-amps in an internal interface.

◆ **Bus power:** Both USB and FireWire buses carry a little extra current along with the data stream, which can be used to provide connected devices with power. Bus power can save you from having to lug around yet one more item of equipment: the power brick.

◆ **MIDI connectors:** If you plan to record to both Real and Software Instrument tracks in your GarageBand compositions, having MIDI connectors built into your audio interface saves you from the need to acquire one more box.

◆ **Drivers:** Okay; they're not really amenities but necessities. Before you buy any audio interface, make sure that drivers are available for it that are compatible with the version of Mac OS X you're running. Look for equipment that brags that it supports CoreAudio. That's the component of Mac OS X that handles digital audio data.

Figure 5.8 A MIDI port. For a photo of some MIDI ports, see Figure 5.11.

Hardware for Recording Software Instruments

Recording into a Software Instrument track has simpler hardware requirements than recording into a Real Instrument track. Stripped down to its basics, the process needs:

◆ A MIDI controller.

◆ A MIDI interface.

MIDI controllers are devices that usually mimic the appearance and operation of "normal" musical instruments but output no sound, just MIDI data (see "Real vs. Software Instrument Tracks" in Chapter 3 for an introduction to MIDI). A controller needs another piece of equipment to produce sound—for instance, your Mac running GarageBand. You can also connect a controller to an external *sound module*, which contains circuitry for generating tones from samples or by synthesizing them. MIDI keyboards can also be combined with tone-generating hardware into a single instrument. These *MIDI synthesizers* can be used as stand-alone instruments, but are much more expensive than simple controllers.

MIDI devices and MIDI cables use a distinctive type of connector not found in Macintosh hardware (**Figure 5.8**), so another piece of equipment, the *MIDI interface*, is needed to mediate between the controller and your Mac. A MIDI cable connects the MIDI controller to the MIDI interface, which in turn is connected to your Mac via a USB (or more rarely, a FireWire) cable. It is becoming more common for MIDI controllers to include simple MIDI interfaces. This interface allows you to plug your MIDI keyboard directly into a USB or FireWire port on your Mac, eliminating yet another box from your desk.

HARDWARE FOR SOFTWARE INSTRUMENTS

MIDI controllers

Most MIDI controllers are keyboards, and in fact, keyboards are the only controllers mentioned in GarageBand's documentation or marketing materials. MIDI controllers can take other forms, however; for instance, some MIDI controllers are in the shape of guitars, some look and play just like wind instruments, and others imitate drums. Even though GarageBand is silent on the subject, any controller that complies with the MIDI standard should work with GarageBand, and there are anecdotal reports from a few brave souls who have successfully used non-keyboard controllers with GarageBand.

Keyboards

I'll concentrate on MIDI keyboard instruments since they're usually easier for beginners to handle. They're also cheaper than the other varieties by a long shot. Keyboards come in a range of sizes, with a variety of bells and whistles available (**Figure 5.9**). If you're a two-handed keyboard player, you'll probably want a keyboard with 49 or 61 keys (four and five octaves, respectively). Keyboard controllers that match the piano's range of 88 keys exist, too, but they cost significantly more and take up more of that precious workspace. Beginners who just want a tool for playing simple melodies into GarageBand may be happier with a two-octave model.

No matter how many keys you decide on, be sure that the keys are full-size—that is, the width and depth of piano keys. You'll see a lot of cheap keyboards with synthesizers and speakers built in but with tiny keys. They're frustrating to play, and also they normally don't have MIDI ports, so they're of no use to GarageBand as MIDI controllers.

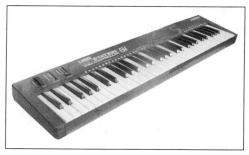

Figure 5.9 A five-octave (61-note) MIDI controller keyboard.

And speaking of keys, MIDI keyboard controllers can have several different types of key action, which provide varying levels of responsiveness (as well as varying levels of cost):

◆ **Synth action:** This is the simplest mechanism. The key is merely a switch and provides no tactile feedback.

◆ **Weighted action:** When you press a key, you feel some resistance, akin to the feeling of playing a piano keyboard. There are different technical means of accomplishing this; the most expensive instruments use actions identical to those in grand pianos.

Other characteristics to look for in a keyboard include:

◆ **Touch sensitivity:** Sometimes called velocity sensitivity; a keyboard with touch sensitivity can record the pressure with which you press the key. In MIDI terms, this is the note's *velocity*, and it translates into volume when played through a Software Instrument. This feature is fairly common in MIDI controllers nowadays.

◆ **Aftertouch:** Some keyboards respond to the pressure of your finger on the key after the note is initially struck or to the way you remove your finger from the key. This response can affect the way the sound changes during a long note, or the end of the sound once the key is released. It's a feature not often found on inexpensive keyboards.

continues on next page

HARDWARE FOR SOFTWARE INSTRUMENTS

Keyboards often have more than just keys. Many have controls that let you add inflection to your performance. GarageBand supports MIDI data for the properties of *pitch bend*, *modulation*, *sustain*, and *expression*, and you can adjust the values for these qualities in the track editor (see Chapter 10 to learn about the track editor). GarageBand also supports data from an additional foot control, whose specific function is set by your keyboard's software or by your MIDI application.

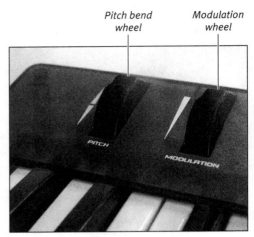

Pitch bend   Modulation
wheel   wheel

Figure 5.10 Pitch bend and modulation wheels on a MIDI keyboard.

◆ **Pitch bend:** Many keyboards include a wheel that allows you raise or lower the pitch by tiny amounts (**Figure 5.10**). This technique is known as *bending* the pitch, and if you bend the pitch of a note while recording a Software Instrument in GarageBand, the amount of bend is also recorded.

◆ **Modulation:** The modulation wheel colors your instrument's sound by adding varying degrees of vibrato (or another kind of tone color) depending on how far you roll the wheel. Some Software Instruments offer sophisticated tonal variations that you can use the modulation wheel to access. For example, in GarageBand Jam Pack 4: Symphony Orchestra, the modulation wheel allows you to choose different styles of articulation in the string section, ranging from legato through staccato all the way to pizzicato, with stops along the way for various kinds of trills. For more about the Jam Packs, see Appendix B.

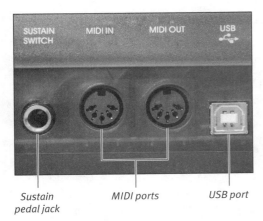

Sustain pedal jack   *MIDI ports*   *USB port*

Figure 5.11 Connectors on the back of a MIDI controller with an integrated MIDI interface, showing MIDI In and MIDI Out ports, a USB port, and a jack for connecting a sustain pedal.

◆ **Sustain:** Most keyboards have a connector that allows you to attach a sustain pedal, which acts just like the pedal of the same name on a piano. If you play a key, hold down the sustain pedal, and then release the key, the note will continue to sound as long as your foot is on the pedal.

◆ **Expression:** More sophisticated keyboards may have one or more additional connectors for foot-operated devices. One of the most common of these is a connector for an expression pedal, which allows you to make subtle volume changes while playing the instrument.

MIDI interfaces

As mentioned earlier, a MIDI interface is a piece of equipment that allows MIDI devices to connect to computers. It can be as simple as a cable with a pair of MIDI In/Out connectors at one end and a USB connector at the other, with some electronics contained in a bulge somewhere around the middle. For GarageBand, that's probably all you need. In fact, chances are good that it's more than you need, because many newer models of MIDI keyboard incorporate MIDI interfaces, so you can connect the keyboard directly to your Mac with a USB cable (**Figure 5.11**).

If you need to connect multiple MIDI instruments to your Mac simultaneously, you can spend more money and get an interface with two, four, or eight sets of MIDI In and Out ports. Some of these devices will connect to your Mac via FireWire, whose greater bandwidth can more easily handle multiple channels of data. Remember, however, that GarageBand can record only one Software Instrument track at a time, so the data from all of your instruments will be condensed into a single track and use the sound of one Software Instrument.

Features to look for in MIDI equipment

When choosing MIDI equipment, look for the following features. Some of these will be familiar from our discussion of audio recording equipment.

◆ **Bus power:** Devices that get their juice from the USB or FireWire bus don't need a separate power adapter.

◆ **Integration with audio:** If you can find a unit that combines a MIDI interface with an audio interface, you have one less piece of equipment to worry about.

◆ **Drivers:** Before you buy a piece of MIDI hardware, check to see that its manufacturer has updated its drivers for compatibility with the version of Mac OS X you're using.

A special note: Look for MIDI devices that say they are "USB-MIDI class compliant." That means that they use the default MIDI driver built into Mac OS X and don't need a separate driver.

Hardware for Playback

By default, when you click the Play button in GarageBand, your song plays back through the speakers built into your Mac. This experience is likely to prove disappointing, as these internal speakers are definitely lo-fi. You won't hear the full spectrum of tonal color produced by GarageBand's instruments, and your own performance will sound wan and anemic.

As long as you've gone to the trouble of adding a good audio interface to your setup, you should also invest in a good pair of speakers and/or headphones. Headphones are especially useful if you often record live performances. They let you monitor the recording without bothering the participants or the audience. They also let you work on your songs late at night and not disturb the neighbors.

Plug your speakers or headphones into the outputs of your audio interface (rather than directly into your Mac) so you can take advantage of the higher-quality audio circuitry. Internal audio interfaces don't always provide headphone jacks, but external interfaces do, almost without exception.

Setting Audio Preferences

After you've hooked up all this great equipment, you have to tell GarageBand to use it. For this task, use the Audio/MIDI pane of the GarageBand Preferences dialog to choose the devices to use for audio input and output. Fortunately, thanks to the native support for MIDI built into Mac OS X, GarageBand finds your MIDI devices automatically.

Preparing Hardware to Recognize GarageBand

Some audio interfaces work only with a specific set of applications. You may have to tell your audio device that it's okay to talk to GarageBand. If you think this may be the case, consult your hardware's documentation for more information.

The Digidesign Mbox is a case in point. Before it will work with GarageBand, GarageBand has to be added to its list of supported applications.

This is easy enough to do. Open the application CoreAudio Setup (it should be in the Digidesign folder along with Pro Tools LE) and click the Supported Applications button in the Digidesign CoreAudio Setup dialog (**Figure 5.12**).

In the Digidesign CoreAudio Supported Applications dialog, click Add New Application (**Figure 5.13**) and navigate to your copy of GarageBand. Select GarageBand and click the Choose button, and GarageBand will be added to the list of supported applications. Click Done two more times, and now you really are done!

Figure 5.12 The Digidesign CoreAudio Setup dialog.

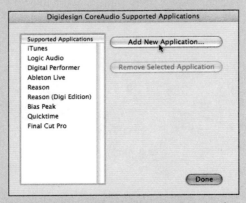

Figure 5.13 The Digidesign CoreAudio Supported Applications dialog.

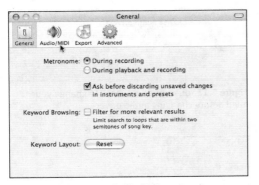

Figure 5.14 The General tab of GarageBand's Preferences dialog.

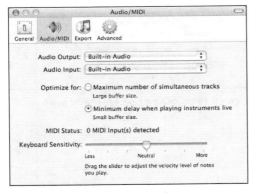

Figure 5.15 Setting audio input and output preferences for GarageBand.

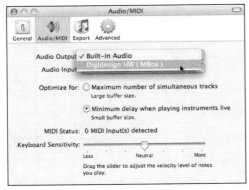

Figure 5.16 Choosing a device to use for audio output.

To choose audio devices:

1. Choose GarageBand > Preferences (Command-,).

   The Preferences dialog opens to the General tab (**Figure 5.14**).

2. Click the Audio/MIDI button to display the Audio/MIDI tab (**Figure 5.15**).

   By default, GarageBand is set to use your computer's built-in audio hardware for input and output.

3. From the Audio Output pop-up menu, choose the device you want to use for output (**Figure 5.16**).

continues on next page

SETTING AUDIO PREFERENCES

4. An alert appears, asking whether you really want to change audio drivers (**Figure 5.17**). Click Yes

After a delay, the new output is ready for use.

5. From the Audio Input pop-up menu, choose the desired input device (**Figure 5.18**).

6. In the Change Audio Driver? dialog, click Yes, and wait while the new driver is prepared.

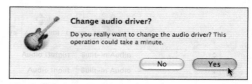

Figure 5.17 You're given a chance to change your mind before changing audio drivers.

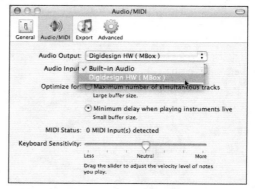

Figure 5.18 Choosing a device to use for audio input.

RECORDING REAL INSTRUMENTS

The process of recording Real Instruments in GarageBand is similar to that for Software Instruments, but different enough that I've provided a separate chapter for each procedure. There is some duplication between the chapters, but I decided it was better to make each one complete rather than use a lot of cross-references.

Once you have your audio equipment set up and connected to your computer, you're ready to record. Recording audio is pretty simple in GarageBand: just click the Record button, and whatever comes in through your audio inputs is captured on your computer's hard disk.

Before you click that button, you should check out some GarageBand features that will help you streamline your recording session. Here's what I cover in this chapter:

◆ Using the metronome to help you keep a steady beat while recording.

◆ Listening to your track while it's being recorded.

◆ Using the new instrument tuner.

◆ Setting the right track recording level.

◆ Recording new regions into Real Instrument tracks.

◆ Using a cycle region to re-record a portion of a recording.

About Recording in GarageBand

As I said, it's easy to record in GarageBand. And it's even easier to make a recording in GarageBand 2 than in the original version. In GarageBand 1, you could record into only one stereo track or two mono tracks at a time. GarageBand 2, on the other hand, lets you record up to eight stereo or mono tracks simultaneously, provided that you have the hardware to support that many tracks.

If you wanted to make a multitrack recording of your band with GarageBand 1, with drums in one track and guitar in another and a vocalist in another, you had to record the tracks one at a time. This took a lot of the fun and spontaneity out of the whole band experience.

Alternatively, you could have set up a pair of microphones in front of the band (or mike each performer individually and run the mikes through a mixer) and recorded the band's performance into a single track. But in that case, which Real Instrument would you have assigned to the track? You could record into a basic track, but then you lost out on one of GarageBand's coolest features: the preset effects settings that define each Real Instrument.

Of course, if your audio interface has only two inputs, which is commonly the case, you're still going to be recording the old GarageBand 1 way. But now, if you can afford the cash for a gizmo with umpteen inputs, you have much more flexibility in setting up your recording. You can record each member of your band onto a different track and assign different effects to each track, but you can do it with everyone playing together in real time. This makes for a much more satisfying musical experience.

But no matter what the class of your audio machinery, and even if your "band" consists of just you and your instruments, GarageBand is an incredibly powerful creative tool. In fact, the program is designed with the solo musician in mind. Thanks to GarageBand's ability to handle several types of musical materials (loops, audio recording, and MIDI data), a musician working alone can have a lot of fun producing richly textured songs with GarageBand. One way to go about it is to start by laying down a percussion track constructed from loops. Next, using a MIDI keyboard, record a bass line into a Software Instrument track. Finally, record a Real Instrument track while playing guitar; or record yourself singing and add piano or guitar chords later, using another Software Instrument track.

GarageBand doesn't assume that you're going to record entire tracks at once. Each time you record a take, you create a *region* within a track (or tracks). A region can be any length, from a few notes to a whole song. You can record as many regions in a track as you want, and you can start recording at any point in the timeline. This gives you tremendous flexibility: you can record small pieces of a song as inspiration strikes and then arrange them into a larger composition when you're ready (you'll learn how to do that in Chapter 8).

ABOUT RECORDING IN GARAGEBAND

Using the Metronome

To help you play or sing in time, GarageBand provides a metronome. While you record, it ticks away at the tempo you set for your song. You can set the metronome to play either only during recording or during both recording and playback.

To give yourself a running start, you can also set the metronome to play for a full measure, or *count-in*, before you start recording.

To use the metronome:

◆ Choose Control > Metronome (Command-U) to place a check mark next to the item (**Figure 6.1**).

The check mark indicates that the metronome is enabled. When you click the Record button, the metronome will play a sound on each beat of your song.

To turn off the metronome:

◆ Choose Control > Metronome (Command-U) to uncheck the item.

The metronome will no longer play during recording.

To have the metronome play a count-in before recording:

◆ Choose Control > Count In to place a check mark next to the command (**Figure 6.2**).

When you click the Record button, the metronome will play for a complete measure before recording begins.

To disable count-in:

◆ Choose Control > Count In to uncheck the item.

The metronome will not play before recording starts.

Figure 6.1 The check mark indicates that the metronome is on.

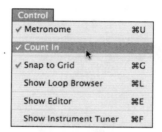

Figure 6.2 Setting the metronome to play a full measure before starting to record.

✔ Tip

■ If you use the metronome while recording, it's best to listen to your Mac's audio output through headphones. Otherwise, your microphones are likely to pick up the sound of the metronome, and its ticking will leak into your recording.

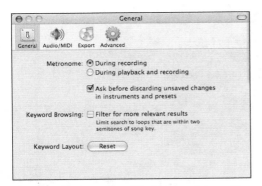

Figure 6.3 The GarageBand Preferences dialog, with the General pane open.

To set preferences for the metronome:

1. Choose GarageBand > Preferences (Command-,).

   The Preferences dialog opens, displaying the General pane (**Figure 6.3**).

2. *Choose one of the Metronome options:*

   ▲ Select During Recording to have the metronome play only while the Record button is pressed.

   ▲ Select During Playback and Recording to have the metronome play both while recording and during playback.

Monitoring

It's very helpful to practice playing or singing your part while listening to the parts of a song that are already assembled. GarageBand also lets you hear yourself, or *monitor* your track, as you play along with the rest of the song. With monitoring turned on, you can hear what your instrument or voice sounds like after filtering through your equipment and into GarageBand. The best part is that you get to hear exactly what is being recorded into the track you have selected.

You can turn monitoring on or off when you first create a track, and you can also change this setting at any time using the Track Info window.

To set monitoring for a track:

1. Select the track into which you want to record (**Figure 6.4**).

2. Open the Track Info window (Command-I) (**Figure 6.5**).

3. Open the Monitor pop-up menu and *do one of the following:*
   - ▲ Choose Off to disable monitoring.
   - ▲ Choose On to enable monitoring.

Figure 6.4 Selecting a track.

Figure 6.5 The Track Info window, showing the Monitor menu.

✔ Tips

- ■ Turn off monitoring while you're not actively recording or rehearsing. If you have a microphone or an instrument connected to your computer while monitoring is on, it can pick up playback from your speakers, resulting in nasty feedback.

- ■ If you're using microphones as part of your recording setup, don't turn on monitoring for the tracks into which the microphones record unless you are going to use headphones, rather than speakers, to monitor your performance. Again, if the microphones pick up the playback from your speakers, you'll hear some wicked feedback.

Figure 6.6 The instrument tuner, showing a large green light in the center; this indicates that the instrument being played is in tune.

Using the Instrument Tuner

A handy new feature included in GarageBand 2 is an instrument tuner. It takes the form of a simple pitch meter that mimics colored LEDs to show whether a note is sharp or flat or in tune (**Figure 6.6**). You can use the tuner to tune any instrument connected to your computer, and a singer can use it with a microphone to polish his or her intonation.

When the tuner is on, it listens for audio input from the selected track. The tuner analyzes the sound and figures out which note is being played and displays it at the left side of the tuner. The meter itself takes up most of the tuner. If the note being played is exactly in tune, a fat green light appears in the center of the meter. If the note is flat or sharp, a skinny red light blinks to the left or right (respectively) of center. The farther the red light is from the center, the more out of tune the note is. The scale is calibrated in *cents* from –50 to +50. There are 100 cents in a semitone, so each end of the scale represents a pitch a quarter-tone out of tune. That's enough to curl your hair!

The tuner works only for Real Instruments, not for Software Instruments. It also works only for individual notes—no chords, please. You can't use the tuner during recording, only when GarageBand is idle or playing back a recording.

To use the Instrument Tuner:

1. Connect the instrument you want to tune to your computer.

2. Select a track whose input is connected to the instrument.

3. Turn off monitoring for the track (see the previous section, "To set monitoring for a track").

continues on next page

USING THE INSTRUMENT TUNER

4. To turn on the instrument tuner, *do one of the following:*

▲ Choose Control > Show Instrument Tuner (Command-F).

▲ Click the tuner icon (the ghostly tuning fork) at the upper left of the time display (**Figure 6.7**).

The tuner icon glows bright blue to show that the instrument tuner is activated.

5. Play a single note on your instrument; observe the lights on the instrument tuner and *do one of the following:*

▲ If a red light appears to the left of center, the instrument is flat (**Figure 6.8**). Raise the pitch of the instrument until the light in the center of the tuner glows green (Figure 6.6).

▲ If a red light appears to the right of center, the instrument is sharp. Lower the instrument's pitch until the center light turns green.

6. When you are finished using the instrument tuner, *do one of the following:*

▲ Choose Control > Hide Instrument Tuner (Command-F) to return the time display to its previous mode (absolute or musical time).

▲ Click one of the time display icons (either the clock or the eighth-note) to switch the time display to a specific mode (**Figure 6.9**).

Figure 6.7 Left: Click this icon to enable the instrument tuner. Right: The glowing tuning fork tells you that the instrument tuner is ready to go.

Figure 6.8 The red light is to the left of center, showing that the instrument is flat.

Figure 6.9 Click one of these icons to restore the time display.

About Setting the Recording Level

A general rule of recording is to record your signal at the highest (or "hottest") level (or volume) possible without causing distortion, or *clipping*. In GarageBand, use the level meters in each track's mixer panel to monitor the track's level. If the level reaches the clipping range frequently, you need to lower your recording level.

In fact, it's a very good idea to set the input level for your track before you start to record. You can test for potential clipping problems by playing or singing a few of the loudest passages from your song and watching the track level meters. Adjust your track's input so that the highest levels cause the red lights to blink briefly, but not to stay lit.

Using the Track Level Meters

The track level meters indicate signal volume levels with a row of colored lights. Low signals activate only a few lights; high signals make the meter light up all the way across. When the signal hits a momentary peak, the light farthest to the right that was activated stays illuminated for an instant longer than the others (**Figure 6.10**), helping you monitor the general strength of the signal without having to pay attention to every tiny fluctuation in the meters.

Most of the lights are green. These indicate that the signal is coming in at a safe level. The lights at the extreme right end of the meter are orange and then red, to alert you that the signal is becoming dangerously high. If the signal reaches the point of distortion, the *clipping indicator* lights up and turns red. This indicator is a separate dot just beyond the end of the meter (**Figure 6.11**). It will stay lit for the rest of the session in case your attention happened to be directed elsewhere when the clipping occurred. Lower the strength of your input signal until the clipping indicators stay dark the whole time (see the next section, "Setting Input Levels").

Once you've fixed the problem that caused the clipping indicators to come on, you should turn the indicators off again, so they can alert you to the next occurrence of clipping.

To reset the clipping indicators:

◆ Click a pair of clipping indicators that have turned red (**Figure 6.12**).
   They go dark.

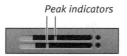

Figure 6.10 The track level meters, showing the peak indicators.

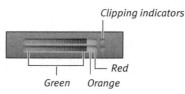

Figure 6.11 The track level meters during an episode of clipping. The extremely high level of the incoming signal has lit up the entire length of the meters, and the clipping indicators have been triggered.

Figure 6.12 Resetting the clipping indicators.

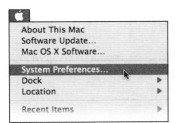

Figure 6.13 The System Preferences command on the Apple menu.

Figure 6.14 The System Preferences application opens.

Input Level indicators

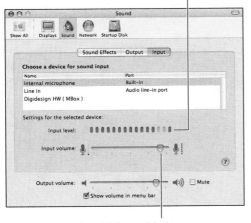

Input Volume slider

Figure 6.15 The Input tab of the Sound pane. The Input Level indicators show that the incoming signal is dangerously close to clipping.

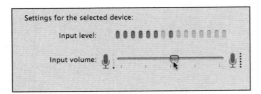

Figure 6.16 Adjusting the Input Volume slider.

Setting Input Levels

Use the controls on your audio interface to adjust the input level of your track. If you have an internal interface (such as a PCI card), you'll probably have to make the adjustment in the software that came with your interface using a control panel or dialog. If you are recording through your Mac's built-in audio-in port (or a PowerBook's internal microphone), use the Sound pane in System Preferences to set your recording level.

To set the input level using System Preferences:

1. From the Apple menu, choose System Preferences (**Figure 6.13**).

   The System Preferences window opens (**Figure 6.14**).

2. Click the Sound button to open the Sound pane.

3. If the Input pane is not visible, click the Input tab (**Figure 6.15**).

4. Play or sing and watch the Input Level indicators. If you notice that the indicators frequently light up all the way across the scale, then clipping is occurring.

5. Adjust the Input Volume slider until the indicators just barely touch the right edge of the scale in the loudest passages (**Figure 6.16**).

6. Close the System Preferences window.

Using the Track Mixer Volume Slider

You may be tempted to use the volume slider in the track mixer to adjust the track's level to compensate for clipping. While recording, however, it's far better to leave the track's volume slider at its 0 dB (zero decibel, or neutral) level and adjust the signal level at an earlier point in the signal path, usually in the audio interface.

Figure 6.17 Preparing to reset the volume slider.

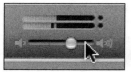

Figure 6.18 The volume slider at the 0 dB level.

The track mixer volume slider is best used later in the process, at the mixing stage. At that point, when you've finished recording all your tracks, use the volume slider to adjust the balance among the individual tracks. I'll show you how to use the track volume slider in Chapter 12.

To reset the volume slider to its neutral level:

◆ In the track mixer, Option-click the volume slider (**Figure 6.17**).

It returns to the neutral (0 dB) gain position (**Figure 6.18**).

✔ Tip

■ The 0 db position is never centered in level meters, but is always fairly close to the high end of the meter. That's because the meter is most useful if it shows many gradations of volume within the range between inaudible and 0 db. Once the signal starts to exceed 0 db, it's getting close to clipping territory, so the meter doesn't need to extend very far beyond the neutral position.

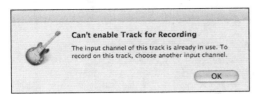

Figure 6.19 This track uses an input that's also connected to another track that you have enabled for recording.

Figure 6.20 The mouse pointer poised over the Record Enable button.

Figure 6.21 Recording has been enabled for this track; the button glows red.

Enabling a Track for Recording

If you plan to do multitrack recording, you will have to enable recording (a new feature in GarageBand 2) for each track that you want to receive an audio signal. You can enable up to eight Real Instrument tracks. If you exceed that number, the track farthest from the last track you enabled will be disabled. If you happen to enable two tracks that share the same input channel, you'll get an alert (**Figure 6.19**). To fix this problem, open the Track Info window for one of the offending tracks and choose a different channel from the Input menu (see "Adding a Real Instrument Track" in Chapter 3). You can enable a track only when GarageBand is idle or playing back a recording, not while recording is going on.

To enable Real Instrument tracks for recording:

1. To enable a track for recording, click the track's Record Enable button (**Figure 6.20**).

   The button glows red to show that it is active (**Figure 6.21**).

2. Click the Record Enable buttons of other tracks you wish to record into, up to a maximum of eight.

✔ Tip

■ To disable a track for recording, click the Record Enable button again, so that the button darkens.

Recording into Real Instrument Tracks

It's almost time to record. Here are the items on your preflight checklist:

Figure 6.22 Recording has been enabled for all four of these tracks.

- Check the amount of free space on your hard drive. Remember that recording audio at CD quality (16-bit resolution, 44.1 MHz sampling rate) requires about 10 MB of disk space per minute of music.

- Check your instruments and/or microphones to make sure they are properly connected to your Mac and that a signal is coming through from each one.

- Open the Track Info window for each track into which you plan to record and check that the input channel and format (stereo or mono) settings are correct. (These are the properties you set when you created the track; see "To add a Real Instrument track" in Chapter 3.) Also make sure that each track uses a unique input channel. While you're there, turn on monitoring as well, if desired.

- Play (or sing) a few loud passages and adjust the strength of the signal from each audio source using the controls on your audio interface to set the recording level for each track (see "About Setting the Recording Level" earlier in this chapter).

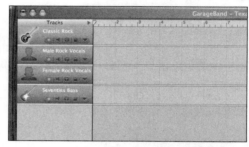

Figure 6.23 Pick a spot to begin recording.

To record into Real Instrument tracks:

1. Click the Record Enable button for each track you want to record into (**Figure 6.22**).

2. Move the playhead to the spot in the song where you want recording to begin (**Figure 6.23**).

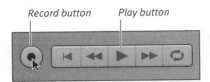

Record button   Play button

Figure 6.24 Click the Record button to start recording and the Play button to stop.

Figure 6.25 New regions appear during recording.

3. To start recording, click the Record button (or press R) (**Figure 6.24**).

The red dot in the center of the button illuminates.

4. Begin your performance.

As you record, the playhead moves down the timeline, leaving a new region in each enabled track in its wake (**Figure 6.25**).

5. To stop recording, click the Play button (or press the spacebar).

The playhead stops at the end of your newly recorded regions (**Figure 6.26**).

6. To make additional recordings, *do one of the following:*

▲ To record more regions in the same tracks, move the playhead to a new location and repeat steps 3 through 5.

▲ To record into different tracks, create new tracks or enable existing tracks and repeat steps 2 through 5.

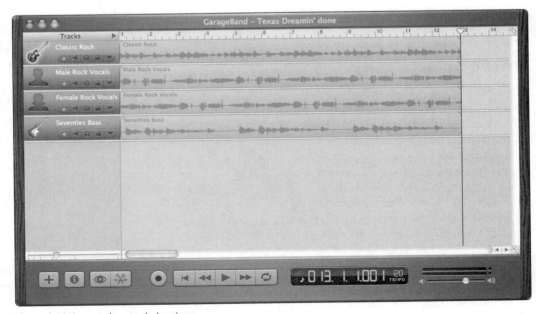

Figure 6.26 Your newly recorded regions.

Re-recording a Section of a Song

Suppose the first take of your recording goes swimmingly, except for one measure where you flubbed a few notes. You don't have to record the whole region over again to fix those notes—GarageBand includes a feature that lets you re-record just a portion of a region.

To re-record a part of a region, you create a *cycle region* that defines the passage you want to record over (**Figure 6.27**). The next time you click the Record button, only the cycle region is recorded. A new region is created in the track, splitting the original region into two parts (**Figure 6.28**).

As you record, the playhead jumps to the beginning of the cycle region and proceeds to the end and then jumps back to the start of the region and plays back the material you just recorded. The playhead continues to cycle through the region, playing the newly recorded material, until you click the Play button to stop playback. Recording is enabled only on the first pass, though. If you don't like what you just recorded, repeat the procedure.

To record over part of a song:

1. Click the Cycle button, in the transport controls below the timeline (**Figure 6.29**).

   A second ruler appears below the beat ruler; a portion of it is colored yellow, indicating the cycle region. If this is the first time you've invoked the cycle region for this song, the cycle region will encompass the first four measures. If you have used the cycle region before in this song, GarageBand displays the cycle region at its previous location.

2. Drag the cycle region so it covers the portion of the timeline you want to record again (**Figure 6.30**).

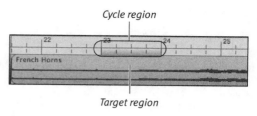

Cycle region

Target region

Figure 6.27 A two-measure cycle region defined, before recording.

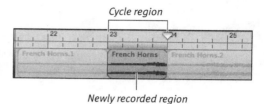

Cycle region

Newly recorded region

Figure 6.28 After recording using the cycle region. A new region has been created in the selected track.

Figure 6.29 The Cycle button.

Figure 6.30 Dragging the cycle region to a new position.

Figure 6.31 Resizing the cycle region.

3. To resize the region, move the mouse pointer over either end of the region. The pointer turns into the Resize tool (**Figure 6.31**). Drag inward or outward on either end of the region to resize it.

4. Click the Record Enable button for the track or tracks into which you want to record.

5. Click the Record button (or press R) to begin recording.

6. Begin playing or singing.

   While you are recording, the playhead moves through the cycle region. A new region appears in the cycled portion of the timeline, containing your newly recorded material (Figure 6.28). When the playhead reaches the end of the cycle region, it jumps back to the beginning and repeats, this time playing back the new region you just recorded.

7. Click the Play button (or press the space-bar) to stop recording.

8. *Do one of the following:*

   ▲ If you want to record over the cycle region again, click Record (or press R) to start the procedure again.

   ▲ If you are satisfied with the new recording, click the Cycle button again to hide the cycle region.

✔ Tips

■ Other audio programs call this technique *punching in* and *punching out* and refer to the ends of the cycle region as *punch-in* and *punch-out points.*

■ When you're satisfied with the results of your cycle recording, you can fuse the newly recorded region with the pieces of the original region to form a single unit. (See "Joining Regions" in Chapter 8.)

Real vs. Software Instrument Cycle Regions

When you record into a Software Instrument track, the cycle region operates differently. As long as the playhead keeps repeating its path through the cycle region, GarageBand stays in record mode. Anything you play during the same recording cycle will be added to the material recorded on the previous passes.

In other words, you can continue to record that difficult passage over and over until you get it right!

RECORDING SOFTWARE INSTRUMENTS

The process of recording Software Instruments in GarageBand is similar to that for Real Instruments, but different enough that I've provided a separate chapter for each procedure. There is some duplication between the chapters, but I decided it was better to make each one complete rather than use a lot of cross-references.

Once your MIDI hardware is set up and connected to your computer, you're ready to record. The act of recording into a Software Instrument track is simple: enable a Software Instrument track for recording, click the Record button, and whatever data comes in through your MIDI interface is captured on your computer's hard disk.

Before you click that button, you should check out some GarageBand features that will streamline your recording session. Here's what I cover in this chapter:

- ◆ General comments about recording Software Instruments.

- ◆ Using the onscreen keyboard and the new Musical Typing feature.

- ◆ Using the metronome to help you keep a steady beat while recording.

- ◆ Recording a new region into a Software Instrument track.

- ◆ Using a cycle region to re-record a portion of a track.

About Recording Software Instruments

GarageBand 2 may allow you to record up to eight tracks of audio at once, but you can still record into only a single Software Instrument track at a time. At least you can record into that single Software Instrument track at the same time that you're recording into all those audio tracks, if your hardware allows it.

Remember that a Software Instrument track can receive input from an external MIDI device (usually a keyboard), but you can also "play" one of GarageBand's built-in input devices: either the onscreen keyboard or the Musical Typing window. Remember also that if you decide after recording a track that you like your performance but you don't care for the specific instrument you used, you can change the instrument at any time using the Track Info window (see "Changing a Track's Instrument" in Chapter 3).

As with Real Instruments, each time you record a take, you create a *region* within a track. A region can be any length, from a few notes to a whole song. You can record as many regions in a track as you want, and you can start recording at any point in the timeline. This gives you tremendous flexibility: you can record small pieces of a song as inspiration strikes and then arrange them into a larger composition when you're ready (you'll learn how to do that in Chapter 8).

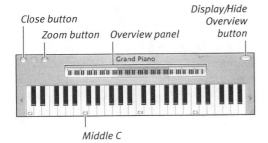

Close button

Zoom button   Overview panel

Display/Hide
Overview
button

Grand Piano

Middle C

Figure 7.1 GarageBand's onscreen keyboard. The name of the currently selected track is displayed at the top.

Figure 7.2 The keyboard is now unavailable for use.

Working with the Onscreen Music Keyboard

For those without MIDI hardware, GarageBand includes a virtual keyboard: a picture of a keyboard, which you play by clicking the keys with the mouse. The onscreen keyboard acts as a substitute for a "real" MIDI keyboard. Any notes you play on it are sent to the selected Software Instrument track. If you are recording, the notes you play are recorded, just as if you had played them on a piece of hardware.

GarageBand 2 lets you enlarge the keys so they're easier to click with the mouse, but the keyboard still feels rather clumsy, and it's not useful for entering lively melodies. It comes in handy, though, if you're trying to get some work done in GarageBand while you're away from your studio—traveling with a PowerBook, for example. It works well for recording long-held notes, and it's useful for trying out unfamiliar Software Instruments to see how they sound.

To display the onscreen keyboard:

◆ With a Software Instrument track selected, choose Window > Keyboard (Command-K).

The onscreen keyboard appears (**Figure 7.1**) bearing the name of the currently selected Software Instrument track.

If you select a Real Instrument track while the keyboard is displayed, the keyboard dims and becomes inactive (**Figure 7.2**).

To hide the onscreen keyboard:

◆ If the keyboard is displayed, *do one of
the following:*

▲ Choose Window > Keyboard
(Command-K).

▲ Click the Close button in the upper-
left corner of the keyboard.

The keyboard disappears.

To use the onscreen keyboard:

◆ Click a key on the keyboard (**Figure 7.3**).
GarageBand sounds the note, using the
selected Software Instrument track.

Figure 7.3 Playing the keyboard with the mouse.

Playing Softly and Loudly

GarageBand's onscreen keyboard allows
you to reproduce the effect of applying
varying degrees of pressure to a physical
key to create notes of different volume
levels. And no, it doesn't depend on how
vigorously you press the mouse button.

Click near the key's front edge to produce
a loud tone (**Figure 7.4**). The farther
toward the back of the key you click, the
softer the tone produced (**Figure 7.5**).

The volume of each note is recorded as
velocity data and can be edited using the
track editor (see Chapter 10 for more
information about using the track editor
to edit MIDI data).

Figure 7.4 Clicking
here plays a note
forte, or loudly.

Figure 7.5 Click
here to play *piano*,
or softly.

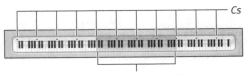

Currently active keyboard range

Figure 7.6 A close-up of the onscreen keyboard overview.

Figure 7.7 Ready to resize the keyboard.

Configuring the Onscreen Keyboard

For a tool of limited practicality, the onscreen keyboard itself is remarkably flexible as a user-interface element. You can resize it (both in terms of compass and key size) and change its pitch up or down to a different octave. It's even touch sensitive (see the sidebar "Playing Softly and Loudly" earlier in this chapter).

By default, the keyboard spans four octaves. In this configuration, the lowest note (labeled "C2") is equivalent to C below middle C on a piano keyboard. The keyboard can expand up to $10\frac{1}{2}$ octaves—far wider than the range of any physical keyboard (ordinary pianos top out at 7 octaves and change). At the default key size, you can reduce its compass to a minimum of 3 octaves.

GarageBand 2 adds a new feature to the onscreen keyboard: the *overview* (**Figure 7.6**). The overview is a miniature representation of the full $10\frac{1}{2}$ octave compass available to the keyboard (with tiny dots above each C to help you to orient yourself). A portion of the overview is colored blue to show the current range displayed by the keyboard. Dragging this blue area left or right moves the keyboard's range down or up by octaves. You can also access notes outside the keyboard's current display by clicking the arrows at either end. The lowest note of the keyboard is always a C. GarageBand 2 also adds the option of enlarging the keys (providing three sizes in all), making them easier to click.

To change the compass of the keyboard:

1. Position the mouse pointer over the lower-right corner of the keyboard (**Figure 7.7**).

continues on next page

2. *Do one of the following:*

▲ To widen the keyboard's range, drag to the right (**Figure 7.8**).

▲ To shrink the keyboard, drag to the left.

To change the range of the keyboard:

◆ *Do one of the following:*

▲ To shift the keyboard's range downward by an octave, click the triangle at the left end of the keyboard (**Figure 7.9**).

▲ To shift the keyboard's range upward by an octave, click the triangle at the right end of the keyboard.

▲ Working in the overview, to move the keyboard's range to a specific octave, click an octave outside the blue area (**Figure 7.10**).

▲ To shift the keyboard's range downward or upward by octaves, drag the blue area in the overview left or right (**Figure 7.11**).

Figure 7.8 After dragging the corner of the keyboard to the right.

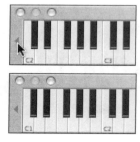

Figure 7.9 Top: Clicking the left-pointing triangle moves the keyboard's range down an octave. Notice that the lowest note of the keyboard is C2. Bottom: After you shift the range, the lowest note of the keyboard is C1.

Figure 7.10 Top: Click an empty part of the overview to have the keyboard shift to cover that octave. Bottom: The keyboard's range now includes the area that was clicked.

Figure 7.11 Top: Starting to drag the blue area to another part of the overview. Bottom: The drag is complete, and the keyboard's range has shifted.

Figure 7.12 Click this button to hide the overview.

Figure 7.13 The overview is hidden.

Figure 7.14 Drag the keyboard from this corner to change the key size.

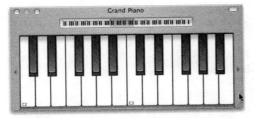

Figure 7.15 Top: Starting from the default (small) key size, the first drag enlarges the keys to the medium size. Bottom: Dragging down from the medium size bumps the keys up to the large size.

To hide or reveal the overview:

◆ *Do one of the following:*

▲ If the overview is visible, click the button at the upper-right corner of the onscreen keyboard (**Figure 7.12**).

The overview disappears (**Figure 7.13**).

▲ If the overview is hidden, click the button at the upper-right corner of the onscreen keyboard to reveal it.

To change the size of the keys:

1. Position the mouse pointer over the lower-right corner of the keyboard (**Figure 7.14**).

2. *Do one of the following:*

▲ To enlarge the keys by one size, drag down (**Figure 7.15**).

▲ To reduce the keys by one size, drag up.

continues on next page

CONFIGURING THE ONSCREEN KEYBOARD

✔ Tip

- To quickly enlarge or reduce the key size, click the Zoom button at the upper left of the keyboard (**Figure 7.16**). When the keyboard is at the small or medium size, clicking the Zoom button bumps up the keys to the next largest size. If the keyboard is at the large size, clicking the Zoom button shrinks it to the medium size.

Zoom button

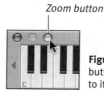

Figure 7.16 Click the Zoom button to snap the keyboard to its full range.

The Piano Keyboard

Here's how to set up the onscreen keyboard to show the full 88-key range of the piano (**Figure 7.17**):

Shift the keyboard downward until the note C-1 is at the bottom of the keyboard's displayed range. The actual lowest note on the great majority of pianos is the A above C-1, but GarageBand always insists on starting the keyboard on a C.

Now grab the lower-right corner of the keyboard and drag to the right until C7 is the topmost note.

There! You have eight octaves showing, a little more than the span of a piano keyboard. By the way, unless you have a very large monitor, this onscreen keyboard will fit on your display only if you use the small key size.

Figure 7.17 The onscreen keyboard, expanded to display the full range of the piano's keyboard.

About Musical Typing

The Musical Typing window is a welcome addition to GarageBand 2. This new feature overcomes some of the limitations of the onscreen keyboard by letting you play and record music into GarageBand by typing on your computer's keyboard. The Musical Typing window itself provides a map to the functions your keyboard can perform (**Figure 7.18**). Musical Typing is rather sophisticated, allowing you not only to enter basic pitch information, but also to control MIDI parameters such as pitch bend, modulation, sustain, and velocity (for more detailed descriptions of these classes of MIDI data, see "The Types of MIDI Controller Data" in Chapter 10). A black-and-white screenshot doesn't do this window justice—the keys that govern MIDI parameters are color-coded according to function.

continues on next page

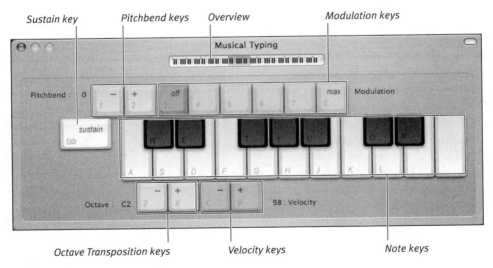

Figure 7.18 The Musical Typing window.

At the heart of the Musical Typing window are, of course, the *Note keys*, which you use to enter actual pitches into your Software Instrument track. The entire middle row of letter keys from A to ' corresponds to an octave and a half of diatonic notes (the white keys on a piano), beginning at C and ending at F. The keys WE, TYU, and OP in the QWERTY row correspond to the chromatic keys (the sharps and flats, or black keys, on a piano). In the Musical Typing window, the keys are drawn as piano keyboard keys, to help you associate each computer key with a note.

By default, the Musical Typing keyboard uses C2 as its lowest note, just like the onscreen keyboard. GarageBand provides several tools for moving the notes to a different octave. At the top of the Musical Typing window is an overview panel; it functions exactly like its counterpart on the onscreen keyboard (see "Configuring the Onscreen Keyboard" earlier in this chapter) as a tool for shifting the keyboard to different octaves. At the lower left of the window, the apricot-tinged *Octave Transposition keys* shift the Note keys up or down in pitch: press Z to move the keyboard down one octave; press X to shift the keyboard up one octave.

The peach-colored *Velocity keys* control the volume of your instrument. Press C to decrease velocity (volume) by 5 units; press V to increase velocity by 5 units. If you press a key and hold it, the velocity will continue to change in 5-unit increments until you bump into one end of the Velocity spectrum (the range of possible values is 0 to 127) or until you play a Note key. To change the volume while holding a Note key, you must click the Velocity key repeatedly.

While we're on the subject of pitch, an indispensable component of any MIDI instrument is the ability to introduce subtle (or not so subtle) inflections in pitch. The number keys 1 and 2 (depicted in a lovely aqua) serve the function of *Pitchbend keys*. Press 1 while playing a Note key to bend the pitch down 20 units; press 2 to bend the pitch up the same amount. The pitch stays bent for as long as you hold down the key. GarageBand supports bending the pitch by more than 20 units but Musical Typing won't go beyond that amount; to bend the pitch by a greater amount, you'll need to use the track editor. Remember that you can always go back later and use the track editor to adjust the pitch bend or any other MIDI parameter.

The number keys from 3 to 8 (tinged with mauve) act as *Modulation keys*, duplicating the effect of the modulation wheel (or Mod wheel) that is a feature of most MIDI keyboards. Usually, the Mod wheel colors the sound of the MIDI instrument by adding vibrato—the farther the wheel is turned, the more of the effect that is added. The specific kind of coloration that is applied to the track by modulation varies according to the way the Software Instrument is designed, and more sophisticated MIDI keyboards allow the user to assign the Mod wheel to control other expressive parameters.

When a Modulation key is pressed, its onscreen representation is darkened, and it remains active until another key is pressed. Thus, there is always one key active—by default it is 3, which turns modulation off. Keys 4 to 8 represent progressively higher amounts of modulation, but the amounts do not increase in a regular fashion. Pressing 4 sets the modulation level at about 33, pressing 5 sets it to about 50, pressing 6 raises it to about 76, pressing 7 moves it to about 98, and pressing 8 jumps it to about 127.

continues on next page

And finally, the Tab key (in a pale lime-green) controls the *Sustain parameter*. When Tab is pressed, a note continues to sound even after its key has been released. On a MIDI keyboard, sustain is normally provided by a pedal switch. Similarly, sustain is a simple on/off switch: when the Tab key is pressed, sustain is on; when the Tab key is released, sustain is off.

To display the Musical Typing window:

◆ Choose Window > Musical Typing (Command-Shift-K).

The Musical Typing window appears.

MIDIKeys

Musical Typing steals most of the thunder from Chris Reed's excellent utility, MIDIKeys, that I recommended in the previous edition of this book (**Figure 7.19**). MIDIKeys not only includes an onscreen keyboard, but, like Musical Typing, it lets you use your computer's keyboard (with its keys of the good old QWERTY variety) as a MIDI keyboard. MIDIKeys still enjoys these advantages over Musical Typing, though:

◆ You can access two full octaves from your computer's keyboard, as opposed to the measly octave and a half you get from Musical Typing.

◆ MIDIKeys takes up only one-sixth the screen space compared to Musical Typing's vast window. This smaller size makes quite a difference if you're working on a small PowerBook screen. In fact, you can even use MIDIKeys when it's in the background, taking up no screen real estate at all!

Download this great (and free!) software from the author's Web site: www.manyetas.com/creed/.

Figure 7.19 The MIDIKeys keyboard.

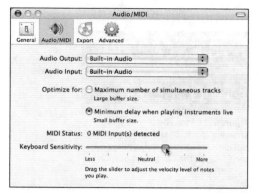

Figure 7.20 Use the slider on the Audio/MIDI tab of the Preferences dialog to adjust keyboard sensitivity.

Adjusting Keyboard Sensitivity

Not all MIDI keyboards are created equal, to coin a phrase. Some respond more deftly to the varying pressure of your skillful fingers than do others. If the lightest touch on your keyboard seems to make GarageBand scream, or if your heaviest pounding produces no more than a whisper, a new feature in GarageBand 2 allows you to do something about it. A Keyboard Sensitivity setting has been added to the Audio/MIDI tab in the GarageBand Preferences dialog. If you choose a higher Sensitivity setting, GarageBand will record a higher velocity level than your keyboard produces, giving every note a little extra oomph. Choosing a lower Sensitivity setting tells GarageBand to soften each of your keystrokes a bit.

To adjust keyboard sensitivity:

1. Choose GarageBand > Preferences (Command-,).

   The Preferences dialog opens.

2. If necessary, choose the Audio/MIDI tab; *then do one of the following:*

   ▲ To increase the keyboard sensitivity, drag the slider to the right (**Figure 7.20**).

   ▲ To decrease keyboard sensitivity, drag the slider to the left.

Using the MIDI Status Light

Buried among the LED-like digits of the time display is a tiny indicator that tells you whenever GarageBand receives a signal from a MIDI instrument. No bigger than a period, this little dot blinks momentarily whenever a key is pressed or released (to MIDI's way of thinking, these are separate events) (**Figure 7.21**).

The MIDI status light can be a useful troubleshooting tool. Everyone who works with MIDI will someday experience the frustrating experience of playing a note on a keyboard and getting no sound. Of course, in any complex system (including your GarageBand setup), there are myriad things that can go wrong, but the MIDI status light helps you isolate the problem. If you press a key and the MIDI status light appears, then GarageBand is getting MIDI data from your keyboard, and you know the trouble lies elsewhere. If the MIDI status light remains dark, then you know it's time to start troubleshooting your MIDI gear.

MIDI status light

Figure 7.21 Top: The time display, showing the MIDI status light on. Bottom: No MIDI signal is being received, so the light goes out.

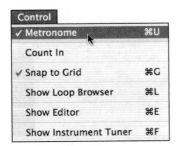

Figure 7.22 The check indicates that the metronome is on.

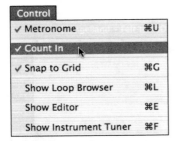

Figure 7.23 Setting the metronome to play a full measure before starting to record.

Using the Metronome

To help you play or sing in time, GarageBand provides a metronome. While you record, it ticks away at the tempo you set for your song. The sound of the metronome itself is not recorded. You can set the metronome to play only during recording or during both recording and playback.

To give yourself a running start, you can also set the metronome to play for a full measure, or *count-in*, before you start recording.

To use the metronome:

◆ Choose Control > Metronome (Command-U). A check mark indicates that the metronome is enabled (**Figure 7.22**).

When you click the Record button, the metronome will play a sound on each beat of the song.

To turn off the metronome:

◆ Choose Control > Metronome (Command-U). The item is now unchecked.

The metronome will no longer play during recording.

To have the metronome play a count-in before recording:

◆ Choose Control > Count In. A check mark appears next to the command (**Figure 7.23**).

When you click the Record button, the metronome will play for a complete measure before recording begins.

To disable count-in:

◆ Choose Control > Count In. The item is now unchecked.

The metronome will not play before recording starts.

To set preferences for the metronome:

1. Choose GarageBand > Preferences (Command-,).

   The Preferences dialog opens, displaying the General tab (**Figure 7.24**).

2. *Choose one of the Metronome options:*

   ▲ To have the metronome play only while the Record button is pressed, select During Recording.

   ▲ To have the metronome play both while recording and during playback, select During Playback and Recording.

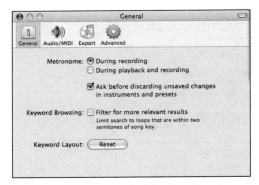

Figure 7.24 The General tab of the GarageBand Preferences dialog.

Figure 7.25 The Record Enable button is turned on for the Jazz Organ track.

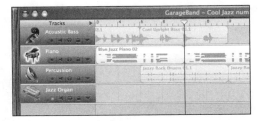

Figure 7.26 Pick a spot to begin recording.

Record button   *Play button*

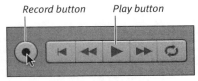

Figure 7.27 Click the Record button to start recording, and the Play button to stop.

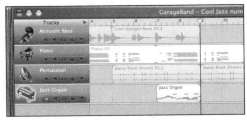

Figure 7.28 A new region appears during recording.

Recording into a Software Instrument Track

It's almost time to record. Here are the items you should have on your preflight checklist:

◆ Check your MIDI instrument and interface (if applicable) to make sure they are properly connected to your Mac.

◆ Decide which Software Instrument track you wish to record into, or create a new one.

◆ Display the onscreen keyboard or Musical Typing window, if you plan to use either of them for your performance.

◆ Play a few notes on your instrument and make sure that the MIDI status light blinks and that sound comes out of your Mac.

To record into a Software Instrument track:

1. Click the Record Enable button for the track in which you wish to record (**Figure 7.25**).

2. Move the playhead to the spot in the song where you want recording to begin (**Figure 7.26**).

3. Click the Record button (or press R) to start recording (**Figure 7.27**).

   The red dot in the center of the button illuminates.

4. Begin your performance.

   Any notes you play on your MIDI keyboard (or enter by clicking the onscreen keyboard) will be recorded. Also, if you use the pitch bend or modulation controller or the sustain pedal, that information will be recorded, too.

   As you record, the playhead moves down the timeline, leaving a new region in its wake (**Figure 7.28**).

continues on next page

157

5. To stop recording, click the Play button (or press the spacebar).

The playhead stops at the end of your newly recorded region (**Figure 7.29**).

6. To make additional recordings, *do one of the following:*

▲ To record another region in the same track, move the playhead to a new location and repeat steps 3 through 5.

▲ To record into another track, create a new track or click the Record Enable button in an existing track and repeat steps 2 through 5.

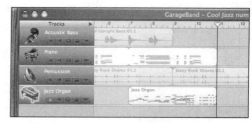

Figure 7.29 Your newly recorded region.

Recording Software Instrument Drums

The job of recording Software Instrument drum kits poses particular challenges. These instruments, like MIDI drum sounds in general, contain many different percussion sounds, each of which is assigned to a different note on the keyboard.

The GarageBand Help file recommends that you make a chart listing the sound or instrument played by each note on the keyboard (**Figure 7.30**), but this is a difficult (not to mention tedious) task. It's also unnecessary. GarageBand's drum kits follow the General MIDI specification pretty closely, so you can use **Table 7.1** as a guide. GarageBand's drums have more sounds than the four octaves defined in the specification, and they do deviate from the spec in places, so you'll still need to do a quick test of the full range of the Software Instrument to find all of its sounds.

The Software Instruments that model acoustic drums (like the Pop Kit and Rock Kit) follow the General MIDI list more closely than the instruments that re-create digital drum pads (like the Dance Kit and Techno Kit). The digital kits use a number of electronic sounds that don't match the General MIDI sounds. You can distinguish the two by their icons:

Acoustic drums: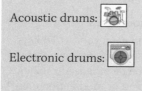

Electronic drums:

Figure 7.30 Part of a map showing the key mappings of percussion sounds.

Table 7.1

General MIDI Percussion Key Map

Keyboard Note	Instrument	Keyboard Note	Instrument
B0	Acoustic Bass Drum	B2	Ride Cymbal 2
C1	Bass Drum	C3	Hi Bongo
C#1	Side Stick	C#3	Low Bongo
D1	Acoustic Snare	D3	Mute Hi Conga
D#1	Hand Clap	D#3	Open Hi Conga
E1	Electric Snare	E3	Low Conga
F1	Low Floor Tom	F3	High Timbale
F#1	Closed Hi Hat	F#3	Low Timbale
G1	High Floor Tom	G3	High Agogo
G#1	Pedal Hi Hat	G#3	Low Agogo
A1	Low Tom	A3	Cabasa
A#1	Open Hi Hat	A#3	Maracas
B1	Low Mid Tom	B3	Short Whistle
C2	Hi Mid Tom	C4	Long Whistle
C#2	Crash Cymbal 1	C#4	Short Guiro
D2	High Tom	D4	Long Guiro
D#2	Ride Cymbal 1	D#4	Claves
E2	Chinese Cymbal	E4	Hi Wood Block
F2	Ride Bell	F4	Low Wood Block
F#2	Tambourine	F#4	Mute Cuica
G2	Splash Cymbal	G4	Open Cuica
G#2	Cowbell	G#4	Mute Triangle
A2	Crash Cymbal 2	A4	Open Triangle
A#2	Vibraslap		

RECORDING A SOFTWARE INSTRUMENT TRACK

Re-recording a Section of a Song

Suppose the first take of your recording goes swimmingly, except for one measure where you flubbed a few notes. You don't have to record the whole track over again to fix those notes—GarageBand includes a feature that lets you re-record just a portion of a track.

You do this by creating a *cycle region* that includes the passage you want to record again (**Figure 7.31**). The next time you click the Record button, only the cycle region is recorded. A new region is created in the track, splitting the original region into two parts (**Figure 7.32**).

When recording starts, the playhead jumps to the beginning of the cycle region and proceeds to the end and then jumps back to the start of the region. The playhead continues to cycle through the region until you click the Play button to stop. To correct a mistake, play during the first time cycling through the region; then listen to the playback on the second cycle.

GarageBand is recording the whole time, so if you play during several repetitions of the cycle, everything you play is recorded. The results can sound like a train wreck if you're not careful, but this feature is useful for building a track by overdubbing (see the sidebar "Using a Cycle Region for Overdubbing" later in this chapter). If you click Record again after stopping, the cycle is wiped clean, and you can begin afresh.

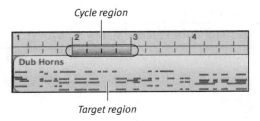

Cycle region

Target region

Figure 7.31 A one-measure cycle region defined, before recording.

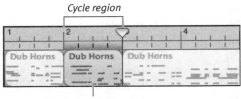

Cycle region

Newly recorded region

Figure 7.32 After recording using the cycle region. A new region has been created in the selected track.

Real vs. Software Instrument Cycle Regions

When you record into a Real Instrument track, the cycle region operates differently. GarageBand records only on the first pass through the region. The subsequent passes allow you to hear what you just recorded, but not to record anything new.

If you want to re-record over the cycle region, you have to stop recording and make a fresh start. See Chapter 6 for more information on recording Real Instrument tracks.

Figure 7.33 The Cycle button.

Figure 7.34 Dragging the cycle region to a new position.

Figure 7.35 Resizing the cycle region.

To record over part of a song:

1. Click the Cycle button in the transport controls below the timeline (**Figure 7.33**), or press C.

   A second ruler appears below the beat ruler; a portion of it is colored yellow, indicating the cycle region. If this is the first time you've invoked the cycle region for this song, the cycle region will encompass the first four measures. If you have used the cycle region before in this song, GarageBand displays it at its previous location.

2. Drag the cycle region so it covers the portion of the timeline you want to record again (**Figure 7.34**).

3. To resize the region, move the mouse pointer over either end. The pointer turns into the Resize tool (**Figure 7.35**). Drag either end of the region to resize it.

4. Select the track into which you want to record.

5. Click the Record button (or press R) to begin recording.

6. Play your instrument.

   While you are recording, the playhead moves through the cycle region. A new region appears in the timeline, containing your newly recorded material. When the playhead reaches the end of the cycle region, it jumps back to the beginning and starts through the cycle region again. This time, you can either listen to the performance you just recorded or keep playing to record fresh material on top of what you've already recorded.

   continues on next page

7. Click the Play button (or press the space-bar) to stop recording.

8. If you are satisfied with the new recording, click the Cycle button again to hide the cycle region.

✔ Tips

■ Other audio programs call this technique *punching in* and *punching out* and refer to the ends of the cycle region as *punch-in* and *punch-out points*.

■ When you're satisfied with the results of your cycle recording, you can fuse the newly recorded region with the pieces of the original region to form a single unit. (See "Joining Regions" in Chapter 8.)

Using a Cycle Region for Overdubbing

Overdubbing refers to the technique of making multiple recording passes over the same part of a track. In GarageBand, it's a good way of constructing a percussion part using Software Instruments, and you can use a cycle region to accomplish it.

A live drummer plays multiple instruments at once to create a rich percussion texture. Usually, the lowest-sounding drums reinforce beats 1 and 2, with brighter sounds on beats 3 and 4. The whole texture is topped by a lively sound moving at a quicker clip, perhaps a cymbal or hi hat playing in eighth or sixteenth notes.

You can reproduce that kind of percussion sound working by yourself in GarageBand. Set up a cycle region in a Sound Instrument percussion track and play a different rhythmic pattern on a different key on each recording cycle (**Figure 7.36**). For example, on the first cycle play C1 (Bass Drum 1) on the strong beats, on the second cycle play F1 (Low Floor Tom) on the weak beats, and on the third cycle play G#1 (Pedal Hi Hat) on every eighth note.

Beware though: If you stop recording and try to overdub more notes later, you'll erase what you just recorded. Overdubbing works only during a continuous series of passes through the cycle.

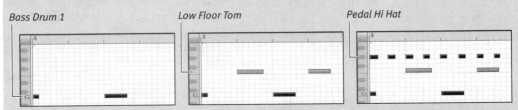

Figure 7.36 Overdubbing a percussion track, using a cycle region (shown here as seen in the track editor, for greater clarity). Left: The first pass through the cycle. Middle: The second pass. Right: The third pass.

Part 2: Polishing Your Song

Chapter 8: Arranging Regions in
the Timeline 165

Chapter 9: Advanced Editing with the
Track Editor 177

Chapter 10: Editing MIDI Data 199

Chapter 11: Applying Effects 217

Chapter 12: Mixing Your Song 249

Chapter 13: Exporting and Importing 267

ARRANGING REGIONS IN THE TIMELINE

Now that you've brought all the pieces of your song into the timeline, it's time to start polishing the composition. Maybe the guitar solo goes on too long, or the background string accompaniment needs to start earlier. What you have at this point is a rough draft; now it's time to refine it.

The first thing to do is to make sure that the general shape of the song is right. Adjusting when parts start and end, arranging sections so they come in the right order, and setting up passages to repeat are all part of the process. This is easily accomplished in GarageBand, because every item you've put into the song is a region, and regions can be arranged (moved, resized, and looped) simply by dragging them.

In this chapter, I discuss:

◆ How regions work.

◆ Selecting regions.

◆ Using the Copy, Paste, and Cut commands.

◆ Moving and resizing regions.

◆ Splitting and joining regions.

About Regions

Each morsel of music that you've placed into a track in the timeline, whether it's a four-minute continuous recording or a four-beat bass loop, is a *region* in GarageBand-speak.

A region is a copy of the original audio or MIDI recording or loop, which is stored as a file on your computer's hard disk. Any edits you make to a region do not affect the original file on which the region is based.

For example, your Apple Loops library consists of hundreds of individual audio and MIDI files. When you drag a loop from the loop browser into the timeline, GarageBand creates a copy of the loop and places it into your song. The original loop file is untouched.

The same principle (though with some differences) operates with regard to recordings you make yourself. When you make an audio recording, for example, the recording is stored as an audio file on your hard disk. If you split the region representing the recording in the timeline into two new regions, each new region can access all of the data in the original audio file.

Color Coding

GarageBand color codes the regions in the timeline so you can tell at a glance what sort of data they contain:

◆ *Purple* indicates Real Instrument regions that you recorded.

◆ *Blue* denotes Real Instrument regions that originated as loops.

◆ *Orange* is used for Real Instrument regions that you imported as audio files (this one's new in GarageBand 2).

◆ *Green* designates Software Instrument regions (including Apple Loops, regions you record yourself, and MIDI files you import into GarageBand).

About Editing Regions

You do your basic editing of regions in the timeline. Regions can be moved within a track, moved to other tracks of the same type, copied and pasted, or deleted from the timeline altogether. Regions can also be resized, split, joined together, and made to repeat (or *loop*). To do more advanced editing, such as editing MIDI note or controller data or transposing regions up or down in pitch, you must use the track editor. I explain how to use the track editor in Chapters 9 and 10.

In general, GarageBand, like many other media-editing programs, employs *nondestructive editing*, which means that when you edit a region, the original disk file from which the region was derived remains unchanged. GarageBand's implementation of nondestructive editing differs significantly from that in other programs, however.

Most programs that incorporate nondestructive editing display a list of all the media available to the program. This list includes all of the recordings you have made, as well as the loops you have added to the project. The list is separate from the timeline, so even if you were to delete all regions based on a single recorded file from the timeline, that recording would still be on your media list and available for use again as a source of new regions.

In GarageBand, your recordings are represented only by the region drawn in the timeline. If all of the regions derived from a recording you made are deleted from the timeline, the original recorded file is deleted from your hard disk.

continues on next page

GarageBand behaves in other unexpected ways. If you split a Real Instrument region into two portions, for example, each portion remains linked to the original audio file. Therefore, you can later enlarge either of the portions and recover the material that was lost in the split (**Figure 8.1**). Unfortunately, this does not work with Software Instrument regions. When a Software Instrument region is split, the resulting regions no longer have access to all the data in the original file (**Figure 8.2**).

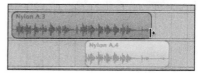

Figure 8.1 Top: A Real Instrument region is split in two. Middle: The region on the right is moved away. Bottom: The region on the left is enlarged, revealing material identical to that lost in the split.

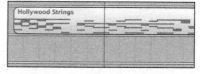
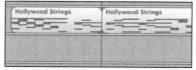
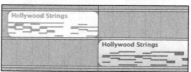
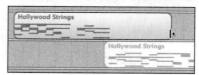

Figure 8.2 Top: A Software Instrument region before splitting. Second: The region is split. Third: The region on the right is moved away. Bottom: The region on the left is enlarged, showing that no data is left in the area split off.

Selected region

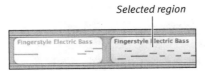

Figure 8.3 Selecting a region changes its appearance.

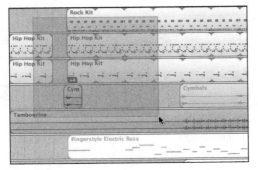

Figure 8.4 Drag-selecting multiple regions.

Figure 8.5 Selecting all of the regions in a track.

Figure 8.6 Click an area free of regions to deselect everything.

Selecting Regions

Before you perform any editing operations on a region, you must select it. You can select single regions or multiple regions, and the regions can be on different tracks. When a region is selected, its color darkens (**Figure 8.3**). You cannot select a partial region in the timeline.

To select regions:

◆ *Do any of the following:*

▲ To select a region, click anywhere within the region.

▲ To add to a selection, click a region; then hold down the Shift key and continue to click regions you want to add to the selection. This technique is useful for regions that are scattered around the timeline.

▲ To select multiple adjoining regions, position the mouse pointer over an empty (gray) area of the timeline and drag a selection rectangle downward and to the right over the regions you want to select (**Figure 8.4**). If you're still dragging when you reach the bottom of the GarageBand display and there are more tracks out of sight, the timeline will scroll upward to bring the hidden tracks into view.

▲ To select all of the regions in a track, click the track header (**Figure 8.5**).

▲ To select all of the regions in the timeline, choose Edit > Select All (Command-A).

To deselect regions:

◆ *Do any of the following:*

▲ To deselect a selected region, Shift-click the region.

▲ To deselect all selected regions, click anywhere in the empty (gray) area of the timeline (**Figure 8.6**).

Basic Editing Functions

GarageBand supports the usual suite of basic editing commands: Copy, Cut, and Paste.

◆ **Copy** places a copy of the selected region into your Mac's Clipboard (a temporary storage area in memory).

◆ **Cut** also places a copy of the selected region into your Clipboard, but the original region is removed from the timeline.

◆ **Paste** places the region stored in the Clipboard into the selected track at the playhead.

You can paste into a different track, as long as it's the same type as the original track. If there is a region in the selected track at the playhead, it will be overwritten by the pasted region. You can continue to move the playhead (and/or select different tracks) and paste the same material into as many different locations as you like. You can also copy a region by Option-dragging it to a new location.

The Delete command works like the Cut command, except the regions cut from the timeline are discarded.

To copy and paste a region:

1. Select the region you want to copy (**Figure 8.7**).

2. Choose Edit > Copy (Command-C).

3. Position the playhead at the point where you want to paste the region (**Figure 8.8**).

4. Choose Edit > Paste (Command-V).

   The region is pasted into the timeline at the new position (**Figure 8.9**).

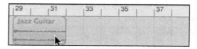

Figure 8.7 This region will be copied.

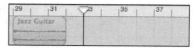

Figure 8.8 The playhead marks the spot where the region will be pasted.

Figure 8.9 The region is pasted at the playhead.

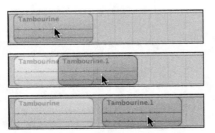

Figure 8.10 Duplicating a region by Option-dragging. Top: Hold down the Option key; then start to drag. Middle: A copy of the original region follows the mouse. Bottom: Release the mouse when the duplicate region is positioned where you want it.

To duplicate a region by dragging:

◆ Option-drag a region to a new location in the same track or in another track of the same type (**Figure 8.10**).

✔ Tip

■ Be sure to press the Option key *before* starting to drag. Otherwise, you will end up moving the region instead of duplicating it.

To cut a region:

1. Select the region you want to cut from the timeline.

2. Choose Edit > Cut (Command-X).

   The region is copied to the Clipboard and removed from the timeline. The cut region is available for pasting.

To delete a region from the timeline:

1. Select the region you want to remove.

2. Choose Edit > Delete or press Delete.

Moving Regions

You can move regions from place to place in the timeline by dragging. Regions can be moved to different locations in the same track or to other tracks of the same type. If you drag a region to a spot already occupied by another region, it overwrites the pre-existing region. As with all operations described in this chapter that involve dragging, the dragged region will snap to the timeline grid if it is enabled (see "About the Timeline Grid" in Chapter 1).

To move a region:

◆ *Do one of the following:*

- ▲ To change a region's position in the track, drag the region left or right.

- ▲ To move a region to a different track of the same kind, drag the region up or down.

Dragging onto Another Region

If you drag a region so it partially overlaps another region, the overlapped region shrinks to make room for the dragged region (**Figure 8.11**). The effect is the same as if you had resized the overlapped region by dragging its end toward its center (see "Resizing Regions" later in this chapter).

If you drag a region onto the middle of a larger region, the larger region is sliced in two, and both portions are reduced in size to accommodate the dragged region (**Figure 8.12**). The effect on the larger region is equivalent to using the Split command (see "Splitting Regions" later in this chapter) and then resizing the resulting fragments.

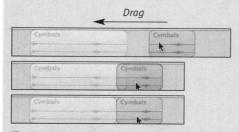

Figure 8.11 Dragging a region so it overlaps another region. Top: Drag the region on the right to the left. Middle: The regions overlap. Bottom: When you release the mouse, the right edge of the left region retreats to make room for the dragged region.

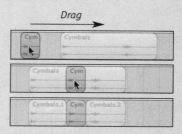

Figure 8.12 Dragging one region into the middle of another. Top: Drag the region on the left toward the middle of the region on the right. Middle: The end of the drag. Bottom: After you release the mouse, the dragged region cuts the larger region in two.

Figure 8.13 The resize pointer, positioned over the right edge of a region.

Figure 8.14 After dragging the right edge toward the left.

✔ Tips

■ The arrow on the resize pointer always points away from the center of the region. It doesn't tell you which way you can drag.

■ Make sure you drag the lower half of the region's boundary. If your mouse pointer strays to the upper half of the right boundary, it will turn into the loop pointer, and dragging the boundary will loop the region rather than extend it (see "Looping a Region" later in this chapter). (Nothing will happen if you drag the upper half of the left boundary of the region.)

Resizing Regions

You can shorten or lengthen a region by dragging one of its ends. Doing this changes only how much of the region is heard in your song—it doesn't change the length of the actual audio or MIDI file.

This means that if you shorten a region and then decide you've gone too far, don't despair—the material you trimmed isn't lost. Just lengthen the region again, and the previous contents of the region are restored. Compare this behavior with what happens when you split a region. Splitting a Real Instrument region results in two regions, each of which can be expanded to recover the material that was lost in the split. If you split a Software Instrument region, however, producing two regions, you cannot recover data by lengthening the regions.

If you extend a Software Instrument region beyond its original length, the extended portion will contain only silence. Real Instrument regions, on the other hand, cannot be extended beyond their original length.

To resize a region:

1. Position the mouse pointer over one of the ends of the region. Make sure the pointer is over the lower part of the region's boundary.

   The pointer turns into the resize pointer (**Figure 8.13**).

2. Drag toward the region to shorten it, or away from the region to lengthen it (**Figure 8.14**).

Looping a Region

If you want a region to repeat, you can copy it and paste it into a track several times in succession. Or you can save a few steps and loop it. Loop a region by dragging its upper-right corner to the right. Instead of lengthening the region with silence, this action appends copies of the region to itself. The upper and lower edges of the region show a notch at each repetition of the original material. The final repetition can end in mid-loop.

To loop a region:

1. Position the mouse pointer over the upper-right corner of the region you want to loop.

   The pointer becomes the loop pointer (**Figure 8.15**).

2. Drag the edge of the region to the right.

   At each repetition of the original region, a notch appears in the upper and lower edges of the region (**Figure 8.16**).

3. Release the mouse when you've created the desired number of repetitions.

✔ Tips

- If you lengthen a Software Instrument region so that silence is added to it and then loop the region, the silence is repeated along with the music in each loop.

- Once you loop a region, resizing it affects all the looped sections as well. Furthermore, you can use the Resize tool only at the edges of the original region (**Figure 8.17**).

Figure 8.15 The loop pointer includes a circular arrow.

Figure 8.16 After dragging the edge of the region with the loop pointer.

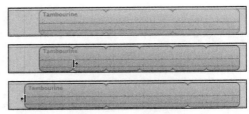

Figure 8.17 Resizing a region that has been looped. Top: The Tambourine region was made to loop twice. Middle: The pointer was placed over the right edge of the original region and dragged to the left to shorten the region. The loops were shortened as well, and more loops were automatically added to fill in the space. Bottom: Here, the left edge of the original region was dragged left, lengthening it. The other loops are similarly lengthened.

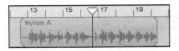

Figure 8.18 The region will be split at the playhead.

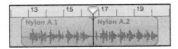

Figure 8.19 One region has become two.

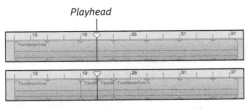

Figure 8.20 Splitting a looped region. Top: The Tambourine region has been extended by looping several times. The playhead is positioned in the middle of the second loop, where the split will occur. Bottom: After splitting, the second loop is separated from the other loops.

Splitting Regions

The Split command divides a region into two new regions at the playhead. Each resulting region can be moved, copied and pasted, or deleted just like any other region.

When you split a Real Instrument region, each of the resulting regions keeps its link with the original audio file. Either of the new regions can be extended to the full length of the original region.

To split a region:

1. Select the region you want to split.

2. Position the playhead at the spot where you want to divide the region (**Figure 8.18**).

3. Choose Edit > Split (Command-T). The region is split in two (**Figure 8.19**).

✔ Tip

■ If you split a region that's looped, GarageBand will separate the new split regions from the existing looped regions. It does this because all the repetitions in a looped region have to be the same length. Since you split one of the loops, it's no longer the same length as the others. To compensate, GarageBand takes the split repetition out of the loop, so to speak (**Figure 8.20**).

SPLITTING REGIONS

Joining Regions

Two regions of the same type can be joined together to form a new region. The two regions must be on the same track. Regions made from Real Instrument loops can't be joined, either to each other or to regions made from Real Instrument recordings.

If you are rejoining two regions that were created by splitting another region, and if you haven't altered either of them, the rejoining is very simple. It's basically equivalent to undoing the original split operation. Otherwise, when GarageBand joins two Real Instrument regions made from recordings, it creates a new audio file on disk, and the resulting joined region represents the new disk file.

To join regions:

1. Select the two regions to be joined (**Figure 8.21**).

2. Choose Edit > Join Selected (Command-J).

   ▲ If you are joining Software Instrument regions, a new Software Instrument region is created.

   ▲ If you are joining Real Instrument regions made from recordings that were not created by splitting another region, an alert dialog appears (**Figure 8.22**). Click Create to continue. A new Real Instrument region is created (**Figure 8.23**).

   The new region takes its name from the region on the left and adds the word *Merged* to the name.

✔ Tip

■ The GarageBand documentation says that to be joined, regions must be touching. This isn't exactly true. You can join regions that are separated by space (**Figure 8.24**); the space between the regions will become a silent zone in the middle of the joined region (**Figure 8.25**).

Figure 8.21 Two regions, ready for joining.

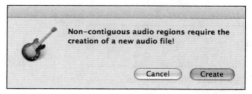

Figure 8.22 An alert warns you that merging these regions will create a new audio file.

Figure 8.23 Joining two Real Instrument regions produces a single region.

Figure 8.24 It shouldn't be possible to join these regions...

Figure 8.25 ...But it is!

ADVANCED EDITING WITH THE TRACK EDITOR

If you're the sort who like to likes to poke around under the hood, fiddle with custom settings, and in general, live dangerously, you'll probably end up using GarageBand's track editor at some point. It's the only window the program provides into the inner workings of the loops and recordings you've added to your song.

But if you're not that sort, don't worry. You can create plenty of great songs without ever firing up the track editor—it's completely optional. Just in case, though, I've stuffed this chapter full of information about:

◆ The anatomy of the track editor.

◆ The difference between using the track editor with Real Instrument tracks and using it with Software Instrument tracks.

◆ Displaying the track editor.

◆ Unlocking the timeline and track editor playheads.

◆ Renaming tracks and regions.

◆ Transposing regions to different keys.

◆ Enhancing the tuning and timing of Real Instrument regions.

◆ Fixing the timing of notes in a Software Instrument region.

About Editing Real Instrument Regions

In GarageBand 1, you couldn't do much to Real Instrument regions in the track editor. You could rename them (and rename tracks as well), and you could transpose regions made from Real Instrument loops but not Real Instrument recordings. GarageBand 2 adds several new features to the Real Instrument track editor, including the ability to transpose Real Instrument regions recorded in GarageBand (you still can't transpose audio files you drag in from the Finder, alas). You can now tweak the tuning or timing of an entire Real Instrument track to make up for inaccuracies in performance.

GarageBand 2 carries over from the original version several undocumented functions, including resizing and looping, that make the track editor potentially much more useful. Because they are undocumented, however, using them entails some risk. See the sidebar "Undocumented Features in the Track Editor" later in this chapter for more details.

About Editing Software Instrument Regions

The track editor is a far more powerful tool for working with Software Instrument regions than for working with Real Instrument regions. When working with a Software Instrument region, you can rename or transpose the region, adjust the timing of the notes in the region, and edit the pitch, loudness, and duration of actual notes in the region. You can also edit a number of MIDI-specific parameters that give you a lot of control over the sound of the notes.

Because editing MIDI data is such a substantial topic, I've given it a chapter to itself (see Chapter 10).

About the Track Editor

The track editor is normally hidden, tucked out of sight at the bottom of the GarageBand window. In fact, it shares the same space as the loop browser. And as with the loop browser, you can bring it out into the open with the click of a button or a simple keystroke. Its controls change depending on the type of track displayed, with more features available to Software Instrument tracks (**Figure 9.1**) than to Real Instrument tracks (**Figure 9.2**).

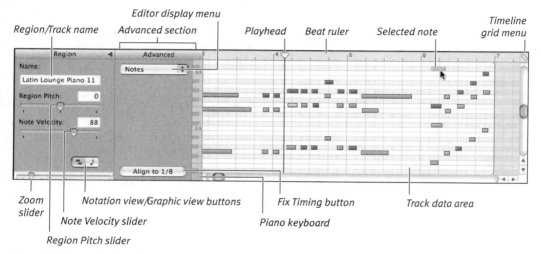

Figure 9.1 The track editor, displaying a Software Instrument region.

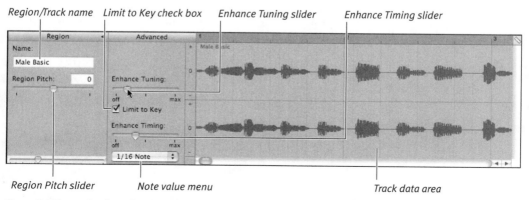

Figure 9.2 The track editor, showing a Real Instrument region.

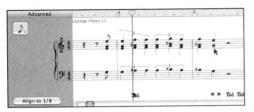

Figure 9.3 The track data area of a Software Instrument region as it appears in notation view.

Some of the track editor's features will be familiar from the timeline (see "The GarageBand Interface" in Chapter 1). The *playhead* and *beat ruler* work just like their counterparts in the timeline, and the playhead's location in the beat ruler is always the same here as in the timeline. The track editor and the timeline always display the same section of a song by default. To change this setting, use the Playhead Lock button (see "Unlocking the Timeline and Track Editor Playheads" later in this chapter). The *timeline grid menu* and *zoom slider* also operate identically to the ones in the timeline, but the settings you choose here are independent of those you make in the timeline.

Most of the track editor is taken up with the *track data area*. Because the two types of tracks in GarageBand record different types of data, the track data area changes appearance drastically from one type of track to the other.

Software Instrument regions are recordings of MIDI data, in which the characteristics of individual notes are recorded. When the track editor is displayed using the default graphic view, each oblong rectangle in the track data area represents a single note. Its horizontal length shows its duration, and its color shows its loudness (*velocity*, in MIDI terminology). A note's vertical position shows its pitch, using the vertical piano *keyboard* along the left edge of the track data area as a reference. Starting with GarageBand 2, you can also view and edit MIDI data as musical notation (**Figure 9.3**).

Because Real Instrument regions are audio recordings, the track data area for Real Instrument tracks uses a *waveform* graph to display the contents of the region. The track shown in Figure 9.2 was recorded in stereo, so there are two waveforms, one for each channel. A mono recording would show only

continues on next page

one waveform. The waveform graphs the loudness (or *amplitude*) of the audio signal over time. Each bulge in the waveform represents a distinct sound event.

The left section of the track editor includes the *Region Name* field, which you can use to change the name of a selected region. If an entire track is selected, this field changes to the *Track Name* field. Both types of track include the *Region Pitch slider* for shifting the pitch of a region up or down, but the rest of the controls in this section are unique to Software Instruments. Use the *Note Velocity slider* to change the loudness of a note (or of several selected notes). The view buttons at the bottom of the track editor allow you to switch between *graphic view* and *notation view*.

The *Advanced section* of the track editor (which can be hidden when not needed) contains editing controls that are unique to each type of track. By default, the Software Instrument track editor shows data for notes, but you can choose to display MIDI controller data as well. Use the *editor display menu* to choose the type of data you want to display and edit (see "Editing MIDI Controller Information" in Chapter 10). The *Fix Timing button* appears only in the Software Instrument track editor. It lets you change the timing of notes that are off the beat by snapping them to the timeline grid. The label on the Fix Timing button shows the timeline grid's current setting.

When you're editing a Real Instrument track, the Advanced section of the track editor contains the *Enhance Tuning slider*, which you use to clean up any intonation faults that may have crept into your recording, and the *Enhance Timing slider*, which you use to fix unintentionally ragged rhythms in the region.

Figure 9.4 The Track Editor button.

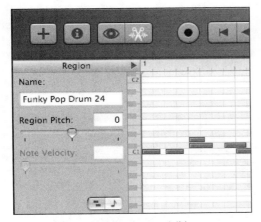

Figure 9.5 The track editor is now visible.

Figure 9.6 Double-clicking this region opens it in the track editor.

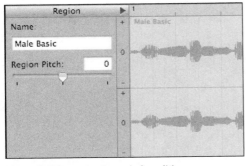

Figure 9.7 The region is ready for editing.

Displaying the Track Editor

When you first start GarageBand, the track editor is hidden, to allow more room for tracks in the timeline, but displaying it is easy.

To display the track editor:

◆ If the track editor is hidden, *do one of the following:*

▲ Click the Track Editor button, near the bottom of the GarageBand window (**Figure 9.4**).

▲ Choose Control > Show Editor.

▲ Press Command-E.

The Track Editor button glows blue, and the track editor itself slides into view (**Figure 9.5**).

To hide the track editor:

◆ Click the Track Editor button or choose Control > Hide Editor (Command-E).

The track editor goes back into hiding.

To display a track in the track editor:

1. Display the track editor.

2. Click the header of the track you wish to edit.

The track appears in the track editor.

To display a specific region in the track editor:

◆ Working in the timeline, double-click the region you want to edit (**Figure 9.6**).

The track editor opens (if it is not already open) and displays the selected region (**Figure 9.7**).

To display the Advanced section of the track editor:

1. Display the track editor.

2. If the Advanced section is not open, click the triangle at the right edge of the track editor header (**Figure 9.8**).

   The Advanced section of the track editor opens (**Figure 9.9**).

3. *Optional:* When you are finished using the Advanced editing controls, click the triangle again to hide the Advanced section of the track editor.

✔ Tip

- Double-clicking a region to open it in the track editor automatically unlocks the playheads (see the next section, "Unlocking the Timeline and Track Editor Playheads").

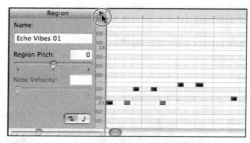

Figure 9.8 Click this triangle to display the Advanced section of the track editor.

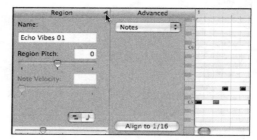

Figure 9.9 The Advanced section of the track editor, revealed in all its glory.

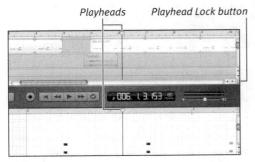

Playheads   Playhead Lock button

Figure 9.10 During normal playback, the playheads in the timeline and track editor both stay centered in their respective areas.

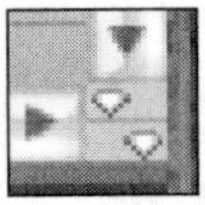

Figure 9.11 When the two triangles in the Playhead Lock button are out of alignment, the playheads are unlocked.

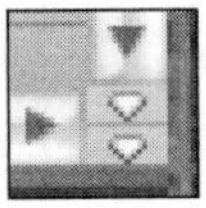

Figure 9.12 When the triangles align, the playheads are locked.

Unlocking the Timeline and Track Editor Playheads

The timeline and the track editor each have their own beat ruler and playhead. The playheads are synchronized: that is, they are both located at the same spot in the song. Normally, when you play a song, the playheads move to the center of the GarageBand window, and the timeline and track editor scroll by in the background so the playheads can stay centered (**Figure 9.10**). If the two areas are at different zoom levels, they will scroll at different speeds to enable the playheads to remain in the center.

Also by default, if you drag one of the playheads, the other moves as well, so the same section of the song is always displayed in both the timeline and the track editor. You can turn off this default behavior by *unlocking* the playheads, allowing the timeline and the track editor to display different parts of the song. When you play a song with unlocked playheads, it is the playheads that move across the display; the timeline and track editor remain stationary, unless you use the scroll bars to move through the song.

To unlock the timeline and track editor playheads:

◆ Click the Playhead Lock button to unlock the playheads (**Figure 9.11**).

You can now scroll to different locations in the song in the two parts of the window.

To lock the timeline and track editor playheads:

◆ Click the Playhead Lock button to lock the playheads (**Figure 9.12**).

Both playheads will now be centered in their respective parts of the GarageBand window.

✔ Tip

■ Using either of the horizontal scroll bars temporarily unlocks the playheads. If the playheads have been unlocked in this manner, starting playback locks them together again.

Renaming Tracks and Regions

When you add a track to your song, it takes its name from the instrument you assign to it in the Track Info window. If your song includes several tracks that use the same instrument, you may want to give them all unique names.

Likewise, when you record a new region, it automatically takes its name from its track. Regions created from loops are named after the loops from which they were made. Again, if your song has several regions with the same name, giving them distinctive names will help you tell them apart.

Use the track editor to rename both regions and tracks. GarageBand 1.1 added the ability to rename a track simply by double-clicking the name in its header (see "Renaming a Track" in Chapter 3), but to rename a region, you'll still have to resort to the track editor.

To rename a track:

1. If the track editor isn't open, open it now.

2. Click the track's header to select the track.

   The track appears in the track editor (**Figure 9.13**).

3. Check the header at the top left of the track editor to make sure it says "Track," not "Region." If it doesn't say "Track," click somewhere in the empty gray area of the track (**Figure 9.14**).

4. In the Name field at the left of the track editor, type a new name for the track (**Figure 9.15**).

5. Press Tab or Return to confirm the new name.

   The name change is reflected in the track header (**Figure 9.16**).

Figure 9.13 This track is ready to be renamed.

Figure 9.14 Click the empty area of the track to select the track, rather than a region in the track.

Figure 9.15 The track has a new, unique name.

Figure 9.16 The track header, showing the new name.

✔ Tip

■ The fact that clicking a track's header in the timeline causes the header in the track editor to say "Region" seemed to be a bug in GarageBand 1, and it still seems like a bug. Perhaps someday Apple will fix this inconsistent behavior.

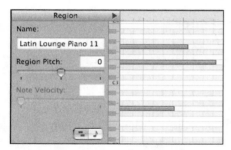

Figure 9.17 The selected region, ready for a new name.

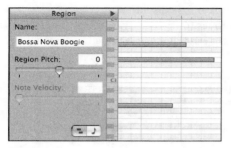

Figure 9.18 Name the region whatever you want.

Figure 9.19 The newly renamed region.

To rename a region:

1. If the track editor isn't open, open it now.

2. Click the region you want to rename to select the region.

   The region appears in the track editor (**Figure 9.17**).

3. Check the header at the top left of the track editor to make sure it says "Region," not "Track." If it doesn't say "Region," try clicking the region in the timeline one more time.

4. In the Name field at the left of the track editor, type a new name for the region (**Figure 9.18**).

5. Press Tab or Return to confirm the new name.

   The name change is reflected in the timeline (**Figure 9.19**).

Expanding the Track Editor

When it first opens, the track editor provides a relatively narrow view of the data contained in a region. It can easily be expanded to display more detail.

Here's how to widen the track editor:

1. Move the mouse pointer to the area that divides the timeline from the track editor. Stay to the left of the Record button or to the right of the time display. The pointer changes into a hand (**Figure 9.20**).

2. Drag upward to widen the track editor (**Figure 9.21**). Its maximum width is more than half again as great as its default width.

Widening the track editor when a Software Instrument region is displayed increases the range of the notes spanned by the editor from 24 semitones (or two octaves) to 38. If a Real Instrument region is displayed, widening the track editor stretches the region's waveform vertically, increasing the detail visible in the waveform.

Figure 9.20 Use this hand-shaped pointer to drag the top of the track editor upward.

Figure 9.21 The hand has dragged as far as it can go.

RENAMING TRACKS AND REGIONS

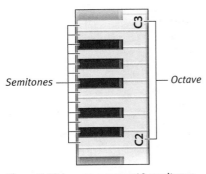

Figure 9.22 An octave spans 12 semitones.

About Transposition

To transpose music is to move it up or down in pitch, so it sounds in a different key. The unit of transposition is the *semitone*, or half-step. This is the distance between two adjacent notes on a piano keyboard: from C to C#, for example, or from E to F. Twelve semitones is equivalent to an octave, or the distance between two notes of the same name, such as C2 and C3 (**Figure 9.22**).

In GarageBand, it's possible to transpose an entire song to a new key using the master track's Track Info window (see "About the Master Track" in Chapter 11). The master track also has a pitch curve that you can use to transpose the whole song or just parts of the song (see "Working with the Master Track Automation Curves" in Chapter 12).

Working with the track editor, you can transpose both Software and Real Instrument regions, though Real Instrument regions can be transposed only if they were made from loops (colored blue) or if they were recorded in GarageBand 2 (colored purple). You can't transpose a Real Instrument region (orange) that you imported into GarageBand from another program. This is because Real Instrument regions that come from outside GarageBand don't include the extra information (the *metadata*) that tells GarageBand what key they are in to start with. Apple Loops and audio recordings you make yourself do include this information, which allows regions made from them to be transposed.

continues on next page

Use transposition sparingly. Keep in mind the relationship between the key of the region you are transposing and the key of the song as a whole. Sometimes you can create a striking effect by shifting a section of a song to a different key from the main song; but you have to be sure that you transpose all the regions that are sounding together, or you'll have cacophony. Another way to use transposition is to fix mistakes, such as to correct a MIDI region that was originally recorded in the wrong key.

You may not be happy with the results if you transpose a Real Instrument region more than a few semitones from its original key. Digitally transposing an audio recording produces only an approximation of the sound that you would get by playing the same passage higher or lower on a physical instrument. Note these possible problems when transposing Real Instrument regions:

◆ Transposing a region alters the color of the sound as well as the pitch. If you transpose an acoustic guitar region down by, say, six semitones, it will likely no longer sound like a guitar.

◆ The more semitones you transpose a region from its original key, the more artificial the sound becomes. The process of digital transposition introduces errors into the data, which can sound like noise.

Because the sound of a Software Instrument is artificially generated to begin with, the instrumental color of a Software Instrument region changes less drastically than does that of a Real Instrument region. That's part of the reason that Software Instrument regions can be transposed farther than Real Instrument regions.

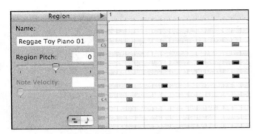

Figure 9.23 The Reggae Toy Piano 01 region is open in the track editor.

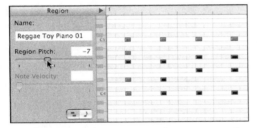

Figure 9.24 The region has been transposed down by seven semitones.

Figure 9.25 This region will be transposed up by six semitones.

Transposing Regions

The process of transposing a region is fairly straightforward: move its Region Pitch slider left or right to shift the pitch down or up. The maximum transposition for Real Instrument regions is 12 semitones (equivalent to one octave), but Software Instrument regions can be transposed three times as far: 36 semitones (equivalent to three octaves) up or down.

To transpose a region:

1. Display a green, blue, or purple region in the track editor (**Figure 9.23**).

2. Working on the left side of the track editor, *do one of the following:*

   ▲ To transpose the region up, drag the Region Pitch slider to the right.

   ▲ To transpose the region down, drag the Region Pitch slider to the left (**Figure 9.24**).

   ▲ To transpose the region by a specific number of semitones, type the number in the Region Pitch text field and press Tab or Return (**Figure 9.25**). Enter a positive number to transpose the region up; enter a negative number to transpose the region down.

continues on next page

TRANSPOSING REGIONS

A small tag appears on transposed regions in the timeline, showing the amount of transposition that has been applied (**Figure 9.26**).

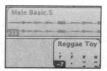

Figure 9.26 The labels in the lower-left corners of these regions show how far they have been transposed.

✔ Tips

■ Option-click the Region Pitch slider to reset its value to 0.

■ There is one "feature" of Software Instrument region transposition that has aggrieved a number of GarageBand users: When a Software Instrument region is transposed, the pitches displayed in the track editor in graphic view do not change. The only way to tell that the region has been transposed is to look at the Region Pitch slider.

When using notation view, however, transposing a Software Instrument region does move the notes to their new pitches. Notation view is a new feature of GarageBand 2 and is described in Chapter 10.

Enhancing Real Instrument Track Tuning or Timing

When making an audio recording, you will likely seldom capture a perfect take. You will, however, usually capture plenty of pretty good takes—the ones that would be just great if the vocalist hadn't sung a phrase flat, or if the drummer hadn't slipped behind the beat ever so slightly.

GarageBand 2 provides a couple of new functions that go a long way toward cleaning up these good takes and making them...well...more nearly perfect. These new functions allow you to enhance the tuning or the timing of a Real Instrument track. The controls for both of these functions live in the Advanced section of the track editor for Real Instruments (see "To display the Advanced section of the track editor" earlier in this chapter).

Each function is controlled by a slider. Use the Enhance Tuning slider to nudge any slightly out-of-tune notes closer to the correct pitch. The farther you drag the slider to the right (toward the end marked "Max"), the greater the correction that's applied. By default, the Enhance Tuning function tries to move the notes toward pitches in the scale of your piece. If your song is harmonically adventurous, however, and uses a lot of chromaticism, you'll find that the Enhance Tuning function will decide that some of your more unorthodox notes are wrong and will move them to different pitches entirely. To avoid this problem, uncheck the Limit to Key option. Now GarageBand will adjust the pitch of each note in the track so it is closer to a note in the full, 12-note chromatic scale.

continues on next page

The Enhance Timing function works similarly. Drag the Enhance Timing slider to the right to bring any rhythmically errant notes in your track back into line. Choose a value from the note value pop-up menu to set the degree of fussiness GarageBand uses in cleaning up your beats. If you choose 1/4 Note, GarageBand will make adjustments at the level of individual beats; but if you choose a smaller value, such as 1/16 Note, the program will make very fine adjustments.

A few words of caution: As with any of the tweaks GarageBand lets you apply to your music, use the enhancement functions judiciously! It's very easy to degrade the sound of your recording by "enhancing" it to the maximum setting. Also, the tuning enhancement really works only with tracks containing melody instruments: that is, an instrument that plays one note at a time, like a flute or the human voice. The timing enhancement, on the other hand, works with melodic and multi-note instruments as well as unpitched percussion. Both of these enhancements affect entire tracks, but work only on blue and purple regions: Real Instrument loops or regions recorded in GarageBand. They don't work on orange regions (audio files imported into GarageBand).

To enhance the tuning of a Real Instrument track:

1. Display a track in the track editor.

2. If the Advanced section of the track editor is not visible, click the triangle at the right edge of the track editor header to open it (**Figure 9.27**).

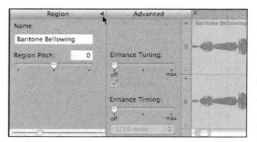

Figure 9.27 We'll apply tuning enhancement to this track.

Figure 9.28 Use this slider to set the amount of tuning enhancement for this track.

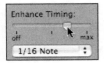

Figure 9.29 Use this slider to set the amount of timing enhancement for this track.

Figure 9.30 The note value menu.

3. Working in the Advanced section of the track editor, *do one of the following:*

   ▲ To increase the amount of tuning enhancement to be applied to the track, drag the Enhance Tuning slider to the right (**Figure 9.28**).

   ▲ To decrease the amount of tuning enhancement, drag the Enhance Tuning slider to the left.

4. *Optional:* Uncheck the Limit to Key check box to allow GarageBand to use all 12 notes of the chromatic scale when correcting the pitch of recorded notes.

To enhance the timing of a Real Instrument track:

1. Display a track in the track editor.

2. If the Advanced section of the track editor is not visible, open it (Figure 9.27).

3. Working in the Advanced section of the track editor, *do one of the following:*

   ▲ To increase the amount of timing enhancement to be applied to the track, drag the Enhance Timing slider to the right (**Figure 9.29**).

   ▲ To decrease the amount of timing enhancement, drag the Enhance Timing slider to the left.

4. *Optional:* Open the note value menu and choose the value to base the timing enhancement on (**Figure 9.30**).

✔ Tip

■ Neither enhancing tuning nor enhancing timing will cause any visible changes in the track data area of the track editor.

ENHANCING REAL INSTRUMENT TUNING OR TIMING

Fixing Software Instrument Region Rhythm

The track editor also includes a tool for tweaking the rhythm of Software Instruments: the Fix Timing button (at the left end of the track editor). Clicking this button snaps all the notes in the region to the timeline grid. If the performance that the region records was fairly stodgy, you can choose one of the Swing options from the timeline grid menu in the track editor and click the Fix Timing button to inject some life into the region.

The Fix Timing button is also handy for shaping up a region recorded by a performer who had trouble sticking with the beat. Choose a timeline grid setting of 1/4 Note and use the Fix Timing button to straighten out the rhythmic framework of the recording.

Note that the Fix Timing button shifts notes to the timeline grid whether or not the Snap to Grid command is checked in the Control menu.

To fix the timing of notes in a region:

1. Working in the track editor, display the Software Instrument region whose timing you want to change.

2. From the timeline grid menu in the track editor (*not* the one in the timeline), choose the grid setting you want to apply to the region (**Figure 9.31**).

   The chosen setting will be displayed at the left of the track editor (**Figure 9.32**).

3. Click the Fix Timing button.

   The notes in the region snap to the nearest gridlines (**Figure 9.33**).

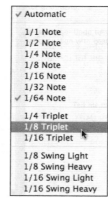

Figure 9.31 The grid is set to 1/8 Triplet.

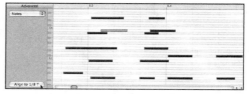

Figure 9.32 Before fixing the timing, notice that the notes don't always align with the gridlines.

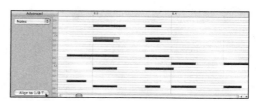

Figure 9.33 After you click the Fix Timing button, the notes all shift to the nearest gridlines.

✔ Tips

■ After clicking the Fix Timing button, listen to the track to see if it sounds the way you want. If you're not satisfied, use the Undo command to restore the region's previous timing. Choose a different setting from the timeline grid menu, click Fix Timing, and audition the region again.

■ The Swing settings will give the region a jazzy feel, while the fractional note values (1/4 note, 1/8 note, and so on) will impose a more rigid, "straight" feel. Be careful about fixing the timing of an entire region—you can very easily take all the life out of a performance this way. It's often better to fix individual notes that are way off and leave a few of the more subtle timing inconsistencies that make a performance sound more real.

FIXING SOFTWARE INSTRUMENT REGION RHYTHM

Undocumented Features in the Track Editor

I wrote in the previous edition of this book that "GarageBand's track editor... (at least in version 1.0.1 of the program) feels in many respects like a work in progress." Well, here we are in version 2.0, and the same statement holds true. If you poke around in the track editor long enough, you'll find features that aren't mentioned anywhere in Apple's Help files. For example, the Resize and Loop tools work on Real Instrument regions just like their counterparts in the timeline do (see "To resize a region" and "To loop a region" in Chapter 8). The track editor also has a tool not found in the timeline (**Figure 9.34**): a pointer that appears when you move the mouse near the upper edge of a region. When this pointer is visible, you can move the region left or right in the track editor by dragging. (However, you cannot move, resize, or loop a Software Instrument region in the track editor.)

Yet Apple's Help file is silent about these features. Perhaps these editing functions were insufficiently tested to warrant official presentation to the world.

The track editor harbors another undocumented feature that is definitely not ready for prime time. Through experimentation, I discovered that, working in the track editor, it's possible to use the Copy, Cut, and Paste commands on just a portion of a region, rather than an entire region. This is exactly the sort of feature that one expects of a track editor: the ability to fine-tune a recording by zeroing in on small portions of a track and trimming them away or slicing them off and moving them elsewhere.

Here's how it works: Move the mouse pointer over a Real Instrument region in the track editor. The pointer turns into a cross. Drag left or right over the passage you want to copy (**Figure 9.35**). The copied part of the region turns dark blue. Cut or copy the selected material; then position the playhead where you want to paste the material and execute the Paste command (**Figure 9.36**).

However, I've found this feature to be extremely unreliable. Sometimes the copied data isn't pasted where I expected, sometimes the track gets fouled up and won't play properly any more, and occasionally using this function crashes GarageBand and corrupts my song file.

We can only hope that Apple will polish this feature and incorporate it into an updated version of GarageBand. In the meantime, all the usual disclaimers apply: Try this at your own risk; your mileage may vary; objects may be closer than they appear.

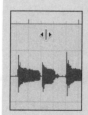

Figure 9.34 The undocumented move pointer.

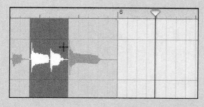

Figure 9.35 Drag with the cross pointed across the data to be cut or copied. The playhead is already positioned where we want to paste the material.

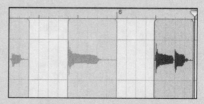

Figure 9.36 A snippet of sound has been cut from its original position and pasted several beats away.

EDITING MIDI DATA

When you record into a Software Instrument track, your performance is saved digitally as MIDI data. A discrete package of information is saved about each note you play, and you can edit this information on a note-by-note basis.

If you hit the wrong key, you can correct the pitch of the offending note. Say you happened to play one note too loudly, so it sticks out of the melodic line—you can change that one note's volume.

In this chapter you'll learn:

◆ How to use the track editor to edit MIDI data for individual notes.

◆ How to display and edit MIDI data using the new notation view.

◆ What MIDI controller data is and how to edit it.

Editing MIDI Data

As explained in Chapters 3 and 5, when you record a Software Instrument region, GarageBand captures data about each individual note played on a MIDI keyboard (or other MIDI controller). The track editor displays this data in graphical form (or as musical notation) and allows you to tweak these properties of any note:

- Length

- Pitch

- Location in time

- Velocity (loudness)

You can also add or delete notes and cut, copy, and paste notes using normal edit commands. You can edit several notes at once by selecting them first. I'll explain editing notes in graphic view first, because that's GarageBand's default display mode; then I'll describe editing in notation view.

To edit individual notes:

1. In the track editor, display the Software Instrument region you want to edit.

2. Display the track editor in graphic view, if necessary, and *do any of the following:*

   ▲ To select a note, click it. To select multiple notes, Shift-click or drag the notes (**Figure 10.1**). Notes turn green when selected.

   ▲ To raise or lower a note's pitch, drag the note up or down (**Figure 10.2**).

   ▲ To change the start of a note, drag the note left or right (**Figure 10.3**).

   ▲ To shorten or lengthen a note, drag the right edge of the note to the left or right (**Figure 10.4**).

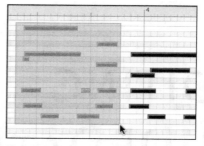

Figure 10.1 Dragging a selection rectangle around several notes.

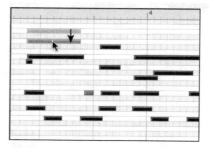

Figure 10.2 This note was dragged downward to lower its pitch by two semitones.

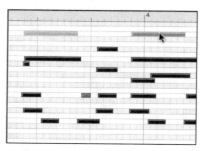

Figure 10.3 This note was dragged right so it will begin two beats later.

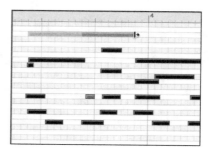

Figure 10.4 The length of this note was almost doubled by dragging.

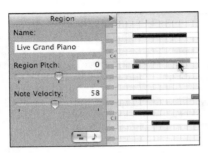

Figure 10.5 The note under the mouse pointer is selected and its original velocity is shown.

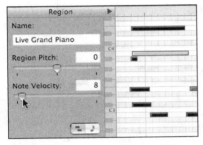

Figure 10.6 The note has turned a light gray, a visual cue that its velocity value is low.

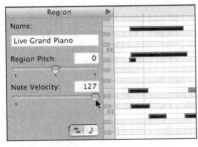

Figure 10.7 The note has darkened, to show that it will now sound as a loud note.

Changing Note Velocity

Velocity is the MIDI term for the loudness or softness of a note. It is a measure of the force with which a key is struck. A note's velocity is indicated in the track editor by its color: the darker the note, the higher its velocity. The range of possible velocity values runs from 1 to 127 (in the MIDI spec, the lowest possible velocity is 0, but for some reason GarageBand doesn't let you achieve absolute silence).

To change a note's velocity:

1. In the track editor, display the region that contains the note whose velocity you want to change.

2. Select the note or notes whose velocity you want to edit (**Figure 10.5**); *then do one of the following:*

   ▲ To make the note quieter, drag the Note Velocity slider to the left (**Figure 10.6**).

   ▲ To make the note louder, drag the Note Velocity slider to the right (**Figure 10.7**).

   The note's color changes to reflect its new velocity value.

✔ Tips

■ An alternative method for changing the velocity of a note is to type a new value in the numerical field above the Note Velocity slider and then press Tab or Return.

■ If you move the Note Velocity slider while multiple notes are selected, each note's velocity value will be raised or lowered by the same amount. The numerical readout above the slider will show the value only for the leftmost selected note.

Adding and Deleting Notes

Ever wish you could go back and erase the flubbed notes from your last piano performance? If you had been playing a MIDI keyboard connected to a Mac running GarageBand, you could do just that. You can delete notes from a Software Instrument region in the track editor, and you can add notes as well.

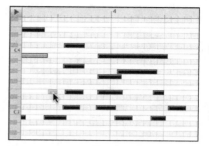

Figure 10.8 The selected note will be removed from the region.

To delete notes from a region:

1. In the track editor, display the region that you want to edit.

2. Select any note (or notes) you want to remove from the region (**Figure 10.8**).

3. Choose Edit > Delete or press Delete.
   The selected note is deleted (**Figure 10.9**).

To add notes to a region:

1. In the track editor, display the region you want to edit.

2. Hold down the Command key.
   The mouse pointer turns into a pencil (**Figure 10.10**).

3. Click the spot where you want to add a note.
   A note one eighth-note long of medium velocity (63) is added to the region (**Figure 10.11**).

✔ Tip

- After you add a new note to the region, you can adjust its length and velocity to taste.

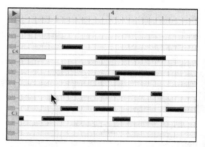

Figure 10.9 The note is gone.

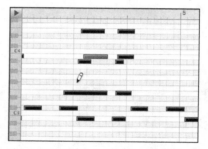

Figure 10.10 Click anywhere with the Pencil tool to add a note to the region.

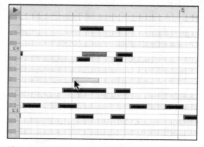

Figure 10.11 A new note appears. You can adjust its length and velocity to suit your needs.

ADDING AND DELETING NOTES

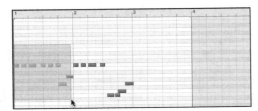

Figure 10.12 Select the notes in one bar of this bass part.

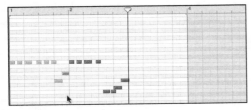

Figure 10.13 The playhead is positioned two measures after the measures previously copied.

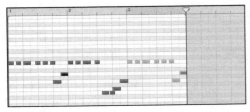

Figure 10.14 The first part of the bass line now repeats. The playhead has shifted to the end of the pasted area.

Using Cut, Copy, and Paste

You can also add, remove, and move notes with those old standbys: the Cut, Copy, and Paste commands. Recall that the Cut and Copy commands place selected notes on the Clipboard, a temporary storage area in your computer's memory. Cut also deletes the notes from their current location in the region. The Paste command places copies of cut or copied notes at the playhead's location. You can paste the notes into any Software Instrument region.

To cut or copy notes from a region:

1. In the track editor, display the region whose notes you want to copy.

2. Select the note (or notes) to be copied (**Figure 10.12**).

3. *Do one of the following:*
   ▲ Choose Edit > Cut (Command-X). The notes are removed from the region and placed on the Clipboard.
   ▲ Choose Edit > Copy (Command-C). The notes are copied to the Clipboard.

To paste notes:

1. Following the procedure outlined in the previous task, use the Cut or Copy command to place notes on the Clipboard.

2. Position the playhead at the spot where you want to paste the notes (**Figure 10.13**).

3. Choose Edit > Paste or press Command-V. The notes are added to the track at the playhead (**Figure 10.14**).

✔ Tip

■ GarageBand 1 allowed you to paste notes into an empty part of a Software Instrument track, creating a new region in the process. This is no longer possible in GarageBand 2. Go figure.

Working with MIDI Data in Notation View

If working with music depicted as little oblong blocks seems unnatural to you, GarageBand 2 offers the option of editing your MIDI data in the form of musical notation. Instead of dragging gray rectangles around on what looks like a piece of graph paper, you can drag actual notes around on a musical staff. Much more intuitive!

Notation view presents your Software Instrument track on a standard grand staff, using the key and time signatures you chose when you created the song or the signatures you chose later using the master track's Track Info window (see Chapter 12) (**Figure 10.15**). A *beat guide* is superimposed on the beat ruler, indicating the beats with large round dots, with beat subdivisions shown with small round dots. The beats are subdivided using the value currently active in the track editor's timeline grid menu (this value is displayed on the *Fix Timing button*). The

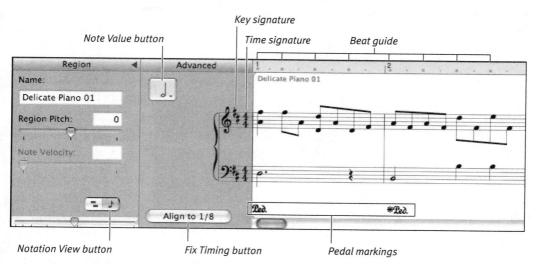

Figure 10.15 The Software Instrument track editor in notation view.

Graphic view

Notation view

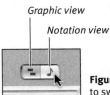

Figure 10.16 Click these buttons to switch between views.

notes' durational values are all adjusted to fit these subdivisions—the effect is the same as clicking the Fix Timing button in graphic view. Any notes you add will take the durational value displayed on the *Note Value button*. Aside from editing the notes in the selected region, you can adjust or delete *pedal markings*.

To display the track editor in notation view:

◆ Working in the left quadrant of the track editor, click the Notation View button (**Figure 10.16**).

To return to graphic view, click the Graphic View button.

✔ Tip

■ When getting ready to record a Software Instrument track, try opening the track in the track editor and switching to notation view. As you play your MIDI instrument, your performance is converted to notation right before your very eyes, in real time!

WORKING WITH MIDI DATA IN NOTATION VIEW

Editing Notes Using Notation View

Using notation view to edit notes in the track editor is much like using graphic view. (In fact, I recommend that you familiarize yourself with the techniques described earlier in this chapter before using notation view.) You select the note or notes you want to work with. When selected, notes display a *duration bar*, which shows how long the note is held. Once a note is selected, you can change its velocity or duration or delete it entirely. Drag a note with the mouse to change its pitch or location in time. Use the mouse plus the Command key to add new notes. The standard cut, copy, and paste editing functions do not seem to work, at least not in GarageBand 2.0.

To edit individual notes in notation view:

1. In the track editor, display the Software Instrument region you want to edit.

2. Display the track editor in notation view, if necessary, and *do one of the following:*

   ▲ To select a note, click it (**Figure 10.17**). To select multiple notes, Shift-click or drag the notes. Notes turn green when selected and display a duration bar.

   ▲ To shorten a note, drag the right side of the note's duration bar left; to lengthen a note, drag right (**Figure 10.18**).

   ▲ To raise or lower a note's pitch, drag the note up or down. As you drag the note, GarageBand plays each new pitch.

   ▲ To change the start of a note, drag the note left or right.

   ▲ To duplicate a note, Option-drag the note.

   ▲ To remove a selected note from a region, press Delete.

Figure 10.17 This note is selected and ready for editing.

Figure 10.18 Drag the right side of the duration bar to change the note's length.

✔ Tips

■ You can also move notes around using the arrow keys. Pressing the up or down arrow key moves the selected note up or down one semitone (but you won't hear the new pitch play). Pressing the left or right arrow key moves the selected note earlier or later in time, to the next point on the timeline grid (the next dot on the beat guide).

■ When you lengthen or shorten a note's duration bar by dragging, the bar's limits snap to the beat guide.

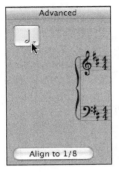

Figure 10.19 The Note Value button.

Figure 10.20 This menu shows the range of note values available.

Figure 10.21 Choose a new note value for notes you will add to your region.

To add notes to a region:

1. In the track editor, display the region that you want to edit.

2. Display the Advanced section of the track editor if it's not already open.

3. Click the Note Value button (**Figure 10.19**).

   The note value menu appears (**Figure 10.20**).

4. Working in the note value menu, choose the value of the note you want to add (**Figure 10.21**).

continues on next page

5. Hold down the Command key and move the mouse pointer over the position in the track data area where you want to add the note (**Figure 10.22**).

Faint notes appear under the pointer as it passes over the lines and spaces in the staff, indicating the note that will be added when you click.

6. When you have found the right spot for your note, click.

A new note will be added to the staff, and other notes in the same beat will be shortened to make room (**Figure 10.23**).

✔ Tip

■ Here's a secret, undocumented shortcut I stumbled across late one night: Control-click anywhere in the track editor (while in notation view), and the note value menu will appear right under your mouse pointer (**Figure 10.24**). This shortcut not only saves you time, but it saves you some screen space as well, because it means that you don't have to keep the Advanced section of the track editor open just to be able to access the Note Value button.

Figure 10.22 As your pointer moves over the F line, an F# note appears to notify you that if you click there, you will add an F# to the region.

Figure 10.23 The new eighth note takes half the value of the quarter note that was already there, reducing the quarter note to an eighth note.

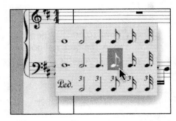

Figure 10.24 The secret note value context menu.

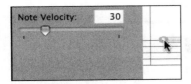

Figure 10.25 Selecting a note before changing its velocity.

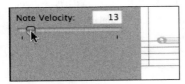

Figure 10.26 Dragging the Note Velocity slider.

Changing Note Velocity in Notation View

I introduced the concept of velocity earlier in this chapter (see "Changing Note Velocity"). Unlike graphic view, notation view provides no visual cue to a note's velocity. All you have to go on is the position of the Note Velocity slider and the text field above it.

To change a note's velocity:

1. In the track editor, display the region that contains the note whose velocity you want to change.

2. Select the note or notes whose velocity you want to edit (**Figure 10.25**); *then do one of the following:*
   - ▲ To make the note quieter, drag the Note Velocity slider to the left (**Figure 10.26**).
   - ▲ To make the note louder, drag the Note Velocity slider to the right.

✔ Tips

- ■ An alternative method for changing the velocity of a note is to type a new value in the numerical field above the Note Velocity slider and then press Tab or Return.

- ■ If you move the Note Velocity slider while multiple notes are selected, each note's velocity value will be raised or lowered by the same amount. The numerical readout above the slider will show the value only for the note selected last.

About Pedal Markings

"Real" pianos—analog, acoustic pianos—incorporate a *sustain* pedal. This is a foot-operated device that, when engaged, prevents the piano strings from being damped when a key is released, allowing the strings to continue to vibrate. MIDI instruments duplicate this effect digitally, recording a parameter called, surprisingly enough, Sustain. (For more information, see Chapter 5 and "Editing MIDI Controller Information" later in this chapter.)

If a Software Instrument region contains sustain data, it will appear as *pedal markings* in the track editor when it's displayed in notation view. Pedal markings are the symbols used in printed piano music (always below the bass, or bottom, staff) that instruct the performer when to depress and release the sustain pedal (**Figure 10.27**). The *pedal down* and *pedal up* symbols correspond to the MIDI sustain values of 1 and 0, respectively. You can edit these marks for a region in notation view; you can also delete them.

To edit pedal markings:

1. Display in the track editor the region whose pedal markings you want to edit.

2. Switch the track editor to notation view, if necessary.

3. *Do one of the following:*
   ▲ Drag the pedal down marker left or right to the desired position (**Figure 10.28**). While you are dragging, a dotted line connects it to its corresponding pedal up marker.
   ▲ Drag the pedal up marker left or right until it is positioned where you want it.

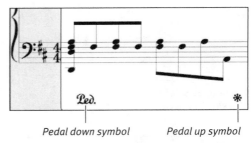

Pedal down symbol   Pedal up symbol

Figure 10.27 GarageBand's pedal markings.

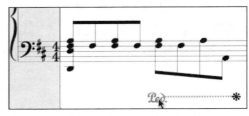

Figure 10.28 The pedal down marker has been dragged to the right.

Figure 10.29 The pedal up marker will be deleted.

Figure 10.30 The pedal up marker is gone.

Don't Start the Presses Just Yet

When Steve Jobs demonstrated GarageBand 2 at the January 2005 Macworld show, he gave those of us in the audience a fleeting glimpse of the notation view. I, along with the other GarageBand fans in the crowd, jumped to one conclusion: Wow! We can print our songs and get into the sheet music business!

But when I visited the Apple booth later that day and played around with the program, I discovered the sad reality: notation view was for editing only, and it displayed just one track at a time. The new program didn't even have a Print command. To print music, I was cheerfully informed by an Apple employee, I would need to pony up the $299 fee to upgrade to Logic Express.

Thanks. Thanks a lot. Way to dash a young man's dreams...

To delete pedal markings:

1. In the track editor, display the region containing the pedal markings you wish to delete.

2. Switch the track editor to notation view, if necessary.

3. Select the pedal marking you wish to delete (**Figure 10.29**) and press Delete.

   The pedal marking is deleted from the region (**Figure 10.30**).

✔ Tip

■ Apple's Help file for GarageBand 2 says that you can add pedal markings to a region by Command-clicking below the note where you want the down pedal to begin and dragging to the point where you want the pedal to go up again. Unfortunately, I couldn't get this to work. And it doesn't make sense: Command-clicking is already used for adding notes to the region. If you try to Command-click below the staff, you'll just add a bunch of very low, growly notes to your song.

I tried many other combinations of key presses and clicks, but nothing worked. You'll have to add pedal marks the old-fashioned way: change to graphic view and add sustain data points to your region (see "Editing MIDI Controller Information" later in this chapter). Then switch back to notation view, where the sustain data points will magically appear as pedal markings, and fine-tune the placement of the markings.

Editing MIDI Controller Information

As explained in Chapter 5, many MIDI keyboards include controllers for performance elements such as pitch bend, modulation, sustain, and expression. GarageBand records any input from these controllers during a performance, and you can use the track editor to edit this data. You can even enter controller data into the track editor, in case your keyboard lacks these hardware amenities.

A pop-up menu in the Advanced section of the track editor provides access to the various sets of controller data (**Figure 10.31**). The control points themselves are represented as dots connected by lines; each control point records a change in the physical state of the controller. Editing these control points is much like editing MIDI note data: you can move, cut, copy, paste, and delete the control points, and you can add new control points in the region, causing the lines that connect the control points to be redrawn in new shapes. The process of editing control points is the same for all types of controller data. Copying and pasting is most useful for transferring controller data from one region to a similar region in the same song.

To display MIDI controller data for a region:

1. Display in the track editor the region whose MIDI controller data you want to edit.

2. Click the triangle in the track editor's header to display the Advanced section of the editor, if it is not already visible.

3. From the Display pop-up menu, choose the type of controller data you want to edit (Figure 10.31).

   The MIDI controller data in this region is now available for editing.

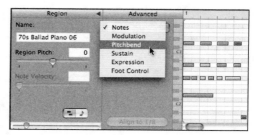

Figure 10.31 The Display pop-up menu, showing the types of MIDI controller data that can be edited in GarageBand.

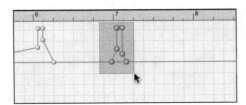

Figure 10.32 Drag-selecting a group of control points.

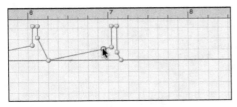

Figure 10.33 This control point was dragged upward.

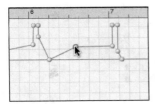

Figure 10.34 This control point was dragged to the left.

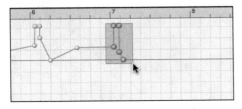

Figure 10.35 A group of points is selected.

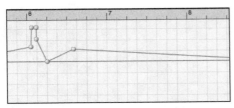

Figure 10.36 The selected points are deleted.

To edit controller information:

◆ Display the MIDI controller data for a region; *then do any of the following:*

◆ To select a control point, click it. To select multiple control points, Shift-click or drag around the points (**Figure 10.32**). Control points enlarge slightly when selected.

◆ To alter a control point's value, drag the control point up or down (**Figure 10.33**).

◆ To change a control point's position in time, drag the control point left or right (**Figure 10.34**).

To delete control points:

1. In the track editor, display the region whose control points you want to edit.

2. Select any point (or points) you want to remove from the region (**Figure 10.35**).

3. Choose Edit > Delete or press Delete. The selected control point is deleted (**Figure 10.36**).

To add control points to a region:

1. In the track editor, display the region whose control points you want to edit.

2. Hold down the Command key.

   The mouse pointer turns into a pencil (**Figure 10.37**).

3. Click the spot where you want to add a control point. (**Figure 10.38**).

   GarageBand adds a control point; a line connects it to the other control points in the region.

To cut or copy control points from a region:

1. In the track editor, display the region whose control points you want to copy.

2. Select the control point (or points) to be copied (**Figure 10.39**).

3. *Do one of the following:*

   ▲ Choose Edit > Cut (Command-X). The control points are removed from the region and placed on the Clipboard.

   ▲ Choose Edit > Copy (Command-C). The control points are copied to the Clipboard.

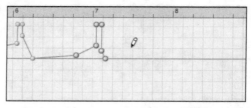

Figure 10.37 Use the Pencil tool to add control points to the region.

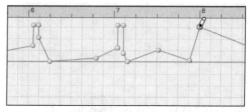

Figure 10.38 After adding several control points.

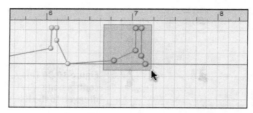

Figure 10.39 These control points will be copied.

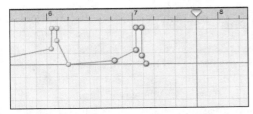

Figure 10.40 The playhead is at the spot where the copied control points will be pasted.

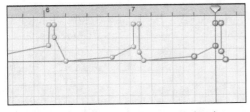

Figure 10.41 The control points are pasted at the playhead.

To paste control points:

1. Following the procedure outlined in the previous task, use the Cut or Copy command to place control points on the Clipboard.

2. Position the playhead at the spot where you want to paste the control points (**Figure 10.40**).

3. Choose Edit > Paste or press Command-V. The control points are added to the region at the playhead (**Figure 10.41**).

✔ Tip

■ The track editor is a handy tool for editing MIDI controller information that you've already programmed into a track, but using it to enter a lot of data by hand is a slow and cumbersome process. There's an easier way, if your MIDI keyboard is equipped with controllers for pitch bend, modulation, and sustain: add the controller data by overdubbing (see the sidebar "Using a Cycle Region for Overdubbing" in Chapter 7).

■ Set up a cycle region that covers the passage to which you want to add controller data; then start recording. While the passage plays, don't touch the keys on the keyboard, but use the keyboard's hardware controllers to create the effect you want. Use a different controller on each pass through the cycle: manipulate the modulation wheel on one pass, twiddle the pitch bend wheel on another pass, and pump the sustain pedal on yet another pass. This process is much more intuitive than clicking and dragging with the mouse!

The Types of MIDI Controller Data

GarageBand is aware of the classes of MIDI controller data that correspond to the physical controllers most commonly integrated into MIDI keyboards: pitch bend, modulation, and sustain data. GarageBand 2 adds support for two less-common controllers: expression and foot control. Pitch bend and modulation are normally adjusted by wheel controls and are capable of recording smoothly varying data points. Expression and foot control are operated by pedals that are also capable of registering a spectrum of data. Sustain, on the other hand, is normally controlled by a simple on/off switch operated by a pedal; thus, its data points always have the value 0 (for off) or 1 (for on) (**Figure 10.42**).

Values for pitch bend are graphed differently from those for modulation, expression, and foot control, as you can see by the different scales at the left end of the track editor when the different data types are displayed.

The pitch bend scale places 0 at the center and measures positive values above and negative values below that point (**Figure 10.43**). The scale (which runs from −64 to +64) is calibrated in arbitrary units. A pitch bend of 30 units on this scale corresponds approximately to a semitone. If a control point has a pitch bend value of +15, therefore, the pitch has been shifted upward about halfway to the next note (for example, halfway from F to F#).

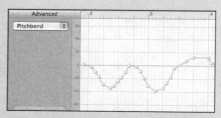

Figure 10.42 Sustain data for a passage in which the sustain pedal is held down continually (sustain value of 1), but is released briefly (sustain value of 0) on the first beat of each measure.

The modulation scale is also calibrated in different arbitrary units, and it starts with 0 at the bottom and rises to 127 (**Figure 10.44**). The modulation controller usually adds color to a note (most commonly in the form of vibrato), and the value of a control point represents the depth of the vibrato at that point. To my ear (that's all I have to go on, because Apple has provided no documentation for this feature), a modulation setting of 127 (the maximum) creates a vibrato that fluctuates about one half semitone above and one half semitone below the pitch of the note.

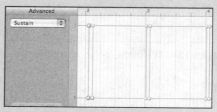

Figure 10.43 A sample of pitch bend data, showing the scale at the left end of the graph.

The newcomers to this list, namely expression and foot control, were added to GarageBand 2 specifically to work with the ultra-sophisticated Software Instruments in GarageBand Jam Pack 4: Symphony Orchestra (this Jam Pack won't work with GarageBand 1, in fact). I'll save the discussion of these MIDI controllers for Appendix B, where I talk about the Jam Packs.

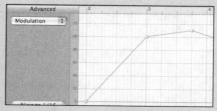

Figure 10.44 A sample of modulation data, showing the scale at the left end of the graph.

APPLYING
EFFECTS

11

One feature that sets GarageBand apart from other inexpensive music programs is its collection of effects. The program includes a couple dozen of these professional-quality audio processing components. A few years ago, effects like these were found only in expensive, high-end audio programs; indeed, GarageBand's effects appear to be derived from those in Apple's flagship music program, Logic Pro.

Adding effects to your song is not a necessary part of composition, but it can make your song sound more professional and add interest—plus they're fun to play with. In this chapter, I discuss:

◆ What effects are.

◆ How to apply effects to individual tracks and to the song as a whole.

◆ How to customize effects and save the settings as presets.

◆ What specific effects do to the sound of your song.

◆ How to edit Software Instrument sounds.

◆ What Audio Units are and how to use them.

APPLYING EFFECTS

217

About Effects

Effects manipulate the sound of a track or a
song electronically to enhance its sound or
change the sound's color. For example, one
of the most common effects is *reverb* (short
for *reverberation*), which electronically alters
the acoustical environment of a sound. A
performance might be recorded in an
acoustically dry setting, for example, like a
recording studio, but with the application of
reverb, the recording can sound like it was
made in a large church or a tiled bathroom.

Until a few years ago, effects (which require
a great deal of audio signal processing) were
produced exclusively by specialized pieces of
hardware. For instance, a recording studio or
a sound system might have a piece of equipment devoted to adding reverb to a signal,
another device might provide equalization,
and still other devices might compress the
dynamic range or add specialized color
effects like tremolo or flanging. Acquiring
all of these boxes cost serious money, and
carting them around and storing them was
a huge inconvenience.

Today's personal computers are powerful
enough to emulate the functions of these
hardware effects generators in software
alone, which means that a Mac running
GarageBand can take the place of quite a
few of those old boxes.

In GarageBand, you use the Track Info window to apply effects to each track. I described
the Track Info window for Real Instrument
and Software Instrument tracks in Chapter
3 (see "About the Track Info Window"). To
add effects to the entire song, you use a
third type of track: the master track.

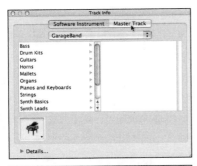

Details pane disclosure triangle

Figure 11.1 Displaying Track Info for the master track. Top: Click the Master Track button at the top of the Track Info window. Bottom: The window now displays info for the master track.

Change your Song's Key, Tempo, or Time Signature

The master track's Track Info window contains the same controls as the dialog you used when you first created your song. You can use these controls to change the tempo, time signature, or key signature of your song at any time (see "Creating a New Song" in Chapter 2 for a full description of these features).

Keep in mind, however, that these changes will *not* affect any audio files you might have imported from the Finder. Only Real Instrument regions you recorded in GarageBand, Real Instrument loops, and Software Instrument tracks will be changed.

About the Master Track

The master track is different from the tracks into which you record or into which you place loops. Unlike Real and Software Instrument tracks, it does not contain music, but it is the repository for a number of settings that affect your song as a whole. If you decide, after working on a song for a while, that you need to change any of its fundamental characteristics (its tempo, time signature, or key signature), you can do this in the master track's Track Info window. You use the master track's Track Info window to apply effects to the entire song. You can also use the master track to add volume or pitch changes over the course of a song by displaying and adjusting its track volume curve or its pitch curve (see "Working with the Master Track Automation Curves" in Chapter 12).

To display the Track Info window for the master track:

1. Display the Track Info window for any track.

2. Click the Master Track button at the top of the window.

   The Track Info window displays information for the master track (**Figure 11.1**).

✔ Tip

■ If the master track is visible, you can display its Track Info window by choosing Track > Show Master Track (Command-I) or by double-clicking its track header.

The Track Info Window Effects Controls

The effects controls reside in a part of the Track Info window that is hidden by default. Click the Details disclosure triangle at the bottom of the window (Figure 11.1) to reveal the effects controls (**Figure 11.2**).

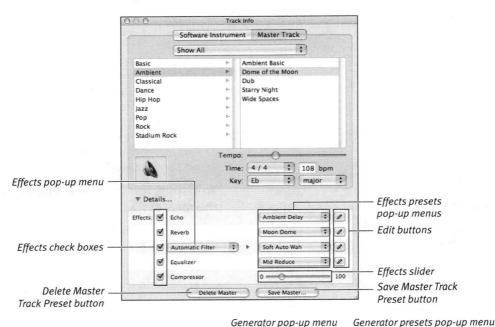

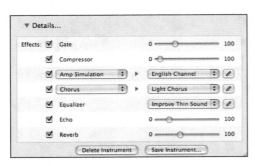

Details pane for a Real Instrument track

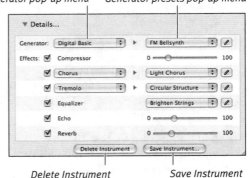

Details pane for a Software Instrument track

Figure 11.2 Top: The Track Info window for the master track, with effects controls now revealed. Bottom left: The Details pane for a Real Instrument track. Bottom right: The Details pane for a Software Instrument track.

You can apply effects to each track individually or to the song as a whole. To add effects to the entire song, apply them to the *master track* (see "About the Master Track" earlier in this chapter). Real Instrument and Software Instrument tracks access the same set of effects, with a few significant exceptions; a subset of these effects is available to the master track.

There are four basic effects available to all tracks: echo, reverb, equalizer (EQ), and compressor. Echo and reverb must be turned on and configured in the master track before they can be applied to any of the instrument tracks. A fifth effect, gate (short for *noise gate*), can be used only with Real Instrument tracks. The Track Info window also has a pair of pop-up menus that offer a long list of optional effects (the master track has only one menu) that may be added to the track.

The Software Instrument Track Info window includes an item that stands apart from the other effects settings. The Generator pop-up menu (together with its attendant presets menu) allows you to alter the track's basic instrumental sound. You can even replace the sound with an entirely different one. Because this procedure is somewhat different from that for adding effects, I discuss it in a separate section at the end of the chapter.

THE TRACK INFO WINDOW EFFECTS CONTROLS

Applying Effects

Applying effects to a track is not simply a matter of flicking a switch. Each effect has parameters that need to be adjusted. GarageBand takes some of the guesswork out of choosing effects settings by providing *presets* for most effects. The presets for each effect appear in a pop-up menu to the right of the effect's listing in the Track Info window. Next to each effect's presets menu is an Edit button, which opens the settings window for that effect so you can customize the effect. You can save your customized settings as a preset, and it will appear on the preset menu. Some of the simpler effects (gate and compressor, for example) are adjusted with a slider. Effects controlled with a slider do not use presets.

While you're just learning to use GarageBand, it's a good idea to stick with the presets. After you're more experienced and you've developed a more sensitive ear, then it's time to dig in and start customizing effects settings to your taste.

To apply an effect to a track:

1. Open the Track Info window for the track to which you want to add an effect.

2. Click the Details button to open the Effects pane of the window and *do one of the following:*

   ▲ Check the box next to the name of the effect you want to add (**Figure 11.3**).

   ▲ Choose an effect from one of the Effects pop-up menus (**Figure 11.4**).

Figure 11.3 The check box shows that this effect is enabled.

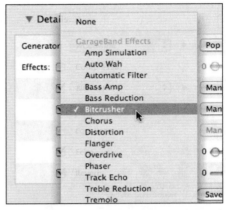

Figure 11.4 This pop-up menu is home to some of the more exotic effects offered by GarageBand.

Figure 11.5 Some effects are controlled by a simple slider.

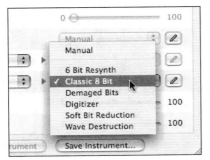

Figure 11.6 GarageBand's presets often have colorful names.

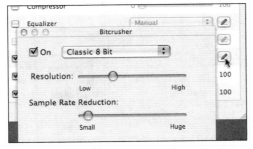

Figure 11.7 Clicking the Edit button for an effect opens a window like this.

3. Adjust the settings for the effect *using one of the following methods:*

▲ Drag the slider (**Figure 11.5**).

▲ Open the effect's presets pop-up menu and choose a preset value (**Figure 11.6**).

▲ Click the Edit button next to the current preset to open the settings window for the effect and drag the sliders (**Figure 11.7**).

4. To add more effects, repeat steps 2 and 3.

✔ Tips

■ If you customize one of the presets, the presets menu will display "Manual" until you save your changes as a new preset (see "Saving Effects Presets" later in this chapter).

■ You can also use the settings window to turn an effect on and off or choose a preset.

Choosing Which Presets Are Displayed

GarageBand ships with a great many instrument and effects presets, and if you purchase one or more GarageBand Jam Packs, or download collections of presets made by third-parties, or create presets of your own, your preset menus can grow to be unmanageably large.

To help you deal with your vast preset library, GarageBand 2 provides a menu similar to the one I discussed in Chapter 4 (see "Choosing the Loops the Loop Browser Displays"). This pop-up menu, situated near the top of the Track Info window, allows you to choose whether all of your presets will be displayed in the Track Info window, or only the presets in individual collections.

Here are the choices on the menu:

Show All (the default): All of the presets installed on your Mac will be displayed.

My Settings: Only the presets created by the user will be shown.

GarageBand: Only those presets originally installed with the program will appear in your search.

Jam Pack 1, 2, 3, or 4: Choosing any of these limits the display to presets contained in that Jam Pack.

Other: Folders of third-party presets that you've imported into GarageBand.

To choose which presets are displayed in the Track Info window:

1. Open the pop-up menu at the top of the Track Info window (**Figure 11.8**).

2. Choose the collection of presets you want to see in the Track Info window (**Figure 11.9**).

   The Track Info window now displays presets from that collection only.

Figure 11.8 Use this pop-up menu to choose a preset collection.

Figure 11.9 After you make this selection, only presets from GarageBand Jam Pack 1 will be displayed in the Track Info window.

What Happened to My Presets?

One consequence of choosing any preset collection other than Show All or My Settings is that presets that you created will not be listed. GarageBand reminds you of this fact when you create a new preset while your own presets are invisible by showing the Your Preset Will Be Hidden dialog (**Figure 11.10**).

Figure 11.10 The Your Preset Will Be Hidden dialog.

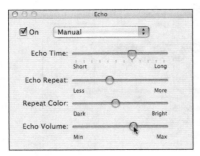

Figure 11.11 The settings window for the echo effect.

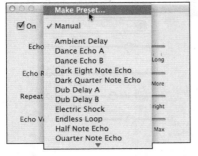

Figure 11.12 The Make Preset command is at the very top of the effects presets pop-up menu.

Figure 11.13 Name your new preset.

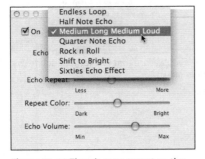

Figure 11.14 There's your preset on the presets pop-up menu.

Saving Effects Presets

You can save effect settings that you want to keep for later use by saving them as presets. Any presets you save will be available in all of your GarageBand songs, not just the one in which you created the preset.

To save a preset for an effect:

1. Click the Edit button for a preset to open its settings window.

2. Adjust the sliders until the effect is configured the way you want it (**Figure 11.11**).

3. From the presets pop-up menu in the settings window, choose Make Preset (**Figure 11.12**).

4. In the Make Preset dialog that appears, type the name you want to give the new preset (**Figure 11.13**).

5. Click OK.

   The new preset is added to the presets menu (**Figure 11.14**).

To delete a preset:

1. Working in the effect's settings window, choose the preset you want to delete (**Figure 11.15**).

2. From the presets pop-up menu, choose Delete Preset (**Figure 11.16**).

3. In the confirmation dialog that appears, click Remove (**Figure 11.17**).

   The preset is removed from the menu.

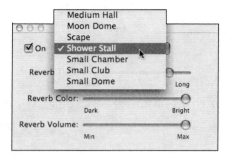

Figure 11.15 The checked preset will be deleted.

Figure 11.16 Choosing the Delete Preset command.

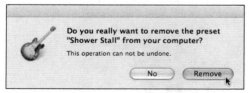

Figure 11.17 If you're sure that you want to delete the preset, click Remove.

Figure 11.18 If you want, choose a different category in which to save your new instrument preset.

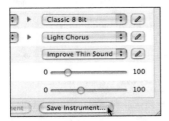

Figure 11.19 The Save Instrument button.

Figure 11.20 The Save Instrument dialog.

Figure 11.21 Your new preset appears in the top half of the Track Info window.

Saving Instrument Presets

Any changes you make to settings in the Details pane of the Track Info window are considered changes to the instrument assigned to that track. You can save your customized effect settings as a new instrument preset. By default, your new preset will be saved in the same category as the instrument you started with. You can save your new instrument preset in a different category by clicking the category in the left column of the upper part of the Track Info window. Choosing a different category won't affect the actual sound of your instrument; the categories merely help to keep the instruments organized.

To save an instrument preset:

1. If you want to save a preset to a different category, click that category's name in the list in the top half of the Track Info window (**Figure 11.18**).

2. Click the Save Instrument button at the bottom right of the Track Info window (**Figure 11.19**).

3. In the Save As field in the Save Instrument dialog that opens, type a name for the new instrument and click Save (**Figure 11.20**).

   The new preset is added to the instrument list in the Track Info window (**Figure 11.21**).

SAVING INSTRUMENT PRESETS

To delete an instrument preset:

1. Working in the instrument list in the top half of the Track Info window, select the instrument you want to delete (**Figure 11.22**).

2. Click the Delete Instrument button at the bottom left of the window (**Figure 11.23**).

3. In the confirmation dialog that appears, click Remove (**Figure 11.24**).

   The instrument is deleted from the Track Info window list.

✔ Tips

■ You can delete only user-created instruments. The instrument presets that ship with GarageBand and the GarageBand Jam Packs cannot be removed.

■ The procedures in these tasks can also be used to save and delete master track presets. When you work with the Track Info window for the master track, every occurrence of the word *instrument* on a button or in a dialog is replaced by the word *master*.

Figure 11.22 Mark an instrument preset for deletion.

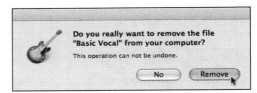

Figure 11.23 The Delete Instrument button.

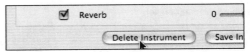

Figure 11.24 You're given one last chance to change your mind.

The Confusing "You Have Made Changes to the Current Instrument Setting" Dialog

Often when working in the Track Info window, you will encounter a puzzling dialog (**Figure 11.25**). It can be puzzling for a couple of reasons:

◆ It's triggered when you switch from the Manual effect setting to a saved preset, even if you didn't make any changes to the customized setting.

◆ The same message appears whether you change to a different effects preset or to a different instrument preset.

The dialog is somewhat misleading, because it implies that, when working with effects, if you switch from the Manual setting to a saved preset, you will lose your customizations. This is not true. The Manual setting retains your customized settings until you change them yourself. Even if you save and close the song, the next time you open it, the Manual effects setting will be intact. The dialog is merely trying to remind you that your customization hasn't been saved as a preset.

If you want to save your special setting as a preset, go ahead and click Save. If you are changing effects settings, you will be presented with the Save Preset dialog, which works like the Make Preset dialog (Figure 11.13). If you are changing to a different instrument preset, the Save Instrument (or Save Master) dialog will appear (Figure 11.20).

Or you can check the Never Ask Again box to turn off the nagging. With that box checked, it's up to you to remember to save as presets the customizations you want to keep.

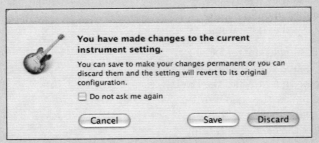

Figure 11.25 The You Have Made Changes to the Current Instrument Setting dialog.

Using the Echo Effect

Echo is one of the most basic effects. The echo effect causes the source sound to repeat after a delay. To use echo, you must first make sure that it's turned on and choose a setting in the master track's Track Info window (the echo and reverb effects share this restriction). Then open the Track Info window for each instrument track to which you want to add echo and enable it there. Use the master track to set the maximum amount of echo in the song; then use the sliders in the Track Info windows for the individual instrument tracks to choose the portion of that maximum you want in each track. Echo has the following parameters (**Figure 11.26**):

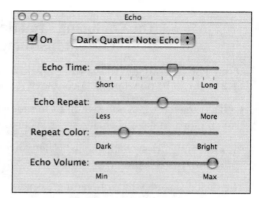

Figure 11.26 Drag these sliders to fine-tune the settings for the echo effect.

◆ **Echo Time:** Adjusts the length of the delay between the original sound and the echo.

◆ **Echo Repeat:** Adjusts the number of times the echo repeats. If you drag the slider all the way to the More end, the echo keeps repeating for a very long time. This echoing can build up and cause feedback if you're not careful.

◆ **Repeat Color:** Changes the tone color of the echo compared with the original sound. Moving the slider toward the Dark end of the scale makes the echo muffled and indistinct, while moving it to the Bright end makes the echo sound tinny and thin. Setting the slider in the middle gives you a nice balance between the two.

◆ **Echo Volume:** Adjusts the volume of the echo relative to the original sound. Dragging the slider toward Min makes the echo softer, and dragging toward Max makes it louder. Remember that you can also control the amount of echo in the individual instrument tracks, so don't set this level too low.

Figure 11.27 The echo effect has been enabled for this song.

Figure 11.28 This slider sets the amount of echo that will be applied to this track.

To use the echo effect:

1. Open the Track Info window for the master track and click the Details pane to reveal the effects controls.

2. Click the Echo check box to turn on the echo effect for the song (**Figure 11.27**).

3. Choose a setting from the presets pop-up menu or click the Edit button and choose your own settings.

4. With the Track Info window still open, select a track in the timeline to which you want to apply the echo effect.

5. Make sure the Echo box is checked and then drag the slider to determine how much of the effect from the master track is applied to the instrument track (**Figure 11.28**).

✔ Tip

■ GarageBand 2 includes another version of the echo effect, called Track Echo (the feature was actually added with the GarageBand 1.1 update). As its name implies, Track Echo is track specific and does not depend on the Echo setting in the master track (see "Track Echo" in the section "About the Other GarageBand Effects" later in this chapter).

Using the Reverb Effect

Reverb is short for *reverberation*, which is what happens to sound in an enclosed space. The sound bounces off the surfaces of the space, decaying a bit at each bounce. It's like a long, smeared-out echo, without any distinct repetition of the original sound. A judicious amount of reverb can sweeten any recording. It creates a sort of acoustic glow that can create just the right atmosphere for a song, and it can cover up some of the imperfections in a mediocre performance. In the real world, reverberation depends on the size and shape of the room and the materials the walls and ceiling are made from. GarageBand's reverb effect can mimic the reverberation you would hear in a variety of real performing spaces.

Like the echo effect, reverb must be turned on in the master track before it can be applied to any instrument track. Use the master track to set the upper limit for the amount of reverb in the song; then use the sliders in the Track Info windows for the individual instrument tracks to choose how much reverb you want in each track. These are the parameters for reverb (**Figure 11.29**):

◆ **Reverb Time:** Adjusts the length of time it takes for the reverberation to die out completely.

◆ **Reverb Color:** Changes the tone color of the reverberation compared with the original sound. Moving the slider toward the Dark end of the scale favors the low frequencies by making the high frequencies die out faster, while moving it toward the Bright end favors the high frequencies.

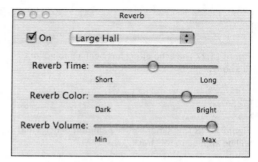

Figure 11.29 These sliders define the characteristics of the reverb effect that will be applied in this song.

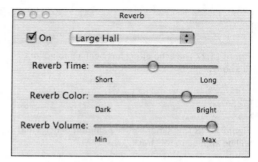 content (as shown in figure): Reverb / On / Large Hall / Reverb Time: Short — Long / Reverb Color: Dark — Bright / Reverb Volume: Min — Max

Figure 11.30 Reverb has been turned on for this song and a preset has been chosen.

Figure 11.31 Reverb will be applied to this track at about half the intensity defined for the master track.

◆ **Reverb Volume:** Adjusts the volume of the reverb relative to the original sound. At the Max setting, the reverb starts at the same volume as the original sound before beginning to decay. Dragging the slider toward Min causes the reverb to start at lower volumes.

To use the reverb effect:

1. Open the Track Info window for the master track and click the Details pane to reveal the effects controls.

2. Click the Reverb check box to turn on the reverb effect for the song (**Figure 11.30**).

3. Choose a setting from the presets pop-up menu or click the Edit button and choose your own settings.

4. With the Track Info window still open, select a track in the timeline to which you want to apply the reverb effect.

5. Make sure the Reverb box is checked and drag the slider to determine how much of the reverb from the master track is applied to the instrument track (**Figure 11.31**).

Turn Off Effects You're Not Using

Some GarageBand users have reported that dragging an effect's slider to 0 is not the same as turning it off—that is, just having echo or reverb enabled appears to sap some of your computer's processing power, even if the values are set to 0. If you are having trouble getting your song to play on your machine, try unchecking any effects you're not actually using. You may free up enough processor cycles to let your song be heard in all its glory. If you're not using echo or reverb on any of your tracks, turning the effect off on the master track saves you the trouble of disabling it on every instrument track.

USING THE REVERB EFFECT

Using the Equalizer Effect

The equalizer effect (often referred to as EQ) allows you to increase or decrease the volume of different parts of the audio spectrum. To bring out a bass line, for instance, you might boost the low-frequency part of the spectrum, while to make percussion sizzle, you might boost the high frequencies (or treble). Alternatively, if one of your tracks has an annoying rumble or other low-frequency noise, you can cut the bass to try to diminish it.

When applied to individual tracks, the equalizer effect is a helpful tool in the mixing process. Each instrument has a distinctive sound color, which is created by a unique mixture of sounds of various frequencies. But if you have tracks with several different sounds overlapping at once, the different colors are likely to merge into a sort of gray cloud. Use the equalizer effect to increase the color contrast among the different instruments in your song to open up the texture and make it more transparent. A good way to learn about equalization is to experiment with the presets provided with GarageBand. The name of each gives a clear idea of what it's designed to do.

The equalizer settings for each instrument track are independent of the master track setting. Each of the three gain sliders controls a different range of frequencies (**Figure 11.32**). Drag each slider to the left to weaken the frequencies in that range, and drag to the right to strengthen them.

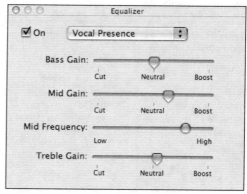

Figure 11.32 Use these sliders to set the equalizer parameters for a song or for a single track.

Figure 11.33 The equalizer effect will be applied to the selected track.

The Mid Frequency slider lets you pick the range affected by the Mid Gain slider. This range is singled out for special treatment because this is the range to which the human ear is most sensitive. The main notes of melodies and most voices fall in this range. For example, when using the equalizer with the main vocal track in your song, drag the Mid Gain slider to the right (while the track is playing) and then adjust the Mid Frequency slider until the vocal line acquires prominence without becoming shrill or distorted.

- **Bass Gain:** Adjusts the strength of low-frequency sounds.

- **Mid Gain:** Adjusts the strength of mid-range frequencies, as determined by the Mid Frequency slider.

- **Mid Frequency:** Determines the specific part of the middle range of frequencies affected by the Mid Gain slider.

- **Treble Gain:** Adjusts the strength of high-frequency sounds.

To use the equalizer:

1. Open the Track Info window for the track to which you want to apply the equalizer effect and click the Details pane to reveal the effects controls.

2. Click the Equalizer check box to enable this effect (**Figure 11.33**).

3. Choose a setting from the presets pop-up menu or click the Edit button and choose your own settings.

Using the Compressor Effect

Figure 11.34 The compressor effect will be applied to the selected track.

The compressor effect reduces the dynamic range of a track (or of a song, if applied to the master track). It's especially useful for individual tracks that have a wider dynamic range than the rest of the song: for example, a vocal track that gets extremely soft in places and very loud in others. Such a track is very difficult to balance with other tracks, because if you boost its lowest volume so it can be heard above the rest of the song, its loudest passages will cause distortion (not to mention deafness!).

You can fix this problem by applying the compressor to the track to reduce the difference between the softest and loudest parts of the song. You might apply compression to an entire song if you knew it was going to be played back on a device with limited dynamic range, such as any portable music player with earbuds.

The compressor setting in the instrumental tracks is independent of the setting in the master track.

To use the compressor effect:

1. Open the Track Info window for the track to which you want to apply the compressor effect and click the Details pane to reveal the effects controls.

2. Click the Compressor check box to enable this effect (**Figure 11.34**).

3. Drag the slider to the right to increase the amount of compression applied to the track, or drag to the left to reduce the amount.

Figure 11.35 The check box turns on the gate effect, and the slider specifies the cutoff volume.

Using the Gate Effect

The gate effect is a simple filter that stops sounds below a certain volume from being heard. It can be useful for blocking quiet background noises that intrude upon audio recordings such as the buzz of an amplifier or a guitar pickup.

The gate effect can be applied only to Real Instrument tracks.

To use the gate effect:

1. Open the Track Info window for the Real Instrument track to which you want to apply the gate effect and click the Details pane to reveal the effects controls.

2. Click the Gate check box to enable this effect (**Figure 11.35**).

3. Drag the slider to the right to raise the minimum volume allowed through the gate. Drag the slider to the left to lower the minimum volume allowed.

   A setting of 100 filters out all sound. A low setting allows all but the quietest sounds through, and a setting of 0 admits all sounds.

About the Other GarageBand Effects

In addition to the basic effects already discussed, GarageBand includes another dozen or so effects (GarageBand 2 added three new ones), listed as GarageBand effects in the top half of the pop-up menus on the left side of the Details pane of the Track Info window (**Figure 11.36**). (I'll touch briefly on the Audio Unit effects listed in the bottom half of those menus a little later, in "About Audio Units.")

You can apply one of the effects from this menu to the master track; instrument tracks generously provide two identical effects menus per track. Keep in mind that every effect you use adds to the load on your computer's processing power, so unless you have a powerful Mac, use effects sparingly. To add one of these effects to your song, see "To apply effects to a track" earlier in the chapter.

Complete explanations of these effects would be highly technical and are beyond the scope of this book; you can learn a great deal by trying the presets and experimenting with the sliders for each effect. However, since Apple's documentation for GarageBand passes over these effects in silence, here are thumbnail descriptions of each:

◆ **Amp Simulation:** This effect makes your track sound like it has been connected to an electric guitar amplifier. This effect is especially useful when recording an electric guitar through a direct connection to your Mac, bypassing the guitar's own amp. Indeed, all of the Real Instrument electric guitar settings, and most of the Software Instrument electric guitar settings, include amp simulation. But it's not just for guitars; this effect works on any instrument, allowing you to play any of your tracks through a virtual guitar amp (**Figure 11.37**). If you

Figure 11.36
The contents of the effects pop-up menu.

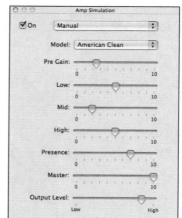

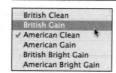

Figure 11.37 Top: The Amp Simulation controls, showing a setting that uses the American Clean model. Bottom: Using the Model pop-up menu to switch to the British Gain model.

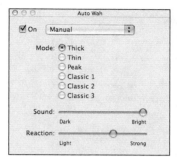

Figure 11.38
The Auto Wah controls.

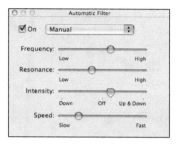

Figure 11.39
The Automatic Filter controls.

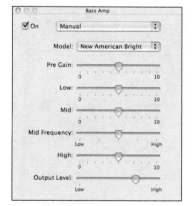

Figure 11.40 Top: The Bass Amp controls showing a setting using the New American Bright model. Bottom: Choosing the American Scoop model from the Model pop-up menu.

plan on creating your own presets, start by choosing a basic sound source from the Model menu. The choices with "Gain" in their names use much more distortion than the "Clean" models. Then fine-tune your instrument's sound with the sliders in the lower part of the dialog.

- **Auto Wah:** In the physical world, an auto wah is a device (usually pedal controlled) that converts a change in volume to a change in color. For example, when attached to an electric guitar, it can translate each pluck of a string into a sort of vowel sound (*wah*); changing the intensity of the pluck changes the vowel sound, or color, of the note. GarageBand's auto-wah effect is meant to imitate this device (**Figure 11.38**).

- **Automatic Filter:** The automatic filter creates special effects by filtering out high frequencies (set by the Frequency slider) and setting the filtering frequency to resonate with itself (set by the Resonance slider). This resonance manifests itself as a wobble or wah in the sound, whose intensity and speed are controlled by two more sliders (**Figure 11.39**).

- **Bass Amp:** New in GarageBand 2, the bass amp effect is designed especially to work with electric basses. It's equivalent to Amp Simulation (which is designed for electric guitars), and its operation is pretty much the same. Choose a model from the Model menu (the choices are somewhat different than for Amp Simulation); then use the sliders to get just the right sound (**Figure 11.40**).

continues on next page

- **Bass Reduction:** This effect cuts the volume of frequencies in the bass (or low) range. Use this filter to get rid of low-frequency noises that afflict live recording or to attenuate excessively boomy bass instruments or drums. It is also effective for thinning guitars and percussion instruments so they don't muddy the mix as much. Use the Frequency slider to choose the portion of the track's low frequencies that are attenuated. Drag the Frequency slider to the left to affect only the lowest frequencies. Drag it to the right to affect a wider range of frequencies (**Figure 11.41**).

- **Bitcrusher:** A purely digital distortion module (that means there's no analog in the analog world), the bitcrusher lets you create bizarre effects (**Figure 11.42**). Digital distortion is harsher and more unpleasant than the other distortion modules, but it does have its place. Try out the presets and then experiment on your own.

- **Chorus:** The chorus effect layers copies of the original sound over itself. The copies are slightly delayed in time compared to the original, making it sound like several instruments or voices are performing the same part together (**Figure 11.43**). Use this effect to thicken a track and make it stand out in the mix.

- **Distortion:** This effect mimics the crackling, grating sound (some would say "noise") created when a stronger signal is sent through an audio circuit than the circuit can handle. Electric guitars often have pedal-operated distortion modules; add this effect to your electric guitar tracks or use it to make an acoustic guitar sound electric (**Figure 11.44**). Warning: It takes only a little bit of this effect to send your song into clipping territory! Use the track's volume level slider to bring the signal down to a manageable level.

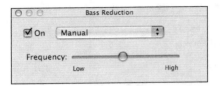

Figure 11.41 The Bass Reduction control.

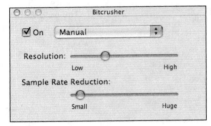

Figure 11.42 The Bitcrusher controls.

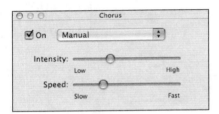

Figure 11.43 The Chorus controls.

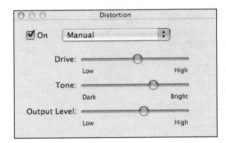

Figure 11.44 The Distortion controls.

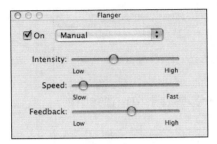

Figure 11.45 The Flanger controls.

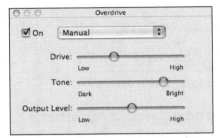

Figure 11.46 The Overdrive controls.

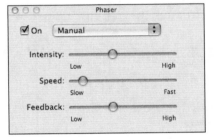

Figure 11.47 The Phaser controls.

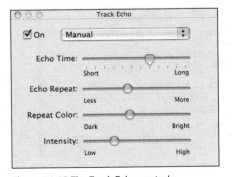

Figure 11.48 The Track Echo controls.

◆ **Flanger:** The flanger effect is similar to the chorus effect, but more extreme. You can achieve some wild effects with the flanger (**Figure 11.45**).

◆ **Overdrive:** This is another effect that imitates the sound of an audio circuit pushed beyond its limits. Overdrive is a kinder, gentler relative of distortion (**Figure 11.46**).

◆ **Phaser:** Another relative of the flanger and chorus effects, the phaser plays the copies of the original sound later in time and also out of phase with the original (that is, the peaks and troughs of its waveforms do not coincide with those of the original). The effect makes the track sound like it is pulsating or whooshing back and forth (**Figure 11.47**).

◆ **Track Echo:** One more of the new effects in GarageBand 2, track echo works like the regular echo effect, but you apply it on a track-by-track basis. Remember that if you use the echo effect from the master track, the same echo settings will apply to every track that uses echo (see "Using the Echo Effect" earlier in this chapter). With track echo, you can tailor individual echo settings for one or more tracks. The controls are essentially the same as for the master track echo—the Intensity slider seems to do the same thing as the Echo Volume slider in the main Echo window (**Figure 11.48**).

continues on next page

ABOUT THE OTHER GARAGEBAND EFFECTS

◆ **Treble Reduction:** As its name implies, this effect lowers the volume of frequencies in the treble (or high) range. Use it to rid a poorly engineered recording of hiss or to tone down any track that seems shrill. You can also use it in conjunction with reverb to make an instrument seem more distant. Use the Frequency slider to choose the portion of the track's high frequencies that are attenuated. Drag the Frequency slider to the right to affect only the very highest frequencies. Drag it to the left to affect a wider range of frequencies (**Figure 11.49**).

◆ **Tremolo:** The tremolo effect adds *vibrato*, a wavering quality, to the sound. Check the Auto Panning box to have the sound bounce back and forth between the left and right stereo channels (**Figure 11.50**).

◆ **Vocal Transformer:** The vocal transformer is the third of the new effects included with GarageBand 2, and it is certainly the one that got the most exposure in marketing materials. Apple's Web site gushes that the vocal transformer effect can change "the apparent gender of recorded voices." Well, the effects presets do include items like Female to Male and Male to Female, but the results are more amusing than convincing. The effect's Pitch slider lets you shift the pitch of the fundamental voice up or down by two octaves, and the Sound slider lets you adjust the voice's overtones, changing its color. To emphasize the upper overtones and brighten the voice, drag the Sound slider to the right. To darken the voice, drag the slider to the left (**Figure 11.51**).

ABOUT THE OTHER GARAGEBAND EFFECTS

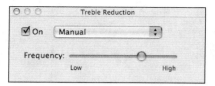

Figure 11.49 The Treble Reduction control.

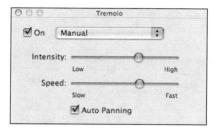

Figure 11.50 The Tremolo controls.

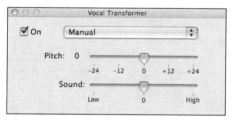

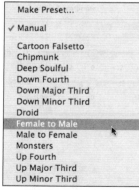

Figure 11.51 Top: The Vocal Transformer controls. Bottom: The factory presets for the vocal transformer effect.

Figure 11.52 The Track Info window for a Software Instrument, showing the Generator pop-up menu.

Software Instrument Generators by Type

The sampled generators are as follows:

- Bass
- Drum Kits
- Guitar
- Horns
- Hybrid Basic
- Hybrid Morph
- Piano
- Tuned Percussion
- Woodwind

The synthesized generators are as follows:

- Analog Basic
- Analog Mono
- Analog Pad
- Analog Swirl
- Analog Sync
- Digital Basic
- Digital Mono
- Digital Stepper
- Electric Clav
- Electric Piano
- Tonewheel Organ
- Voice

Editing Software Instruments

For Software Instruments, the Details pane of the Track Info window contains one more item: the Generator pop-up menu, with its attendant presets pop-up menu (**Figure 11.52**). These two menus don't define an effect; rather, they define the instrumental sound of a Software Instrument track.

The checked item on the Generator menu is the basic source of the sound for the instrument. Some of the generators in the list produce their sounds from recordings, or samples, of actual instruments. The rest of the generators rely on synthesized sounds, meaning that GarageBand creates their sounds entirely through mathematical calculations (see the sidebar "Software Intrument Generators by Type").

Your generator choice defines the instrument's basic characteristics. To get a specific instrumental sound, you need to choose a setting from the Generator presets menu. For sampled instruments, the generator acts as a basic model of the instrument in software. When you choose a preset from the Generator presets menu, you tell GarageBand to use a specific folder of samples (bearing the same name as the preset) to create the actual sound of the instrument. These samples reside in the folder /Library/Application Support/GarageBand/Instrument Library/Sampler/Sampler Files.

This presets menu works differently from the effects presets menus in GarageBand. In those menus, a preset is a saved combination of the settings chosen in the effect's settings window. The settings for a generator always consist of the adjustments you make in the settings window *in addition to* the information contained in one of the presets that ships with GarageBand. These factory

continues on next page

presets can be neither edited nor deleted (because they are tied to a folder of instrument samples); you can create your own presets, but they will always be based on one of the factory presets.

Here's an example: **Figure 11.53** shows the settings windows for two different instrument presets I created using the Woodwind generator. The sliders in both windows are in exactly the same positions; but even so, the two instruments sound very different. That's because I based each of my presets on a different factory preset, so that each preset draws upon a different set of sampled files (**Figure 11.54**). The settings window for any Software Instrument using a sample-based generator always displays the name of the factory preset that the current settings are based on.

For synthesizer-based generators, editing presets is much more straightforward. The parameters shown in the settings window are the only adjustments available for the generator, so the presets that come with GarageBand have no greater importance than presets you create.

Factory presets used as the basis for these custom settings

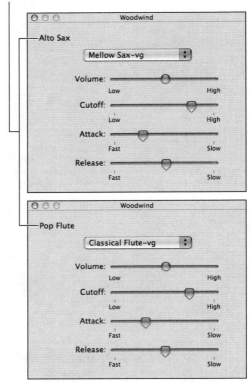

Figure 11.53 Settings windows for two custom instruments based on the Woodwind generator. The slider positions in each are almost identical, but the instruments sound very different, because they are based on different factory presets.

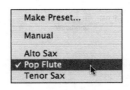

Figure 11.54
The factory presets for the Woodwind generator.

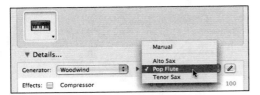

Figure 11.55 The presets pop-up menu for the Woodwind generator.

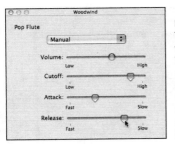

Figure 11.56 The settings window for the Woodwind generator. This example shows a customized setting based on the Pop Flute preset.

To edit a Software Instrument:

1. Select a Software Instrument track whose instrument you want to edit.

2. Open the Track Info window and *do any of the following:*

   ▲ To change to a completely different instrumental sound, choose a new generator from the Generator pop-up menu (Figure 11.52); then choose a preset from the Generator presets pop-up menu (**Figure 11.55**).

   ▲ To make a less drastic change in the instrument's sound, leave the generator alone and choose a preset from the Generator presets pop-up menu (Figure 11.55).

   ▲ To make a subtle change in the instrument's sound, click the Edit button and adjust the controls in the settings window (**Figure 11.56**). Save your settings as a preset, if desired.

3. Click the Save Instrument button at the bottom of the window to save your edited instrument (see "To save an instrument preset" earlier in this chapter).

About Audio Units

Software effects are often distributed as *plug-ins* so they can be loaded into the program on an as-needed basis. To facilitate the sharing of plug-ins among music applications, several standardized plug-in formats have been established. As part of the specification for Mac OS X, Apple introduced yet another plug-in format, the *Audio Unit*. The Audio Unit format is attractive to music software developers because, unlike other plug-in formats, it is supported at the system level, which enables programmers to very easily create music applications compatible with it.

GarageBand, being an Apple product, supports the Audio Unit format and comes with a number of Audio Unit effects. You'll find them listed in the bottom half of the effects pop-up menus (**Figure 11.57**). GarageBand also (in theory) accepts third-party Audio Units. Anecdotal evidence from users indicates that not all Audio Unit plug-ins work with GarageBand, but the majority do.

Many of GarageBand's built-in Audio Units are more complex versions of the program's standard effects. Compare, for example, the interface for the standard equalizer effect, with its three frequency ranges (Figure 11.32), with that for AUGraphicEQ, a plug-in that also functions as an equalizer (**Figure 11.58**). The AUGraphicEQ effect breaks the audio spectrum into a whopping 31 frequency ranges. **Table 11.1** lists some other Audio Units that can substitute for standard GarageBand effects.

Explaining the operation of all of the included Audio Units is beyond the scope of this book. M. Danielson has written a fine tutorial on the use of the Audio Unit effects that are supplied with GarageBand. You'll find it on the Web at www.macjams.com; the title of the article is "GarageBand Tutorial: Built-in Audio Unit Effects."

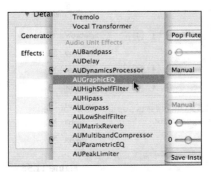

Figure 11.57 The Audio Unit effects that ship with GarageBand.

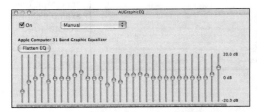

Figure 11.58 The interface for the AUGraphicEQ Audio Unit.

Table 11.1

Audio Unit Equivalents of Standard GarageBand Effects

AUDIO UNIT	STANDARD EFFECT
AUDelay	Echo
AUMatrixReverb	Reverb
AUGraphicEQ	Equalizer
AUParametricEQ	
AUMultibandCompressor	Compressor
AULowpass	Treble reduction
AUHighShelfFilter	
AUHpass	Bass reduction
AULowShelfFilter	

Using Audio Unit Instrument Plug-Ins

Not all Audio Units are effects plug-ins; there are also Audio Unit instrument plug-ins. AU instruments work like the Software Instrument generators that are included with GarageBand.

There are many third-party AU instrument plug-ins, and most (but not all) seem to work as expected in GarageBand. Normally, they are provided with an installer program; simply run the installer to add the plug-in to your collection. Some plug-ins, however, need to be installed by hand, using the following procedure:

1. Quit GarageBand, if it's running.

2. Open the folder containing the Audio Unit you wish to install (**Figure 11.59**).

3. Locate the item with the suffix .component and drag it to the folder /Library/Audio/ Plug-Ins/Components (if you want it to be available to all users of your computer) or to ~/Library/Audio/Plug-Ins/Components (if you want it to be available only to you) (**Figure 11.60**).

4. Restart GarageBand. The Audio Unit will now be ready for use.

Figure 11.59 The Finder icon for Buzzer2, a free-ware plug-in by alphakanal multimedia gmbh (www.alphakanal.de/snipsnap/space/Buzzer2) that emulates an analog synthesizer.

Figure 11.60 Installing the Buzzer2.component file by dragging.

continues on next page

Using Audio Unit Instrument Plug-Ins *(continued)*

Once it's installed, use an AU instrument just like you would any other generator:

1. Select the Software Instrument track in which you want to use the Audio Unit instrument and open the Track Info window.

2. From the Generator menu, choose the AU instrument you want to use (**Figure 11.61**).

3. If the instrument's settings window doesn't open automatically, click the Edit button to open it.

4. Adjust the plug-in's settings to taste (**Figure 11.62**).

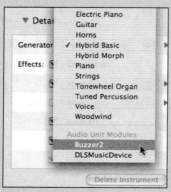

Figure 11.61 Choosing Buzzer2 from the Generator menu.

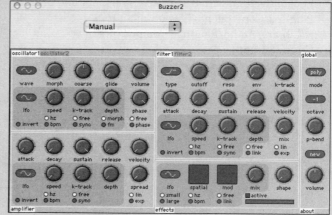

Figure 11.62 The Buzzer2 settings window.

MIXING YOUR SONG

Mixing is the final part of the process of creating a song in GarageBand. You've brought together all of the musical materials you want to use, you've arranged them into just the right sequence, and now it's time to add the finishing touches that make the song come alive.

Mixing a song involves some or all of these tasks:

- ◆ Setting volume levels for individual tracks so the various instruments balance each other.

- ◆ Adding volume curves to tracks to create changes in volume over time.

- ◆ Setting the pan position for each track, adding pan curves to tracks (new in GarageBand 2) to create changes in the pan position over time.

- ◆ Using the master track volume curve to adjust the overall dynamics for songs.

- ◆ Adjusting the master volume slider so the loudest passages barely turn the master level meters red.

- ◆ Using the master track pitch curve to adjust the overall pitch changes for songs (also new in GarageBand 2).

Choosing a Volume Level for Each Track

The fundamental activity in creating a final mix is setting the output volume level of each track. This process has two goals:

◆ To achieve just the right balance among all the different sounds in your song.

◆ To prevent the total output of all tracks from reaching a level high enough to cause distortion, or *clipping*.

Achieving balance

In your song, you want the percussion to have real punch and the bass line to have presence, but you also want to ensure that the combination of all the parts doesn't swamp the melody line. You can use the volume level sliders to cut back the levels of accompanying tracks to let the more important tracks shine. If you have an instrument that stays mostly in the background but steps forward for one eight-bar solo (a guitar, for example), add a volume curve to that instrument's track. You can use the volume curve to lower the track's level for most of the song, but then boost the volume during the instrument's time in the spotlight. Likewise, if your singer has problems with breath control and can't maintain an even dynamic level, you can use a volume curve to compensate.

Preventing clipping

In Chapter 6, I stressed the importance of watching individual track levels while recording to keep the track from clipping (see "About Setting the Recording Level" in Chapter 6). Even if you scrupulously monitor each track and none of them reaches clipping level, you still may find that when all of the tracks in your song are played together, clipping occurs.

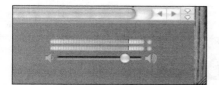

Figure 12.1 The master level meters, showing clipping in progress. Use the master volume slider, just below the meters, to adjust the output level of the song.

To monitor clipping in the song as a whole, watch the master level meters in the lower-right corner of the GarageBand window (see "Setting the Output Volume" later in this chapter). Like the individual track level meters, they include clipping indicators that turn red when clipping occurs (**Figure 12.1**).

There are several possible causes for clipping, and for each cause there is a remedy:

◆ If several of your tracks remain at a high volume throughout, use their respective volume level sliders to reduce their overall levels (see "Setting the Volume Level for a Track" later in this chapter).

◆ If two or more tracks have simultaneous loud passages, add volume level curves to those tracks and back off the volume during those passages (see "About Track Automation" later in this chapter).

◆ If you're sure you've found the perfect balance among all of your tracks and you don't want to adjust one or two of them to get rid of clipping, use the master volume slider to lower the output level of the whole song (see "Setting the Output Volume" later in this chapter).

◆ If you added effects to some of your tracks, the effects may have boosted the tracks' volume enough to cause clipping. Open the Track Info window for each of those tracks and reduce the strength of the applied effects (see Chapter 11), or reduce the track's volume.

Setting levels for each track in a song and then a final output level for the entire song is not a linear process. You set individual track levels, then adjust the master volume slider, then perhaps open the Track Info window and tweak the effects for a track or two, then adjust the master volume slider again, and so on. The ultimate guide in this process is your own musical taste. Keep fiddling with the controls until the song sounds right.

CHOOSING A VOLUME LEVEL FOR EACH TRACK

Setting the Volume Level for a Track

Use the volume slider in the track mixer to set the basic volume level for a track. Later, I'll show you how to program volume changes into a track, so some sections play more loudly or softly than others (see "About Track Automation" later in this chapter).

To set a track's volume level:

1. Working in the main GarageBand window, if the track mixer is hidden, click the triangle at the top right of the Tracks column (Command-Y).

   The track mixer appears (**Figure 12.2**).

2. *Do one of the following:*

   ▲ To increase the track's volume level, drag the volume slider to the right.

   ▲ To decrease the track's volume, drag the volume slider to the left (**Figure 12.3**).

   Continue to the next track and set its level until you have taken care of all the tracks in your song.

✔ Tip

■ All of the volume sliders in GarageBand are set by default to their neutral positions, meaning that they cause no change in volume, or *gain*. This setting is also called "0 dB gain," because the gain is adjusted by 0 dB. The term *dB* is the abbreviation for *decibel*, a unit of sound intensity. To reset the volume level slider to its neutral position, Option-click the slider (see "Using the Track Mixer Volume Slider" in Chapter 6).

Figure 12.2 Clicking the triangle reveals the Mixer column.

Figure 12.3 Drag the track volume slider to adjust its output level.

Setting the Pan Position

Modern stereophonic recording captures the positions of the musicians in the studio relative to each other. When such a recording is played back through two (or more) speakers, the listener hears the performers distributed throughout the aural space, or *stereo field*, which adds a sense of presence and space to the recording.

By default, all of your GarageBand tracks sound like they're centered in front of the listener—a pretty uninteresting mix. Fortunately, you can give each track its own *pan* (for *panorama*) *position* so it has a specific left-to-right placement in the recording's stereo field. Drag the pan wheel in the track mixer to set a track's pan position. The white dot on the perimeter of the wheel shows the track's current pan setting.

Customarily, vocals and drums are positioned more or less centrally, with other percussion instruments and bass placed a short distance either side of center. Guitars and other harmony or melody instruments are then located farther to the left or right. What you are striving for in a good stereo mix is an *overall* balance—there may be moments when there's more going on in the left or right speaker, but the song as a whole should feel balanced in the stereo field.

To set a track's pan position:

◆ Display the track mixer if it's not already open; *then do one of the following:*

  ▲ Place the pointer over the center of the pan wheel and drag down or up to move the track to the right or left, respectively, in the stereo field.

  ▲ Place the pointer over the outer edge of the pan wheel and drag left or right to move the track to the left or right, respectively. When you use this method, the wheel snaps to each of the white tick marks around the perimeter (**Figure 12.4**).

  ▲ To choose a setting directly, click a point around the edge of the pan wheel (**Figure 12.5**).

✔ Tip

■ Option-click the pan wheel to reset it to the default center position.

Drag up or down   Drag left or right

Figure 12.4 The pan wheel reacts differently to dragging depending on where the dragging begins.

Figure 12.5 Clicking at the 3 o'clock position causes the pan wheel to point to the right.

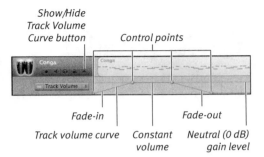

Show/Hide
Track Volume
Curve button

Control points

Fade-in

Fade-out

Track volume curve

Constant volume

Neutral (0 dB) gain level

Figure 12.6 A simple track volume curve showing a fade-in and a fade-out.

About Track Automation

The track mixer volume slider provides an easy way to set the output level for a track, but this method is also inflexible. The level you set is maintained unwaveringly throughout the song. If you add a *volume curve* to a track, on the other hand, you can create volume changes over time, or *fades*. Raising a track's volume level from silence is called a *fade-in*, and bringing it back down to silence is called a *fade-out*. A more sophisticated effect is the *crossfade*, in which one track fades in while another track fades out.

Likewise, the pan wheel lets you place your instruments precisely in 3-D space, but it leaves them in one position for the length of the song. GarageBand 2 allows you to vary the pan position of a track as the song progresses by adding a *pan curve*.

Volume curves and pan curves are examples of *track automation*—they provide the means to program GarageBand to make changes during a song that normally you would have to implement by hand.

Editing automation curves is much like editing MIDI controller data (see "Editing MIDI Controller Information" in Chapter 10): set control points along the curve at spots where you want the volume or pan to change; then drag each point up or down to adjust the volume or pan at that location. GarageBand automatically adjusts the curve to follow your control points (**Figure 12.6**).

Parts of volume curves that slope upward to the right represent increases in volume, or *crescendos*; parts that slope downward to the right represent decreases in volume, or *decrescendos*. In the case of a pan curve, an upward slope represents a pan to the left, and a downward slope represents a pan to the right.

continues on next page

You can add automation curves to any instrument track. Doing so disables both that track's volume slider and its pan wheel. You can also add a volume curve to the master track (but not a pan curve) to make volume changes that apply to the song as a whole (see "Working with the Master Track Automation Curves" later in this chapter).

When you first display an automation curve, it is dimmed to show that it's disabled. When enabled for the first time, the curve appears as a straight horizontal line at the level corresponding to the current track volume slider setting (**Figure 12.7**). The curve also initially has a single control point at its left end. Drag this control point up and down to adjust the overall volume for the track. This is equivalent to adjusting the volume slider or pan wheel. In fact, if you display the volume or pan curve without enabling it, you'll see that the curve moves up or down if the volume slider or pan wheel is moved.

✔ Tip

■ The term *automation curve* is a bit of a misnomer, because GarageBand lets you use only straight lines in your "curve" (unlike pricier audio applications, which allow you to draw curves that actually… well…curve).

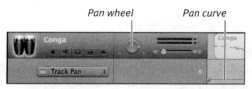

Pan wheel   Pan curve

Figure 12.7 This is how the pan curve looks when first enabled.

Using an Automation Curve

Figure 12.8 Click this button to reveal the automation curve area.

Figure 12.9 The automation controls appear, but are dimmed.

Figure 12.10 Use the track curve pop-up menu to choose which track automation curve will be displayed.

Figure 12.11 The track volume curve has been chosen.

If you don't want a track's volume or pan position to remain constant throughout a song, enable its automation curves and add control points to the curve wherever you want volume or pan changes to begin or end. Editing automation curves is much like editing MIDI controller data (see "Editing MIDI Controller Information" in Chapter 10). You can drag control points up or down to adjust the volume level, and left or right to move them to different points in time. You can select control points so you can change several at once, and you can copy, paste, or delete them altogether.

When you turn on automation, you enable both volume and pan curves, disabling the track volume slider and the pan wheel in the track mixer. You can display only one of the curves at a time, however.

To display the automation curves:

1. Select the track whose automation curves you want to display.

2. Click the Show Track Volume or Pan Curve button or press A (**Figure 12.8**).

   The track's automation curve area pops into view under the track throughout the length of the timeline (**Figure 12.9**).

3. Open the track curve pop-up menu and choose whether to display the track volume curve or the pan curve for the track (**Figure 12.10**).

   The automation curve you chose is displayed (**Figure 12.11**).

To edit a track volume curve:

1. Display the track volume curve for the track you wish to edit.

2. Click the button next to the track curve menu to enable the automation curves for the track (**Figure 12.12**).

   The button glows blue.

   When first turned on, the track volume curve is a straight line representing the current value of the track volume slider.

3. To set the track's initial volume, drag the control point at the left end of the curve up or down (**Figure 12.13**).

   A tool tip shows the numerical value of the curve at that point.

4. Click the track volume curve at the spot where you want the track's volume to start to change (**Figure 12.14**).

   A control point is added to the curve.

5. Place another control point at the spot where you want the volume to stop changing; then drag up or down to the new volume (**Figure 12.15**).

6. Continue adding and adjusting control points until you're satisfied with the track's volume changes.

7. To hide the track volume curve, again click the Show Track Volume or Pan Curve button or select the track and press A.

Figure 12.12 The button glows blue to show that the track's automation curves are now enabled.

Figure 12.13 The guitar will enter at high volume.

Figure 12.14 Click to place the first control point where you want the fade to begin.

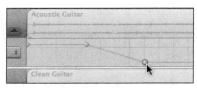

Figure 12.15 Click to place the second control point and drag to the new volume. Here, the guitar track will fade out over the course of four beats.

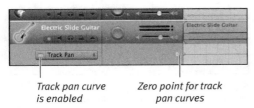

Track pan curve   Zero point for track
is enabled   pan curves

Figure 12.16 The button glows blue to show that the track's automation curves are now enabled. The default control point is at the zero line, indicating that the track is centered.

Figure 12.17 At the start of the song, the slide guitar will be heard coming from the left side.

✔ Tip

■ If you've created a complicated volume curve for a track and you want to hear the track at full volume temporarily, click the button next to the track curve menu to disable your volume curve (the blue light on the button will go out; note that if you've added a pan curve to the track, it will be disabled, too). This procedure is useful if you've faded out a portion of a track and you want to hear what it sounds like without changing the complex volume curve you just created. When the volume curve is disabled, you can adjust the track volume using the volume slider, but once you enable the volume curve again, the slider will follow the levels set in the volume curve.

To edit a pan curve:

1. Display the pan curve for the track you wish to edit.

2. Click the button next to the track curve menu to enable the automation curves for the track (**Figure 12.16**).

   The button glows blue.

   When first turned on, the pan curve is a straight line representing the current value of the pan wheel. If the curve's value is 0, the track is perfectly centered in the stereo field.

3. To set the track's initial pan position, drag the control point at the left end of the curve up or down (**Figure 12.17**).

   A tool tip shows the numerical value of the curve at that point. Positive numbers (below the zero line) indicate a position to the right, and panning left (so the control point is above the zero line) produces negative values.

   continues on next page

USING AN AUTOMATION CURVE

4. Click the pan curve at the spot where you want the track's pan position to start to change (**Figure 12.18**).

A control point is added to the curve.

5. Place another control point at the spot where you want panning to stop changing; then drag up or down to the new pan position (**Figure 12.19**).

6. Continue adding and adjusting control points until you're satisfied with the track's pan changes.

7. To hide the pan curve, again click the Show Track Volume or Pan Curve button or select the track and press A.

Figure 12.18 Click to place the first control point where you want the track to start to pan.

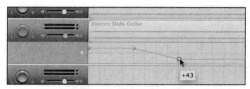

Figure 12.19 Click to place the second control point and drag to the pan position. Here, the slide guitar track will move from the left side of the stereo field to the right side over the course of four beats.

Figure 12.20 The first step in making a two-measure crossfade is to create a two-measure overlap between the regions involved.

Figure 12.21 The track volume curves are enabled.

Solo button

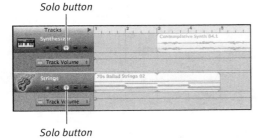

Solo button

Figure 12.22 The tracks are set to solo mode.

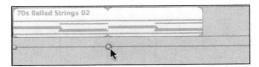

Figure 12.23 The fade-out will start at this control point.

Figure 12.24 The fade-out will end at this control point.

Creating a Basic Crossfade

A *crossfade* is a common audio effect: one track fades out as another track fades in. This simple yet sophisticated effect creates a seamless transition from one instrument or musical phrase to another.

GarageBand lacks a specific tool for creating crossfades (a common feature in more expensive music programs), but you can easily duplicate the effect with track volume curves. Simply set the control points of one track's volume curve to fade to silence (*fade out*) over a period of time, and use the other track's curve so that the track increases in volume (*fades in*) during the same period.

To create a crossfade:

1. Make sure the two regions you want to use for the crossfade overlap by at least the amount of time you want the cross-fade to last (**Figure 12.20**).

2. Enable the track volume curves for the two tracks involved in the crossfade by clicking the button next to the track curve menu for each track (**Figure 12.21**).

3. If your song contains other tracks, you may want to set the tracks involved in the crossfade to solo mode by clicking each track's Solo button (**Figure 12.22**). Setting the tracks to solo lets you hear the crossfade by itself.

4. Working in the track that will fade out, place a control point on the volume curve at the location where you want the fade to begin (**Figure 12.23**).

5. Place another control point where you want the fade out to end (**Figure 12.24**).

continues on next page

CREATING A BASIC CROSSFADE

6. Drag the second control point down as far as it will go (**Figure 12.25**).

At this point, the track's gain is –144.0 dB, and the track is essentially inaudible.

This completes the fade-out.

7. Working in the track that will fade in, place a control point at the location where you want the fade-in to begin; then drag the point down as far as it will go (**Figure 12.26**).

The fade-in will begin from silence.

8. Place another control point at the location where you want the fade-in to end; then drag up to the desired level (**Figure 12.27**).

The crossfade is now complete (**Figure 12.28**).

✔ Tips

■ To select all of the control points on a curve in a single stroke, click anywhere in the automation curve header (the empty space surrounding the track curve menu) (**Figure 12.29**). This trick comes in handy when you want to delete all the control points on a curve at once.

■ Note that the left end of the track volume curve in Figure 12.26 rises up to a significant level. In this case, it doesn't disturb our fade-in because that part of the track is empty. If there were a region in the track to the left of the region we wanted to fade in (as there might be if our crossfade were in the middle of a piece), we would probably have to add more control points and adjust more of the track to a lower volume to ensure a silent start to the fade-in.

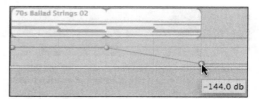

Figure 12.25 The track now fades to silence at the second control point.

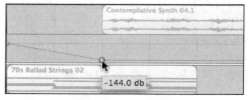

Figure 12.26 The first control point has been dragged down so the fade-in can begin from silence.

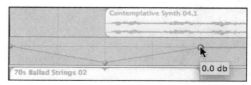

Figure 12.27 At the end of the fade-in, the track's gain is now set to 0 dB, or full volume .

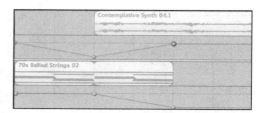

Figure 12.28 The upper track fades in as the lower track fades out.

Figure 12.29 Click in this area to select all of the control points on the curve.

Working with Master Track Automation Curves

To apply effects and to set an overall volume for your song or to make global pitch changes in it, use the master track (introduced in Chapter 11). The master track not only has its own collection of effects presets, accessible by way of the Track Info window; it also has its own automation curves, which appear at the very bottom of the timeline when the track is displayed (**Figure 12.30**).

The master track's automation curves are a bit different from those of instrument tracks. The master track doesn't have a pan curve, but it does have a *master pitch curve*. You can use the master pitch curve to transpose the entire song (with some exceptions) up or down from one to 12 semitones. The master pitch curve affects only certain kinds of regions: green Software Instrument regions (except those using drum kits) and blue Real Instrument loops. Purple recorded Real Instrument regions and orange regions (audio files imported into GarageBand) are not affected—all of which reduces the

continues on next page

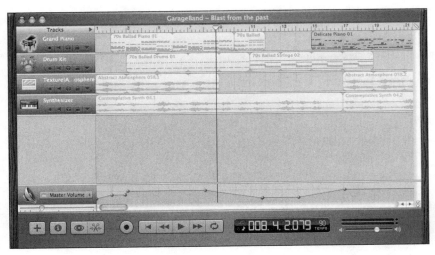

Figure 12.30
The master track is displayed, showing the master track volume curve.

appeal of the feature. As with other curves, you can add control points to the master pitch curve to introduce key changes at various points in the song. The master pitch curve is even less curvy than the other automation curves: the curve always makes abrupt cliff-like changes from one level to another—no intervening slopes allowed. And there's one other oddity: you can't turn off the master pitch curve (contrary to what Apple's documentation says), so you can't disable the effect without deleting all of your control points. Sounds like a bug to me...

The *master volume curve*, on the other hand, works just like the volume curves for ordinary tracks (see "About Track Automation" earlier in this chapter). The first time you display the master track for a newly created song, its volume curve is dimmed to show that it is disabled (I've noticed that almost all GarageBand 1 songs open in GarageBand 2 with their master tracks enabled). By default, the curve is a straight line at the neutral (0 dB) gain volume level and represents a constant volume setting for the entire song. If you enable the master volume curve, you can drag it up or down to adjust this constant volume. Alternatively, if you want the dynamics of your song to change from time to time, add control points to the master volume level curve and adjust them up or down. You can use the master track volume curve to end a song with a fade-out, for example.

To add volume changes to a song:

1. Choose Track > Show Master Track (Command-B).

   The master track is displayed along the bottom of the timeline (**Figure 12.31**).

2. Open the master track curve pop-up menu and choose Master Volume, if it's not already selected (**Figure 12.32**).

   The master track volume curve is dimmed by default.

Figure 12.31 The master track automation area, before any changes have been made.

Figure 12.32 Choose which of the master track automation curves to display.

Figure 12.33 The button turns blue to show that the master track volume curve is now ready for action.

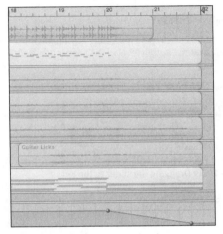

Figure 12.34 The master track volume curve was used to create a fade-out at the end of this song.

Figure 12.35 Use this menu to display the master pitch curve.

Figure 12.36 This control point has been dragged upward, raising the pitch of the song five semitones above its normal key.

Figure 12.37 Starting at this control point, the song will be heard eight semitones below its normal key.

3. To enable the master track's volume curve, click the button to the left of the master track curve menu (**Figure 12.33**).

The button turns blue. The curve has a single control point, located at its extreme left end.

4. Set control points along the master track volume curve and create fade-ins and fade-outs (**Figure 12.34**).

To add pitch changes to a song:

1. Display the master track.

2. Open the master track curve menu and choose Master Pitch, if it's not already selected (**Figure 12.35**).

By default, the master pitch curve has a single control point, located at its extreme left end.

3. To change the pitch of your song, *do one of the following:*

▲ To transpose the entire song up in pitch, drag the single control point up (**Figure 12.36**); to transpose the song down, drag the control point down. The tool tip shows how many semitones you have changed the pitch relative to the normal key of the song.

▲ To introduce pitch changes in the middle of a song, add control points wherever you want the pitch to change; then drag each control point up or down (**Figure 12.37**).

✔ Tips

■ To hide the master track, again choose Track > Show Master Track or press Command-B.

■ To transpose purple Real Instrument regions (audio recordings you made yourself), use the Region Pitch slider in the track editor (see "Transposing Regions" in Chapter 9).

Setting the Output Volume

The last step you need to take before exporting your song to iTunes is to use the master volume slider to set the song's output level. Even if you've been assiduously tweaking track levels and the master volume curve to rid the song of clipping, listen to the entire song one more time while keeping a close eye on the master level meters. The master level meters work identically to the individual track level meters and include a clipping indicator that lights up red when clipping is encountered (see "Using the Track Level Meters" in Chapter 6). Adjust the master volume slider until the clipping indicators no longer come on while the song is playing.

To set the output volume for a song:

◆ Play the song from the beginning and watch the track level meters for clipping (**Figure 12.38**); *do one of the following:*

▲ If the clipping indicators light up, drag the master volume slider left to lower the output level until the song no longer clips (**Figure 12.39**).

▲ If the song seems too quiet, drag the master volume slider right to raise the output level. Be sure not to raise it so much that clipping occurs.

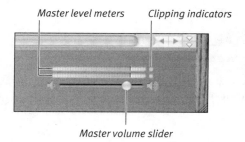

Master level meters   *Clipping indicators*

Master volume slider

Figure 12.38 The clipping indicators are illuminated, showing that the output level of the song is too high.

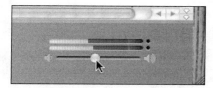

Figure 12.39 Dragging the slider to the left lowers the output volume, preventing clipping.

EXPORTING AND IMPORTING

Sure, it's fun just to play around in GarageBand, but eventually you'll accumulate a repertoire of finished songs. You may want to share some of the fruits of your creative endeavors with friends. Or perhaps your songs are intimate diary musings that you want to keep to yourself, but you want to copy them to your iPod to take with you wherever you go.

And creative work isn't just about output. You may want to assemble pieces of music from bits of sound collected from a variety of sources. Is there any way to bring these nuggets into GarageBand?

GarageBand is extremely limited in its relations with the rest of the world—that's one characteristic that distinguishes it from pricier music programs. But there are a few things you can do to get music into and out of GarageBand. In this chapter I discuss:

◆ Exporting GarageBand songs to iTunes.

◆ Using iTunes to convert songs into more portable formats.

◆ Using GarageBand songs in the other iLife applications.

◆ Importing audio files into GarageBand.

◆ Importing MIDI files into GarageBand (new in GarageBand 2).

GarageBand and Other Applications

It's not easy to share native GarageBand files with the wider world. The only programs that can open native GarageBand song files (other than GarageBand itself, of course) are Logic Express 7 and Logic Pro 7, Apple's prosumer and professional music programs. The two Logic programs include the same Software Instruments and Apple Loops as GarageBand, so your songs should usually sound the same when played in Logic. If you plan on opening your GarageBand songs in Logic on a different computer than the one on which they were created, you need to make sure the same extra instruments and loops are installed on that computer. One way around this restriction is to export your song as an archive, which saves the song in a bundle with all the loop files used in the song (see "Saving a Song as an Archive" in Chapter 2).

If you want to distribute your immortal compositions beyond the world of GarageBand and Logic users, you'll have to export them to iTunes first. Once a song is in iTunes, you can save it in a popular format like MP3, which not only makes the file smaller but renders your song playable on almost every computer and iPod-like device now in existence.

Likewise, GarageBand can't open project files from other music programs. You can, however, drag audio (and as of GarageBand 2) MIDI files into GarageBand from the Finder. Dragging an audio file into GarageBand creates a new Real Instrument region, which you can treat just as you would treat any Real Instrument region you recorded in GarageBand yourself. In GarageBand 2, regions made from imported audio files are colored orange, to distinguish them from audio regions you recorded in GarageBand, which are purple. Importing a MIDI file creates a new Software Instrument track, which will, naturally, adopt the color green.

Steppin' on Up

If you do decide to break down and spend the money to upgrade from GarageBand to one of the Logic programs, you'll find a very helpful document waiting for you on the Logic installation disc. It's the imaginatively named PDF called "Logic for GarageBand Users," and it does a nice job of showing you which of Logic's tools and features correspond to those you've learned to love in GarageBand. You'll find it in the folder /Documentation/English.

Exporting a Song to iTunes

One way of sharing your songs with your friends and the world is to hand out your GarageBand file. This gets cumbersome pretty quickly, because anyone who wants to listen to your song has to have a copy of GarageBand and a Mac, and that Mac must be powerful enough to process in real time all the tracks and effects you've included in your composition.

Fortunately, you can also export your songs to iTunes, which is freely available to any Mac or Windows user and has far more modest hardware requirements. Better still, you can use iTunes to compress the exported song file, making it even more portable. And once you've built up a repertoire of immortal compositions, you can use iTunes to burn your works onto a CD.

In addition, all of the songs in your iTunes library are automatically made available to other iLife programs on your Mac, so they can be used as background music in an iPhoto slideshow, an iMovie film, or an iDVD menu or slideshow.

The process of exporting is fairly straightforward, though not without its pitfalls. The exported song will be placed in a special iTunes playlist, which you choose in GarageBand's Preferences dialog. In the same dialog, you can also choose the names of the composer and album that will be saved with the song.

The exported song file, however, will have the same name as your GarageBand project—GarageBand doesn't let you save the exported file under another name. This becomes awkward if you export the same song more than once. You then end up with a bunch of identically titled songs in your iTunes playlist. You can give each song a

continues on next page

new name in the iTunes library by selecting the song, waiting a second and then clicking the song title, and then typing a new name. And don't worry—if you export a song more than once, a number is appended to the name of the exported file, and this number is incremented each time, so the most recent file doesn't overwrite previous files.

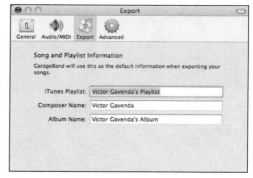

Figure 13.1 Default settings in the Export pane of the GarageBand Preferences dialog.

To set export preferences:

1. Choose GarageBand > Preferences (Command-,).

   The Preferences dialog opens.

2. Click the Export button to display the Export pane (**Figure 13.1**).

   By default, GarageBand derives the playlist name, composer name, and album name from the name of the currently logged-in user.

3. If you want to customize these entries, type new names in the fields (**Figure 13.2**).

4. Close the Preferences dialog.

Figure 13.2 Custom names have been entered in some of the fields.

Choosing How Much of Your Song Is Exported

When you create a new song, its length is automatically set to 90 measures (see "About Song Length" in Chapter 2). But if you don't fill up all 90 bars with music, GarageBand doesn't insist on exporting the empty measures along with the occupied ones. By default, when you export a song, GarageBand ends the export after the end of the final region of the song.

You can choose to export a smaller portion of the song by dragging the end-of-song marker to the point where you want the export to end, but note that you can't drag the marker any farther left than measure 32.

Using the end-of-song marker to define the part of the song to be exported works only if the part you want to export begins at the start of the song. If you want to export a portion of the middle of the song, turn on the cycle region (see "Re-recording a Section of a Song" in either Chapter 6 or Chapter 7) and adjust the cycle region to encompass only those measures that you want to export.

Figure 13.3 The Export to iTunes command.

Figure 13.4 The Creating Mixdown progress bar.

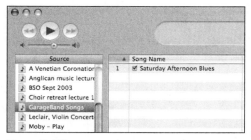

Figure 13.5 The exported song appears in a new playlist in iTunes.

To export a song to iTunes:

1. Choose File > Export to iTunes (**Figure 13.3**).

   The export process begins, and the Creating Mixdown dialog appears (**Figure 13.4**). Click the Cancel button if you want to halt the export process.

   When the progress bar reaches its end and the Creating Mixdown dialog vanishes, the process is complete.

2. Start iTunes.

   Your exported song file will be added to the playlist you specified in GarageBand's preferences. If a playlist with that name didn't exist before, it will be created (**Figure 13.5**).

✔ Tips

- If you use echo or reverb on one of your tracks, you may find that the last bit of the effect gets cut off when you export your song because the effect lingers after the final region has been played. To solve this problem, add a new track and drag a loop into the timeline at the end of the song. Loop it so it extends a few measures past the end of the other regions and turn its track volume to zero. When you export the song, GarageBand doesn't stop recording until this region ends, even though the track is inaudible.

- Be sure to save your song file before starting the export process. That way if something goes wrong in the exporting process (heaven forbid!), you won't have lost the last bit of work you did.

Using iTunes to Compress Your Song

GarageBand exports songs as uncompressed (that is to say, large) *AIFF* (Audio Interchange File Format) files. AIFF is a high-quality format, similar to the format used to store music data on CDs, but AIFF files also have correspondingly large file sizes. This makes AIFF inconvenient as a file-sharing medium. You can use iTunes to rip the file to a compressed format, reducing its size by a factor of 10 in the process. You can then e-mail your song to friends, or download it to a portable music player (such as an iPod), or post it on a Web site.

iTunes 4.71 gives you a choice of several compression schemes when exporting songs from iTunes—MP3, AAC, and Apple Lossless—and for two of them, you can choose a quality setting. The quality setting has a direct effect on the size of the resulting file: the higher the quality, the bigger the file. AAC produces higher-quality files than MP3 when the files are encoded at the same data rate, but the MP3 format is compatible with a far wider range of players. Use AAC if you are encoding files for your own use or for copying to an iPod, or if you know that the recipients of your files all have QuickTime 6.2 or later installed. For distribution to a wider audience or for copying to MP3 players other than an iPod, use MP3.

The relatively new Apple Lossless encoder provides the highest quality. It compresses the file without losing any information, so it preserves essentially the same quality as the original AIFF file, meanwhile taking up only half the storage space. Unfortunately, that's still about five times the size of MP3 or AAC files. Keep in mind also that Apple Lossless files can be played in ordinary iPods, but not in the iPod shuffle.

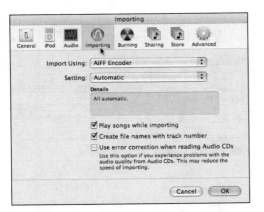

Figure 13.6 The Importing pane of the iTunes Preferences dialog.

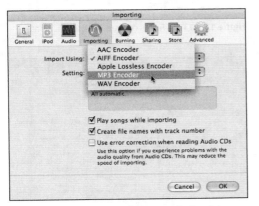

Figure 13.7 The encoding choices on the Import Using menu.

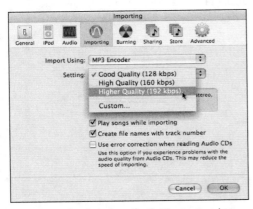

Figure 13.8 The choices on the Setting menu when the MP3 encoder is in use. This menu will look different if you choose another encoder.

Note that iTunes exports files in the same format you choose for importing files, so you (counterintuitively) choose the export format from the Import Using menu in the iTunes Preferences dialog.

The encoding process does not affect your original song file; rather, a new file is created. One slightly annoying feature of the process is that iTunes doesn't keep the encoded file in the same playlist. It just dumps the file into the library with all the rest of your iTunes songs. If you want to keep a song with the rest of the songs you exported from GarageBand, you must put it in the GarageBand playlist manually. One more thing: the encoded file will appear in iTunes lists with the exact same name as the original song, so you'll need to rename one of the files if you want to tell them apart.

To compress your file in iTunes:

1. Choose iTunes > Preferences (Command-,) to open the iTunes Preferences dialog and then click the Importing button.

   The Importing pane appears (**Figure 13.6**).

2. From the Import Using pop-up menu, choose an encoding method (**Figure 13.7**).

3. From the Setting pop-up menu, choose a quality setting (**Figure 13.8**); then click OK to close the dialog.

   continues on next page

4. Working in the main iTunes window, select the file or files you want to encode (**Figure 13.9**).

5. Choose Advanced > Convert Selection to [*chosen format*].

    A progress bar at the top of the iTunes window tracks the conversion process for each song (**Figure 13.10**). If you want to cancel conversion, click the X to the right of the progress bar.

    A tone sounds when the conversion process is complete.

6. Working in the Source list on the left side of the iTunes window, click Library to display all the songs you've added to iTunes and find your newly converted song (**Figure 13.11**).

7. If you wish, rename the converted file and drag it to your GarageBand playlist.

✔ Tip

■ The fifth choice in the Import Using menu is WAV. WAV is the Windows equivalent of AIFF—a high-quality, uncompressed audio format native to the operating system. If you are sharing songs with Windows users who may not have MP3 software (but those are rare indeed), you should export your songs in WAV format. Another reason to use WAV is if you intend to convert your songs to loops in the common (among Windows users) Sony ACID format.

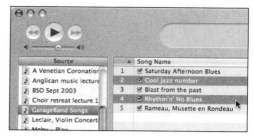

Figure 13.9 Files selected for encoding.

Cancel button

Figure 13.10 The iTunes conversion progress bar.

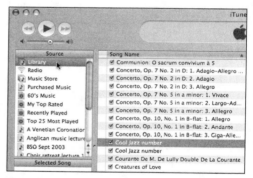

Figure 13.11 The newly converted file joins the original file in your iTunes library.

Figure 13.12 To set options for an iPhoto slideshow, start by selecting the slideshow in the Source list.

Figure 13.13 Top: To display a list of available songs, first click the Music button in the lower-right corner of the iPhoto window. Bottom: Select an iTunes playlist in the top part of the dialog; then select a specific song in the lower part of the dialog.

Using GarageBand Songs in Other iLife Programs

A great feature of Apple's iLife application suite is the ease with which the programs can share media assets. One of the best examples of this is the ready availability of your entire iTunes library in each application. I can't provide a complete introduction to each program, but I can show you how to access your iTunes library and playlists in the other three applications in iLife '05.

To add a GarageBand song to a slideshow in iPhoto 5

1. Working in the main iPhoto window, select a slideshow in the Source list (**Figure 13.12**).

   The slideshow options are displayed in the main iPhoto window.

2. Click the Music button to display the music dialog (**Figure 13.13**).

3. To enable background music during your slideshow, check the Play Music During Slideshow box.

4. Choose your GarageBand playlist from the list at the top of the dialog.

5. Select a song from your GarageBand playlist and *do one of the following*:

   ▲ To close the dialog without saving any settings, click Cancel.

   ▲ To confirm your song choice, click OK.

   When you next play the slideshow, the song you selected will play in the background.

To add a GarageBand song to the soundtrack of an iMovie HD project:

1. Working in the timeline viewer in the iMovie window, place the playhead in the movie where you want your song to begin playing.

2. Click the Audio button to display the Audio pane (**Figure 13.14**).

3. From the Audio Source pop-up menu, choose your GarageBand playlist (**Figure 13.15**).

4. Click the Place at Playhead button to insert your song into the movie at the playhead's position (**Figure 13.16**).

   When the movie is played, your song will be heard in the soundtrack at the playhead's current position.

Audio pane *Audio Source pop-up menu*

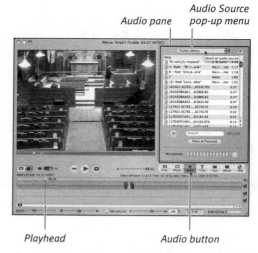

Playhead *Audio button*

Figure 13.14 The iMovie window, displaying the Audio pane.

Figure 13.15 Choosing the GarageBand playlist.

Place at Playhead button

GarageBand song inserted into movie

Figure 13.16 The song is added to the movie at the playhead.

GarageBand Songs in Other iLife Programs

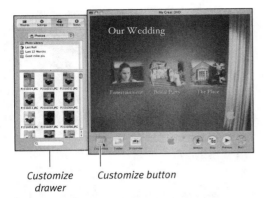

Customize   Customize button
drawer

Figure 13.17 Clicking the Customize button opens the Customize drawer.

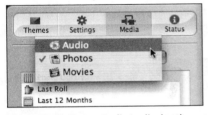

Figure 13.18 Choose Audio to display the songs in your iTunes library.

Figure 13.19 The GarageBand playlist.

To play a GarageBand song in the background of an iDVD 5 menu:

1. Working in the main iDVD window, display the menu in which you want your song to play.

2. Click the Customize button to open the Customize drawer (**Figure 13.17**).

3. Click the Media button at the top of the Customize drawer to switch to the Media pane, if it's not already open.

4. Choose Audio from the pop-up menu at the top of the Media pane to display the contents of your iTunes library (**Figure 13.18**).

5. In the top part of the Audio list, click the playlist that contains your GarageBand songs.

   The contents of the playlist are displayed in the bottom part of the Audio list (**Figure 13.19**).

6. Select a song from the playlist to play in the background of the DVD menu.

   When a DVD burned from this project is played, the song you chose will play in the background when this menu is on the screen.

GARAGEBAND SONGS IN OTHER iLIFE PROGRAMS

To play a song in the background of an iDVD slideshow:

1. Double-click a slideshow button in the menu currently displayed in iDVD (**Figure 13.20**).

    The slideshow opens in the slideshow editor.

2. Follow steps 1 through 4 of the previous task to display the iTunes playlist containing your GarageBand songs.

3. Drag a song from your playlist to the Audio well at the bottom of the slideshow window (**Figure 13.21**).

4. Click the Return button to close the slideshow editor and return to the previous menu.

    The song will now play in the background during the slideshow.

Slideshow buttons

Figure 13.20 Double-click a slideshow button to open the slideshow editor.

Figure 13.21 Dragging a song to the Audio well.

---

iTunes and iLife Resources

For information about iTunes and the rest of the iLife '05 suite of products, here are some suggestions for further reading (all from Peachpit Press, of course):

iTunes 4 for Macintosh and Windows: Visual QuickStart Guide by Judith Stern and Robert Lettieri.

Apple Training Series: iLife '05 by Michael Rubin.

The Macintosh iLife '05 by Jim Heid.

Robin Williams Cool Mac Apps: A Guide to iLife '05, Mac.com, and More, 2nd Edition, by John Tollett and Robin Williams.

Bringing Audio Files into GarageBand

You can add an audio file to your GarageBand song merely by dragging it into the timeline from the Finder. The file can be stored anywhere on your hard disk or on an audio CD inserted into your computer. You can drag the file to an existing Real Instrument track, and the imported file will appear as a new region. The imported file replaces any pre-existing regions that it overlaps. You can also drag the file to the empty area below the tracks already in the song, and a new Real Instrument track will be created for the file. You can drag multiple files at once; each file will be placed in its own track.

This drag-and-drop method of bringing material into GarageBand works for these file formats: AIFF, WAV (including Sony ACID loop files), MP3, Apple Lossless, and AAC (the last two are newly supported in GarageBand 2). If you import any file other than an AIFF file, GarageBand will convert it to AIFF before adding it to the song. This may take some time, so be prepared to wait.

And in these litigious times, we feel compelled to offer these words of wisdom: If the file you drag into GarageBand was not created by you, be sure to get its author's permission before distributing the song beyond the confines of your own personal computer. In addition, you can't import files in "protected AAC" format. The songs you purchase and download from the iTunes Music Store are compressed in this format and can be played only in iTunes on computers you authorize or in your iPod.

To drag an audio file into GarageBand:

1. In the Finder, locate the file (or files) you want to bring into GarageBand. Arrange your Finder and GarageBand windows so you can see both the file and the GarageBand timeline at the same time (**Figure 13.22**).

2. Drag the file from the Finder into the GarageBand timeline; a vertical bar shows you where the new region will begin (**Figure 13.23**).

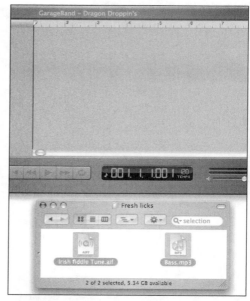

Figure 13.22 These files are ready to be dragged into GarageBand.

Vertical bar; the new region will begin here

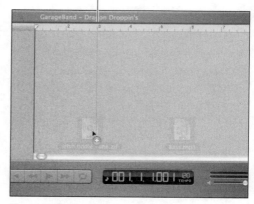

Figure 13.23 The files are poised over the timeline.

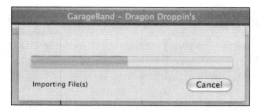

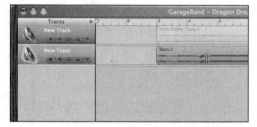

Figure 13.24 The Importing File(s) progress bar.

Figure 13.25 Dragging two files into the GarageBand timeline results in two new tracks.

3. When the file is in position, release the mouse button.

The Importing dialog lets you track the progress of the operation (**Figure 13.24**; if you dragged an MP3 file into the timeline, the dialog says "Converting" instead). If you want, you can click Cancel to stop the procedure.

A new region is added to your song for each file you dragged into the timeline. If you dragged the files over the blank area of the timeline, new tracks are created as well (**Figure 13.25**).

4. If you want, click the header of each track and give the tracks distinctive names.

✔ Tip

■ Remember that audio files you import from the Finder don't include the same cool metadata that your home-grown recorded regions do (or that Apple Loops do) and so will not cooperate when you use the master track to change the tempo or key of the song.

8-Bit Files Not Allowed

If you drag an audio file into GarageBand but are greeted with the alert shown in **Figure 13.26**, your file was probably created by an antique piece of software. Today, 16-bit resolution is the norm for audio files (largely because it's part of the audio CD standard), and just about every music program expects 16-bit audio files. GarageBand, obviously, insists upon them.

All is not lost, however. You can open the file in Apple's QuickTime Player application, and if you've paid the $30 for QuickTime Pro, you can export your file as a 16-bit file.

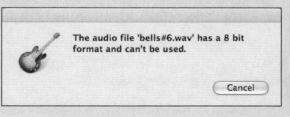

The audio file 'bells#6.wav' has a 8 bit format and can't be used.

Cancel

Figure 13.26 You'll encounter this warning if you try to import an 8-bit audio file into GarageBand.

ReWire

Another way to use the output of another music program in your GarageBand songs is to connect the programs via ReWire technology. ReWire (developed by Propellerhead Software in Sweden) is a protocol for funneling the output of one music program into another. GarageBand will accept the output of any ReWire-enabled application; examples include Reason and ReBirth from Propellerhead, and Ableton Live.

Using ReWire is simple:

1. Start GarageBand and open the song you want to bring ReWire audio into.

2. Start the ReWire-enabled application and open the song you want to connect to GarageBand.

3. Switch back to GarageBand and play your song. The ReWire application also starts to play, and the ReWire song is merged with the tracks of your GarageBand song.

Your ReWire application is synchronized with GarageBand, so GarageBand's transport controls also control the ReWire program. Any effects you have applied to the master track will be applied to the ReWire song as well, just as if it were a track in your GarageBand song. You will have to set the ReWire song's level in the ReWire application, though. If you export the GarageBand song to iTunes, the ReWire song will be saved in the mix.

When you're finished, be sure to quit the programs in the reverse order of starting them: quit the ReWire application first and then GarageBand.

Bringing MIDI Files into GarageBand

One of the new features in GarageBand 2 that induced widespread rejoicing among the GarageBand user base is the ability to import MIDI files. Denied this pleasure by GarageBand 1, many of us resorted to third-party workarounds, such as Bery Rinaldo's excellent utility Dent du Midi (as I described in the first edition of this book).

But now MIDI import is built right into GarageBand itself, and the process couldn't be easier. It works just like importing audio files: simply drag the MIDI file from the Finder over the GarageBand window and drop it into place.

You can drag a MIDI file to the empty space below the tracks in the GarageBand window, and a new track will be created to contain the imported MIDI region. If the MIDI file contains multiple tracks, GarageBand will sort them out and place each MIDI track in its own Software Instrument track. GarageBand will even do its best to match a Software Instrument to the instrumentation of the original MIDI file. Apple's documentation claims that you can drag a MIDI file over a pre-existing Software Instrument track and it will be converted to a region in that track. Alas, I've not been able to make this work. I've tried many different MIDI files, and GarageBand won't let me drop any of them onto a pre-existing track. The workaround is simple: drag the MIDI file to the empty area of the GarageBand window, let a new track be created for it, and then drag the region to the track where you want it.

To drag a MIDI file into GarageBand:

1. In the Finder, locate the file you want to bring into GarageBand. Arrange your Finder and GarageBand windows so you can see both the file and the GarageBand timeline at the same time (**Figure 13.27**).

   This MIDI file was exported from the music notation program Finale. The original file is an orchestral score, with four string parts and two woodwind parts.

2. Drag the file from the Finder into the GarageBand timeline; a vertical bar shows you where the new region (or regions) will begin (**Figure 13.28**).

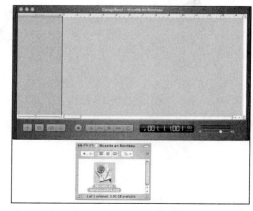

Figure 13.27 The Finder window containing the MIDI file has been brought close to the GarageBand window.

Figure 13.28 Importing a MIDI file by dragging it from the Finder.

Figure 13.29 While you're waiting, this dialog shows you how the import process is going.

Figure 13.30 The MIDI file has been successfully imported and split into six tracks, corresponding to the six instrumental parts in the original file.

3. When the file is in position, release the mouse button.

   The MIDI File Import dialog lets you track the progress of the operation (**Figure 13.29**). If you want, you can click Cancel to stop the procedure.

   A new track is added to your song for each instrument track in the file you dragged into the timeline (**Figure 13.30**). GarageBand will assign a Software Instrument from your library to each track, trying to find the closest match to the instrument information stored in the file.

4. If you want, select each track and assign a different Software Instrument to it.

MIDI Precautions

Here are a few nuggets of wisdom that we hope will contribute to an easy-going relationship between MIDI files and your copy of GarageBand:

Make sure the MIDI files you import into GarageBand have the filename suffix .mid. Various people have reported that GarageBand sometimes refuses to accept MIDI files lacking this common suffix. To be sure, you may need to change your Finder preferences to display file extensions. Working in the Finder, choose Finder > Preferences > Advanced and check the box labeled Show All File Extensions.

Oftentimes the MIDI files you import into GarageBand will have been produced by persons unknown. But if you have anything to do with creating the MIDI file in the first place, be sure to save it as a Format 1 MIDI file. This means that each instrument is contained in a different track, so that when you import the file into GarageBand, each instrument gets its own Software Instrument track.

If you know the tempo, time, or key signature of the song from which the MIDI file was created, change those properties of your GarageBand song (using the Master Track Info window) before importing. Say, for example, that you import a G-major MIDI file into a GarageBand song in C major. You then realize your error and change the key of the song to G major, which is an upward transposition of a fifth. Unfortunately, the tracks that came from the imported MIDI file will also be transposed up a fifth, to D major. If you had changed the key of the song to G before importing the MIDI file, all would have been well.

IMPROVING PERFORMANCE

GarageBand is an immensely complex program; the amount of audio signal processing it can accomplish would have required a roomful of refrigerator-sized mainframe computers a decade or two ago. Not only does it perform massive amounts of sheer number crunching, but it also juggles the demands placed on various bits of hardware, including audio interfaces, sound cards, and MIDI controllers. This is hard work, even for a modern Mac, so don't be surprised if GarageBand sometimes stumbles a bit. What can you do to keep GarageBand running in tip-top shape?

Run the Software Update application (on the Apple menu) periodically to check for new versions of GarageBand. You should also regularly visit the GarageBand support page at Apple's Web site (www.apple.com/support/garageband/) to check for software updates and search Apple's support database for answers to technical questions.

Another good resource for technical advice is the official GarageBand discussion board: discussions.info.apple.com/garageband/. GarageBand users gather here to share tips, report problems, and brainstorm to find solutions to the program's mysteries.

And finally, don't forget to let Apple know what you think of GarageBand. Submit complaints, suggestions, and words of praise to www.apple.com/feedback/garageband.html.

General Performance Tips

What's the one thing you can do that will have the biggest impact on GarageBand's performance?

Get a faster Mac.

No, seriously. The kind of data crunching GarageBand does is extremely processor intensive. The program requires at least a 600-MHz processor, but don't even think about using Software Instruments unless your Mac is powered by a G4 or G5 chip.

If a faster Mac doesn't happen to be in your budget at the moment, add as much RAM to your current machine as it will hold. The number of tracks GarageBand can handle at once is directly related to the amount of RAM installed.

You can also try to ensure that no other software is competing for your Mac's attention while running GarageBand. Here are some basic steps you can take (and what's great is that they don't cost any money):

◆ Make sure no other programs are running in the background while you're working in GarageBand.

◆ Turn off background system processes such as File Sharing.

◆ Disable timed application services that operate in the background, such as utilities that check for new e-mail messages periodically and scheduling programs that set off alarms to remind you of appointments.

◆ Turn off FileVault in System Preferences. If you can't do without the protection afforded by FileVault, you can safeguard your GarageBand songs by storing them somewhere other than in your Home folder (which includes your Documents and Music folders).

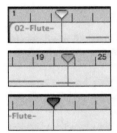

Figure A.1 Top: The color of the playhead at rest is plain white. Middle: The triangle shows a bit of color when playback is just starting to tax the processor. Bottom: The triangle is red, and GarageBand is in danger of coming to a crashing halt.

Monitor processor load with the playhead

The color of the triangle at the top of the playhead acts as an indicator of the amount of stress your hardware is experiencing while playing a song in GarageBand (**Figure A.1**). When the playhead is at rest, the triangle is blank, but during playback of your song, it changes color to alert you to conditions inside your machine. When you play a song with a few tracks, including some Software Instrument tracks, the triangle turns pale orange. The greater the load on the processor, the darker the color of the triangle. Finally, when GarageBand is about to collapse under the weight of the tasks you are asking it to perform, such as playing a song with many Software Instrument tracks and effects enabled, the triangle turns beet red. This is a warning that the program may be ready to stop dead in its tracks.

As your song plays, watch the playhead and note the places where the triangle darkens. Try thinning out the texture at those spots: trim (or delete) some regions from that neighborhood. Turning off effects helps lighten the load, too.

Reduce the graphics processing load

Apple makes beautiful interfaces for its software, but drawing all that eye candy on the screen is expensive in terms of processor cycles. In particular, it's the moving elements that exact the greatest penalty, so turning off or minimizing onscreen animation will gain a bit of breathing room for GarageBand. Here are some things to try:

◆ **Make the GarageBand window as small as possible.** The less of it there is to draw, the less effort it take to draw it, right? To do this, drag the lower-right corner of the screen as far up and to the left as it will go (see "To resize the GarageBand window" in Chapter 1).

◆ **Zoom out until you can see the whole song.** Showing all the different colored regions marching across the screen from right to left takes quite a lot of processor horsepower. If the whole song is visible in the window, then nothing moves except the playhead. Use the zoom slider to accomplish this (see "Zooming in the Timeline" in Chapter 1).

◆ **Hide the track mixer column.** The little colored lights that make the track level meters a delight to watch also gobble up processor time. Click the triangle at the top of the Tracks column to tuck the Mixer column out of view (see "To hide the track mixer" in Chapter 3).

◆ **Hide the entire program while your song plays back.** Select Hide GarageBand from the GarageBand menu (or press Command-H).

Lock tracks

Two of the things that stress your system the most when playing a song in GarageBand are Software Instruments and effects. Both of these components take up a lot of CPU cycles because they are calculated in real time. One way to relieve this stress is to lock tracks that make use of these features. When you lock a track, GarageBand plays through the song saving a version of each locked track to disk. The next time you play the song, the saved version of the locked track is used, freeing up processor time for other functions (see "Locking a Track" in Chapter 3).

The Tips section in GarageBand's Help file suggests converting Software Instrument regions to Real Instrument regions to ease up the load on the processor (simply drag the Software Instrument region into a Real Instrument track). But this method has a drawback: you lose the ability to edit the notes or the effects in the Software Instrument or to change its instrument. If you lock the Software Instrument track, you gain the same benefits as if you had converted it to a Real Instrument track, but you always have the option of unlocking the track later and editing it.

Bounce tracks

Bouncing is a technique from analog recording days. It involves mixing down several tracks into a single track. This single track then takes the place of the tracks that were mixed to create it. The new track lock feature (introduced in GarageBand 2) has rendered bouncing obsolete for the most part, since locking provides most of the same benefits but is much less labor intensive. See "Bouncing Tracks to Improve Performance" later in this chapter for detailed instructions.

Turn off unneeded effects

All instrument presets, whether Real Instrument or Software Instrument, come with a certain number of effects turned on by default. Each of these enabled effects saps some of your processor cycles. If your song won't play smoothly, open the Track Info window and examine the settings in the Details pane for each track (see "Applying Effects" in Chapter 11). Turn off effects that aren't absolutely necessary.

Be especially vigilant for effects that are turned on, but are turned all the way down (**Figure A.2**). These effects cost you processor time, too, even if their values are set to zero.

Allow fewer simultaneous notes in Software Instrument tracks

All Software Instrument tracks are not created equal when it comes to stressing your Mac during playback. A Software Instrument track used for a melody instrument, like a saxophone or bass, usually plays back only one note at a time. Keyboard and guitar tracks, on the other hand, frequently contain chords, which are stacks of notes sounding together.

Processing chords in a Software Instrument track makes GarageBand work harder than when it processes single-note tracks. You can set a limit on the number of notes an instrument can play at once using the Voices per Instrument pop-up menu in the Advanced pane of the GarageBand Preferences dialog. The default setting is Automatic, meaning that GarageBand decides how many voices to allot to each instrument based on the speed of your computer's CPU. To set a different limit, choose a setting from the Voices per Instrument

Figure A.2 These effects aren't doing you any good, but they're consuming valuable system resources.

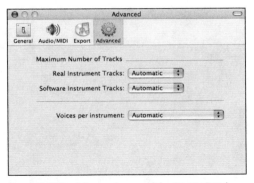

Figure A.3 The Advanced pane of the GarageBand Preferences dialog.

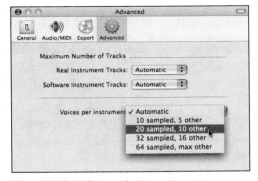

Figure A.4 The Voices per Instrument pop-up menu.

menu. Notice that each of the choices allows twice as many notes for sampled instruments as for "other" (meaning synthesized) instruments. To read about the distinction between sampled and synthesized instruments, see "Real vs. Software Instrument Tracks" in Chapter 3.

To change the maximum number of voices per Software Instrument:

1. Choose GarageBand > Preferences (Command-,) to open the Preferences dialog.

2. Click the Advanced tab to switch to the Advanced preferences pane (**Figure A.3**).

3. From the Voices per Instrument pop-up menu, choose a different setting (**Figure A.4**).

   Settings allowing fewer notes improve GarageBand's playback performance, and settings allowing more voices per instrument are likely to degrade performance.

4. Close the Preferences dialog.

Bouncing Tracks to Improve Performance

Bouncing is a workaround that dates back to the days of analog tape recording. For example, if an engineer was working on a project that required 12 recorded tracks but had only 8-track equipment available, the solution was to combine, or *bounce*, some of those tracks into a single track. The bounced tracks could then be erased, leaving enough empty tracks for the rest of the song.

In GarageBand, bouncing comes in handy if your song uses more tracks than your Mac can gracefully handle. Start by building your song with a few tracks. Adjust the mix, save the file, and then export the song to iTunes (see "Exporting a Song to iTunes" in Chapter 13). Next, save the song under a new name, delete the tracks that you just exported, and find the exported song in the Finder and drag it into GarageBand. The material that required several tracks before now occupies only a single track.

In the previous edition of this book, I recommended bouncing Software Instrument tracks as a way to increase GarageBand's performance, but the new track lock feature does just as much good, takes less work, and is reversible (you can unlock a track, edit it, and then lock it again). See "Locking a Track" in Chapter 3 for the details.

To bounce tracks:

1. Refine the mix of your song and save the file (**Figure A.5**).

2. Use the Save As command to save a copy of your song under a new name.

   This is the copy you'll use to export tracks to iTunes (**Figure A.6**).

3. Solo the tracks that you want to include in the bounced file (**Figure A.7**).

Figure A.5 This song has 10 Software Instrument tracks. Four of them are strings.

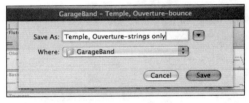

Figure A.6 Saving the file under the name we want the exported song to have.

Figure A.7 The four string tracks (which will combined into a single track) have been set to Solo mode.

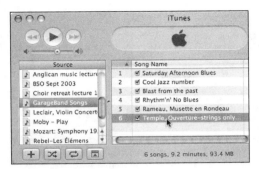

Figure A.8 The exported song is included in the GarageBand Songs playlist.

Figure A.9 The exported song file's Finder icon.

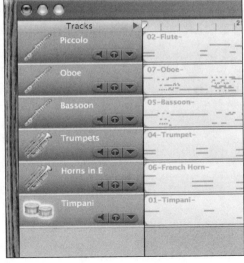

Figure A.10 The original file after deleting all four string tracks.

4. Choose File > Export to iTunes and wait while GarageBand mixes and exports the tracks.

   When the export process is complete, iTunes opens in the background.

5. Click the iTunes window to bring it to the foreground; then find the song you exported in your GarageBand export playlist (**Figure A.8**).

6. Select the song and Choose File > Show Song File (Command-R) to reveal the song file in the Finder (**Figure A.9**).

7. Working in GarageBand, delete the tracks you set to Solo mode in step 3 (**Figure A.10**).

continues on next page

8. Drag the exported song file (which contains the music from the deleted tracks) into the GarageBand window (**Figure A.11**).

9. GarageBand creates a new track to hold the exported song (**Figure A.12**).

The bounced tracks have been combined into a single Real Instrument track, reducing the total number of tracks in the song without losing any of the musical content in the bounced tracks. Because you saved your original song in step 1, you can return to it later and refine the mix if you want and create a new bounce file.

10. Save the song under a new name, using the Save As command, if you want.

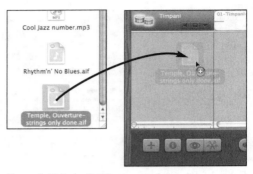

Figure A.11 Dragging the exported song into GarageBand.

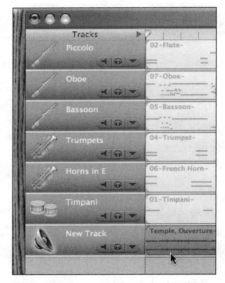

Figure A.12 The exported song is placed in a new Real Instrument track.

GARAGEBAND JAM PACKS

Released simultaneously with GarageBand, the original GarageBand Jam Pack was the first collection of add-ons for GarageBand released by Apple. Apple described the package as "more than 2,000 additional Apple Loops in a variety of instruments, moods and genres, more than 100 new Software Instruments, over 100 audio effects presets and 15 new guitar amp settings."

Apple followed that first Jam Pack several months later with a pair of sequels, Jam Pack 2: Remix Tools and Jam Pack 3: Rhythm Section. At the same time, the original Jam Pack was rechristened Jam Pack 1: Instruments, Loops, and Effects.

Each of the new collections, like the first one, contains over 2,000 Apple Loops and scores of new Software Instruments. The Remix Tools set is designed for creating music in club dance, urban, and electronica styles. New instruments include a variety of dance and urban beat kits, with turntable effects like scratching and needle drops. The loops in the Rhythm Section collection are divided more or less equally between drum beats and bass guitar licks (as the name implies). The same theme continues in the list of Software Instruments, which include acoustic and electronic basses, guitars—and yes, more drums.

continues on next page

And finally (so far, at least), in January 2005 Apple released yet another Jam Pack alongside GarageBand 2, titled Jam Pack 4: Symphony Orchestra. This collection stands somewhat apart from the others, and I'll talk about it more in a minute.

In the first edition of this book, I devoted this appendix to a rather detailed description of the instrument presets bundled in the first Jam Pack. But now that there are four Jam Packs, it's impractical to provide equal coverage for all of them in these pages. Fortunately, listings of the contents of the Jam Packs are not hard to find online. The intrepid duo of M. Danielson and Peter J. Hill at Macjams.com posted a condensed listing of the loops, with descriptions, at www.macjams.com (see the article "In Depth: Apple GarageBand Jam Pack"). Descriptions of Jam Packs 2, 3, and 4 can be found at icompositions.com—go to the archives page (www.icompositions.com/news/music_archives.php) and search within the page for the words *Jam Pack* to find the individual articles.

Jam Pack 4: Symphony Orchestra bears further scrutiny because of its features that set it apart from its forebears—features that are much more interesting to read about than pages-long lists of instrument presets. For starters, it's huge. It comes on two DVDs, and once installed, it gobbles up 10 GB of hard drive space. Much of that space is devoted to the obligatory 2,000+ Apple Loops, but if you look closely, you'll see that they're installed in /Library/Audio rather than in /Library/GarageBand like the rest of your loops. Not only is Jam Pack 4 a glutton for disk space, but it's hungry for other resources, too: its RAM requirements are twice that of GarageBand alone (512 MB minimum, with 1 GB recommended). All of these details are indicative of a structural shift in GarageBand's relationship to loops and instruments—an observation confirmed by the fact that Jam Pack 4 works only in GarageBand 2 (and Logic 7 Express and Logic 7 Pro), not with the original version of the program.

The most impressive thing about Jam Pack 4: Symphony Orchestra is its instrument collection. It includes a full array of high-quality sampled orchestral instruments—and not just individual instruments, but whole sections. It also offers excellent keyboard and tuned percussion instruments as well as a full panoply of unpitched percussion. The principal instruments in the collection (the ones with the word *Orchestra* in their names) use actual recorded samples of every note in the original instrument's range (no wonder the Jam Pack takes up so much disk space!). Furthermore, many of the Orchestra instruments include a variety of sounds for each note, which you access by way of your MIDI keyboard or the virtual Musical Typing keyboard. You can also edit the corresponding attribute in the Software Instrument track editor.

Many of the instruments respond to changes in *velocity* (how hard you strike the key) with variations in the sound of their attack or the volume of the sound they produce. But if you want to introduce subtle changes in volume in the course of a melodic phrase or during a held note, the string, wind, and brass instruments can be made to produce *crescendos* or *diminuendos* (gradual increases or decreases in volume). Use the pitch bend controller on your MIDI keyboard (real or virtual) to create these inflections during performance, or enter them later by editing the Expression parameter in the track editor.

Another characteristic of instrumental sound is *articulation*. This refers to the quality of the connection between notes: whether one note leads smoothly to another (*legato*)

continues on next page

GARAGEBAND JAM PACKS

or ends abruptly before the next note begins (*staccato*). Other articulations include *pizzicato* (plucking the string of a string instrument), *tremolo* (agitated repetition of a single note), and quick *trills* (alternation of a note with the note above). Many of the instruments in Jam Pack 4 support a variety of articulations, which you access by means of the modulation wheel on your MIDI device (or by editing the Foot Control parameter in the track editor).

The documentation that accompanies the GarageBand Jam Pack 4 package spells out the precise MIDI controller values for the articulations supported by each instrument. The documentation also includes an excellent survey of the instruments of the orchestra, covering their history and the uses to which they have been put over the centuries. It even advises you on how to set the pan control for each instrument so it will sound like it's in the right place in the orchestra (there's a nice little map for this purpose).

The Orchestra instruments, with their full gamut of samples and their extensive selection of articulations, are resource hogs and demand a machine with a lot of RAM. Combining several of these instruments in a song can drag a computer to its knees. Apple thoughtfully provided a substitute set of instruments for use in just such a situation. These instruments, which use the word *Xtra* in their names, are constructed from fewer samples than their Orchestra cousins and have only a single articulation each. If, for example, your composition includes a flute track, you could assign to it the standard Orchestra Flute, which has two articulations (legato and staccato). But if the track doesn't require two articulations—perhaps it would sound best played legato throughout—you could assign the Xtra Flute Legato instrument to the track, lightening the computer's processing load.

INDEX

~ (tilde), 5
0 dB gain, 252
8-bit files, 281
16-bit resolution, 281
24-bit resolution, 111–112
96-kHz sampling rate, 111–112

A

AAC format, 272, 279
Ableton Live, 282
absolute time, 16
access permissions, loop, 94
ACID format, 274, 279
ACID loops, 96
acoustic drums, 158
ADCs, 108, 109, 111–112
Add Loop dialog, 97
Add to Loop Library command, 96, 97
Add Track button, 8, 9, 53
Advanced section, track editor
    editing controls, 182, 184
    illustrated, 180
    and MIDI controller data, 212
    Note Value button, 207–208
    showing/hiding, 184
    track timing controls, 193–195
    track tuning controls, 193–195
aftertouch, keyboard, 115
AIFF files, 100, 272, 274, 279
amp simulation effect, 238–239
analog-digital converters, 108. See also ADCs
Apple
    GarageBand Support page, 287
    iLife suite, 3, 5, 275, 278
    Logic Express, 268
    Logic Pro, 217, 268
    QuickTime, 272, 281
    Soundtrack Loop Utility, 100

Apple Loops. See also loops
    adding to GarageBand, 95
    converting AIFF/WAV files to, 100
    creating your own, 97–100
    and metadata, 72
    shipped with GarageBand, 5, 72, 297
Apple Lossless format, 272, 279
Apple Training Series: iLife '05, 278
Applications folder, 6
articulation, 299
audio
    8- vs. 16-bit, 281
    data, 48
    digitizing, 103, 108
    drivers, 112, 118, 122
    effects (See effects)
    files (See audio files)
    hardware, 3, 101–119
    interfaces, 103, 108–112, 120, 124
    recording (See recording)
    sources, 103, 105–107
audio-digitizing hardware, 108
audio files
    exporting, 269–271
    importing, 279–285
    supported file formats, 279
audio-in ports, 108, 109–110
Audio Input pop-up menu, 122
Audio Interchange File Format, 272. See also
        AIFF files
Audio/MIDI pane, Preferences dialog, 120–122
audio-out ports, 105, 107
audio-playback hardware, 119
audio-recording hardware, 101–118
    advances in, 102
    for audio interfaces, 103, 108–112
    for audio sources, 103, 105–107
    features to look for in, 111–112
    for recording Software Instruments, 113–118
    setting preferences for, 120–122

Audio Units, 246–248
auditioning loops, 89
AUGraphic EQ effect, 246
auto wah effect, 239
automatic filter effect, 239

B

.band filename extension, 29
basic tracks, 56
bass amp effect, 239
Bass Gain slider, 235
bass reduction effect, 240
beat guide, 204
beat ruler, 12, 14, 181, 185
beats
   cleaning up, 194
   grouping of, 34
   and musical time, 10, 16
   and song length, 38
   sorting loops by, 86
   and time display, 16, 17
   and time signatures, 34
   and timeline beat ruler, 12
   up-tempo, 33
beats per minute, 17, 33, 96
bitcrusher effect, 240
bits, 108
blue tracks/regions, 42, 166
bouncing tracks, 291, 294–296
bpm, 17, 33. See also beats
button view, loop browser, 75, 76–78, 87
Buzzer2, 247–248

C

CardBus slot, 110
cents, 129
Change Audio Driver? dialog, 122
chorus effect, 240
Clipboard, 170–171, 203, 214–215
clipping, 11, 131, 250–251
clipping indicators, 132
color-coding, region/track, 42, 166
column view, loop browser, 75, 80, 88
compass, onscreen keyboard, 145–146
.component extension, 247
compressing songs, 272–274
compressor effect, 221, 236
computer music revolution, 3
condenser microphones, 106–107
control points, 212–215, 262
Convert to Real Instrument box, 92
Copy command, 59, 170, 198, 203, 214
CoreAudio, 112, 120

count-in, 126, 155–156
Count In command, 126, 155–156
crescendos, 255, 299
crossfades, 255, 261–262
Cut command, 170, 171, 198, 203, 214
Cycle button, 10, 138, 161
cycle regions, 138, 160, 162, 215

D

Danielson, M., 246, 298
dB, 252
decibel, 252
decrescendos, 255
Delete command, 170, 171
Delete Instrument button, 228
Delete Preset command, 226
Delete Track command, 64
demo songs, 26
Dent du Midi, 283
diaphragms, 106, 107
diatonic notes, 150
Digidesign CoreAudio Setup dialog, 120
Digidesign Mbox, 120
digital pianos, 107
diminuendos, 299
discussion board, 287
Display pop-up menu, 212
distortion, 11, 131, 240, 250
downbeat, 34
drag-and-drop method, 279
drivers, audio, 112, 118, 122
drums, recording Software Instrument, 158, 162
Duplicate Track command, 59
duration bar, 206
DVD menus, 277–278
dynamic microphones, 106
dynamic range, 236

E

Easy Install, 5
echo effect, 221, 230–231, 271
Echo Repeat parameter, 230
Echo Time parameter, 230
Echo Volume parameter, 230
editing. See also track editor
   individual notes, 206
   MIDI controller information, 212–216
   MIDI data, 199–211
   non-destructive, 167
   pan curves, 259–260
   pedal markings, 210
   Real Instrument regions, 178

regions, 167–168, 170–171
Software Instrument regions, 179
Software Instruments, 243–245
undocumented features, 198
volume curves, 258–259
editing commands, 170–171, 198
editor display menu, 182
effects, 217–248
about, 218
applying, 221, 222–223, 238
Audio Unit, 246
descriptions of non-basic, 238–242
producing, 218
purpose of, 218
saving presets for, 225–226
turning off, 233, 292
using basic, 230–237
effects controls, Track Info window, 220–221
effects generators, 218
effects pop-up menu, 238
effects presets, 225–226, 263
electric guitars, 107
electronic drums, 158
eMac, 108
end-of-song marker, 38, 270
Enhance Timing slider, 182, 194, 195
Enhance Tuning slider, 182, 193, 195
equalizer (EQ) effect, 221, 234–235, 246
Export to iTunes command, 28, 271
exporting
compressing songs prior to, 272–273
to iTunes, 268, 269–271
portions of songs, 270
saving songs prior to, 271
setting preferences for, 270
expression pedal, 117, 216
extensions, filename, 29
external audio interfaces, 110–111
eye icon, 9

F

fade-ins/-outs, 255, 261–262
Fast Forward button, 10
Fav column, loop browser, 86
favorites, marking loops as, 87–88
Favorites button, 87
File Sharing, 288
filename extensions, 29
FileVault, 288
FireWire, 111, 112, 113, 118
Fix Timing button, 182, 196–197, 204

flanger effect, 241
foot control, 216
Format 1 MIDI files, 285
freezing tracks, 63

G

gain, 252
GarageBand
adding Apple Loops to, 95
announcement of, 3
bringing audio files into, 279–285
buttons/controls, 8–11
checking for new versions of, 287
color-coding in, 42, 166
complexity of, 287
discussion board, 287
effects (See effects)
exporting to iTunes from, 268, 269–271
getting help with, 7 (See also Help file)
and iLife, 3
importing songs into, 268
improving performance of, 287–296
interface, 3, 8–11
Jam Packs (See Jam Packs)
launching, 6
musical goodies shipped with, 5
and other applications, 268, 275–278
popularity of, 3
recording in (See recording)
sharing files from, 268
submitting feedback on, 287
upgrading to Logic programs from, 268
using ACID loops in, 96
what you can do with, 4
GarageBand folder, 5
GarageBand window, 8, 11
gate effect, 221, 237
General MIDI Percussion Key Map, 159
Generator pop-up menu, 221, 243
generators
classes of, 49
emulating functions of, 218
sampled, 49, 243
synthesized, 49, 243
genre, searching for loops by, 73, 98
Genre pop-up menu, 98
Go to Beginning button, 10
graphic view, track editor, 182, 192, 205
graphics, 290
green tracks/regions, 42, 166
gridlines, 20. See also timeline grid

H

hardware, 101–122
  audio-digitizing, 103, 108
  audio-recording, 103–118
  effects generators, 218
  performance considerations, 288
  for playback, 119
  setting preferences for, 120–122
headphones, 119
Heid, Jim, 278
Help file, 7, 198, 211, 291
Hide Editor command, 183
Hide Extension box, 29
Hide GarageBand command, 290
Hide Instrument Tuner command, 130
hiding/showing
  loop browser, 74
  onscreen keyboard, 143–144
  track editor, 183
  track editor Advanced section, 184
  track mixer, 43, 47
Hill, Peter J., 298
Home folder, 5

I

icompositions.com, 298
iDVD, 277–278
IEEE 1394b, 111
iLife suite
  inclusion of GarageBand in, 3
  Installer program, 5
  recommended books on, 278
  and sharing of media assets, 275
iMac, 108
iMovie HD, 276
importing
  audio files, 279–285
  challenges of, 268
  with Dent du Midi, 283
  with drag and drop, 279–281, 284–285
  and filename extensions, 285
  MIDI files, 283–285
  permissions considerations, 279
Input Level indicators, 133
Input Volume slider, 133
instrument icons, 43, 68
instrument presets, 51, 227–228
instrument tuner, 11, 129–130
instruments. See also Real Instruments; Software
    Instruments
  changing track's assigned, 67–68
  displaying installed, 52

how GarageBand defines, 42
  matching to loops, 98
  searching for loops by, 73
interfaces
  audio, 103, 108–112, 120, 124
  external, 110–111
  GarageBand, 3, 8–11
  internal, 110, 133
  loop browser search, 73, 75
  MIDI, 113, 117–118
internal audio interfaces, 110, 133
iPhoto, 275
iTunes
  compressing songs in, 272–274
  exporting songs to, 268–271
  Music Store, 279
  recommended book on, 278
iTunes 4 for Macintosh and Windows, 278

J

Jam Packs, 5, 216, 224, 297–300
Join Selected command, 176

K

key action, keyboard controller, 115
Key pop-up menu, 37
Keyboard command, 143
keyboard shortcuts
  for GarageBand help, 7
  for moving playhead, 14
keyboard synthesizers, 107
keyboards
  adjusting sensitivity of, 153
  features to look for in, 114–117
  MIDI, 114, 153, 216
  Musical Typing window, 149
  onscreen (See onscreen keyboard)
  piano, 148
  QWERTY, 150, 152
keys
  about, 36–37
  changing, 37, 219
  sorting loops by, 86
Keyword Browsing box, 81
keywords, button, 77–78
kHz, 108
kilohertz, 108

L

legato, 299
Lettieri, Robert, 278
level meters, 131

Library folder, 5
Lock button, 43, 63
locking tracks, 43, 62–63
Logic Express, 211, 268
"Logic for GarageBand Users" (PDF), 268
Logic Pro, 217, 268
loop browser, 73–81
    customizing button view in, 77–78
    dimmed buttons in, 81
    expanding to show more buttons, 79
    finding loops in, 76, 80–82
    illustrated, 9, 73
    marking loops as favorites in, 87–88
    purpose of, 9, 73
    restricting loops displayed in, 83–84
    showing/hiding, 74
    viewing modes for, 75
    working with results list in, 85–86
Loop Browser button, 8, 9, 74
loop-creation tool, 100
loop-management tool, 83–84
Loop Name Already Exists dialog, 99
looping regions, 167, 174
loops, 71–100. See also Apple Loops
    about, 72
    adding to songs, 90–91
    auditioning, 89
    creating your own, 97–100
    defined, 71, 72
    marking as favorites, 87–88
    and metadata, 72
    searching for, 73, 75, 76, 80–82
    setting access permissions for, 94
    sorting, 73, 86
    sources of, 83
Loops menu, 75, 76, 83–84
loudness, 200, 201. See also velocity

M

Mac OS X
    and audio drivers, 112, 118
    and Audio Unit format, 246
    and CoreAudio, 112
    and filename extensions, 29
    folder/path names, 5
    and MIDI, 57, 118, 120
    plug-in formats, 246
Macintosh
    audio-in ports, 108
    getting external audio to work with, 3
    performance considerations, 288
Macintosh iLife '05, The, 278

Macjams.com, 298
Make Preset command, 225
Make Preset dialog, 229
Manual setting, Track Info window, 229
markers
    beat, 20
    end-of-song, 38, 270
    loop, 72
    pedal up/down, 210–211
master level meters, 8, 11
master pitch curve, 263
master track
    about, 219
    applying effects to, 221
    automation curves, 263–265
    illustrated, 8, 12
    purpose of, 13, 219
    Track Info window for, 219, 220
Master Track button, 219
master volume curve, 264
master volume slider, 8, 11, 266
Maximum Number of Tracks settings, 69
measures, 34
memory. See RAM
metadata, 72, 189, 281
metronome, 126–127, 155–156
microphone pre-amps, 112
microphones, 105–107, 124, 128
.mid extension, 285
Mid Frequency slider, 235
Mid Gain slider, 235
MIDI
    bus power, 118
    caveats regarding, 285
    connectors, 112
    controller data, 212–216
    controllers, 113, 114, 212
    data (See MIDI data)
    drivers, 118
    drum sounds, 158
    file import, 283–284
    In/Out ports, 117
    interfaces, 113, 117–118
    keyboards, 114, 153, 216 (See also keyboards)
    meaning of acronym, 48
    and Musical Typing window, 149
    percussion key map, 159
    and pitch bend, 151
    ports, 114
    status light, 154
    synthesizers, 113

MIDI data, 199–211
    adding/deleting notes in, 202, 207–208
    changing note velocity in, 201, 209
    cutting/copying notes in, 203
    editing individual notes in, 200, 206
    and notation view, 204–209
    pasting notes in, 203
    and pedal markings, 210–211
    recording, 102
    vs. audio data, 48, 50, 102
MIDIKeys utility, 152
mini-jacks, 109
mixing, 249–266
    and automation curves, 255–260, 263–265
    and crossfades, 255, 261–262
    defined, 249
    and master track, 263–265
    and output volume, 266
    and pan curves, 255, 257, 259–260
    and pan position, 253–254
    tasks associated with, 249
    and track automation, 255–256
    and volume curves, 250, 255–256, 257, 258–259
    and volume levels, 250–252
Modulation keys, 151
modulation scale, 216
modulation wheel, 116, 216
Monitor pop-up menu, 55, 128
mood, searching for loops by, 73
Mood Discriptors area, 99
movies, 276
MP3 format, 268, 272, 279
multitrack recording, 104, 124
music. See also songs
    jargon/terms, 33, 299–200
    printing, 211
    programs, 3, 217, 246, 267, 268, 282
    recording (See recording)
    transposing, 189 (See also transposition)
Music folder, 5
Music Store, iTunes, 279
Musical Instrument Digital Interface, 48. See also
    MIDI data
musical notation, 204
musical time, 10, 16
Musical Typing window, 142, 149–152
Mute button, 43, 45

N

naming/renaming
    presets, 225
    regions, 93, 178, 182, 186, 187
    tracks, 60, 186–187

New Basic Track command, 56
New Project dialog, 31
New Track dialog, 51–52, 53, 57
noise gate effect, 221
non-destructive editing, 167
notation view, track editor, 182, 192, 204–209
Note keys, 150
Note Value button, 205, 207, 208
Note Velocity slider, 182, 201, 209
notes
    adding/deleting, 202, 207
    changing velocity of, 201, 209
    cutting/copying, 203
    editing individual, 200, 206
    fixing timing of, 196–197
    moving with arrow keys, 206
    pasting, 203

O

Octave Transposition keys, 150
octaves, 114, 145–146, 148, 150, 189
onscreen keyboard, 143–148
    alternatives to, 149, 152
    changing compass of, 145–146
    changing range of, 146
    configuring, 145–148
    displaying full piano keyboard in, 148
    overview feature, 145, 147
    playing, 142, 143, 144
    purpose of, 143
    resizing keys on, 147–148
    showing/hiding, 143–144
Open command/dialog, 25
Open Recent command, 26
orange regions, 42, 166
Orchestra instruments, 300. See also Symphony
    Orchestra
output volume, setting, 266
overdrive effect, 241
overdubbing, 162, 215
overview feature
    Musical Typing window, 150
    onscreen keyboard, 145, 147

P

padlock icon, 63
pan curves, 12, 13, 255, 257, 259–260
pan position, 253–254
Paste command, 59, 170, 198, 203, 215
PC Card slot, 110
PCI card/slot, 110, 133
pedal markings, 205, 210–211

pedal up/down symbols, 210
percussion key map, MIDI, 159
percussion sounds, 158, 159, 162
performance tips, 288–296
permissions
    loop access, 94
    song, 279
phaser effect, 241
photo slideshows. See slideshows
piano keyboard, 148
pitch, 36, 265
pitch bend scale, 216
pitch bend wheel, 116, 216
pitch curves, 12, 13
pitch meter, 129
Pitchbend keys, 150
pizzicato, 300
Play button, 10, 30, 137
playback hardware, 119
Playhead Lock button, 185
playheads
    locking/unlocking, 185
    monitoring processor load with, 289
    moving, 14–15, 17
    purpose of, 12, 181
    timeline vs. track editor, 181
plug-in formats, 246
Power Macintosh, 108
PowerBook, 14, 108
pre-amplifiers, 105, 112
Preferences dialog
    Adding Loops to Timeline setting, 92
    Audio/MIDI settings, 120–122
    Export settings, 270
    Keyboard Sensitivity setting, 153
    Keyword Browsing setting, 81
    Keyword Layout setting, 78
    Maximum Number of Tracks settings, 69
    Metronome settings, 127, 156
    permission settings, 94
    Voices per Instrument setting, 293
presets, 224–228
    deleting, 226, 228
    effects, 225–226
    instrument, 227–228
    managing, 224
    naming, 225
    saving, 227
    setting display options for, 224
previewing loops, 89
projects, 24. See also songs
Propellerhead Software, 282

punch-in/-out points, 139, 162
punching in/out, 139, 162
purple regions, 42, 166

Q

QuickTime encoding, 272
QuickTime Player, 281
QuickTime Pro, 281
QWERTY keyboard, 150, 152

R

RAM, 40, 69, 288, 298, 300
re-recording, 138–139, 160–162
Real Instrument loops. See also loops
    adding to songs, 90–91
    converting Software Instrument loops to, 92
    dragging to timeline, 93
    dragging to tracks, 42, 90
Real Instrument regions. See also regions
    and ACID loops, 96
    color-coding of, 42, 166
    converting Software Instrument loops into, 90, 93
    dragging to loop browser, 97
    editing, 178
    joining, 176
    naming/renaming, 93, 178
    resizing, 173
    splitting, 168, 173, 175
    and track editor, 178, 180, 181
    transposing, 178, 189, 190, 191–192
Real Instrument tracks. See also tracks
    adding, 53–55
    changing instrument assigned to, 67
    enabling for recording, 135
    enhancing timing of, 193, 194, 195
    enhancing tuning of, 193–195
    recording into, 160
    setting input volume for, 54
    Track Info window for, 65
    vs. Software Instrument tracks, 48–50
    when to use, 42
Real Instruments
    recording, 123, 136–139
    setting input levels for, 133
    setting recording level for, 131
    using instrument tuner with, 129–130
Reason, 282
ReBirth, 282
Record button, 10, 137
Record Enable button, 43, 135, 157

recording
about, 124–125
avoiding distortion in, 131
disk space required for, 136
electric guitars, 107
enabling tracks for, 135
hardware (See audio-recording hardware)
multitrack, 104, 124
over part of song, 138–139, 160–162
into Real Instrument tracks, 123, 136–139, 160
regions, 125, 137, 142, 158
Software Instrument drums, 158
into Software Instrument tracks, 141–142, 157–162, 205
turning off monitoring during, 128
using metronome while, 126, 155–156
recording levels, 123, 131, 133, 136
recording studios, 101, 218
Redo command, 39
Reed, Chris, 152
Region Name field, 182
Region Pitch slider, 182, 265
regions, 165–176
about, 166
adding/deleting notes in, 202, 207–208
arranging, 24
color-coding of, 42, 166
copying and pasting, 170
cutting, 171
cutting/copying notes from, 203
cutting/copying notes in, 203
defined, 13, 24, 166
deleting, 171
displaying in track editor, 183
dragging, 172
duplicating, 171
editing, 167–168
editing portions of, 198
fixing timing of notes in, 196–197
illustrated, 12
joining, 176
looping/repeating, 167, 174
moving, 172
naming/renaming, 93, 182, 186, 187
purpose of, 13
recording, 125, 137, 142, 158
resizing, 139, 173
selecting/deselecting, 169
shifting pitch of, 182
splitting, 166, 168, 175
transposing, 178, 189–192
Remix Tools, 297
renaming. See naming/renaming
Repeat Color parameter, 230

resolution
8- vs. 16-bit, 281
ADC, 108
results list, loop browser, 85–86
Reverb Color parameter, 232
reverb effect, 218, 221, 232–233, 271
Reverb Time parameter, 232
Reverb Volume parameter, 233
Revert to Saved command, 39
Rewind button, 10
ReWire, 282
Rhythm Section, 297
Rinaldo, Bery, 283
Robin Williams Cool Mac Apps, 278
Rubin, Michael, 278

S

sampled generators, 243, 244
sampled sounds, 49
sampling rates, 108, 112
Save as Archive command, 28
Save As command/dialog, 27
Save command, 27
Save Instrument button, 227
Save Preset dialog, 229
Scale pop-up menu, 82, 98
scale type, finding loops by, 82
scales, 36, 37, 82, 98, 216
scissors icon, 10
scroll bars, 12, 13
search interface, loop browser, 73, 75
semitones, 129, 189, 190
sheet music, 211
Show All File Extensions box, 29
Show Editor command, 183
Show Instrument Tuner command, 130
Show Master Track command, 219
Show Track Mixer control, 43
Show Volume/Pan Curve control, 43
showing/hiding
loop browser, 74
onscreen keyboard, 143–144
track editor, 183
track editor Advanced section, 184
track mixer, 43, 47
slideshows, 275, 278
SLU, 100
Software Instrument drums, 158
Software Instrument loops. See also loops
adding to songs, 90–91
color-coding of, 42
converting to Real Instrument loops, 42, 92

Software Instrument regions. See also regions
  adding/deleting notes in, 202
  color-coding of, 166
  editing, 179, 206
  joining, 176
  looping, 174
  naming of, 93
  pasting notes into, 203
  and pedal markings, 210
  resizing, 173, 174
  splitting, 168
  and track editor, 179, 180, 181
  transposing, 24, 189, 191–192
Software Instrument tracks. See also tracks
  adding, 57–58
  changing instrument assigned to, 67
  choosing icon for, 58
  and cycle regions, 139
  entering pitches into, 150
  in notation view, 204
  pasting notes into, 203
  processing chords in, 292–293
  recording into, 141–142, 157–162, 205
  Track Info window for, 66, 221, 243
  vs. Real Instrument tracks, 48–50
  when to use, 42
Software Instruments
  changing maximum number of voices for, 293
  editing, 243–245
  hardware for recording, 113–118
  and instrument tuner, 129
  performance considerations, 288
  recording, 141–142, 157–162
  shipped with GarageBand, 5
Software Update application, 287
Solo button, 43, 46
songs, 23–40
  about, 24
  adding loops to, 90–91
  adding pitch changes to, 265
  adding tracks to, 51–58
  adding volume changes to, 264–265
  changing length of, 38
  closing, 26
  compatibility considerations, 28
  compressing, 272–274
  creating, 31–32
  default settings for, 32
  deleting tracks in, 64
  elements of typical, 41
  exporting to iTunes, 268, 269–271
  GarageBand's prebuilt, 26
  maximum length of, 38
  maximum number of tracks in, 69

  mixing, 249 (See also mixing)
  opening, 25–26
  playing, 30
  polishing, 165
  recording over part of, 138–139, 160–162
  refining mix for, 24
  reordering tracks in, 61
  reverting to saved version of, 39
  saving, 27–29
  setting key/scale for, 37
  setting output volume for, 266
  setting tempo for, 33, 219
  setting time signature for, 35
  transposing, 189 (See also transposition)
  undoing actions to, 39–40
  as unit of creation, 23
Sony ACID format, 274, 279
sorting loops, 86
sound, sampled vs. synthesized, 49
sound effects. See effects
sound files. See audio files
sound-pressure levels, 106
soundcards, 110
Soundtrack application, 8, 94
Soundtrack Loop Utility, 100
speakers, 119
Split command, 175
SPLs, 106
staccato, 300
stereo field, 253
Stern, Judith, 278
Sustain parameter, 152
sustain pedal, keyboard, 117, 210
Swing settings, 197
Symphony Orchestra, 298–300
synth key action, 115
synthesized generators, 243, 244
synthesized sounds, 49
synthesizers, MIDI, 113
System Preferences command, 133

T

tempo
  about, 33
  adjusting, 18
  defined, 17, 33
  setting, 33, 219
  and time display, 10
  vs. time signature, 34
Tempo column, loop browser, 86
Tempo slider, 18, 33
text search, finding loops with, 82
tick marks, 20

ticks, 16
tilde (~), 5
time display, 16–18
    changing format of, 17
    how time is presented in, 16
    illustrated, 8, 16
    moving playhead with, 17
    purpose of, 10, 16
Time pop-up menu, 35
time signatures, 34–35, 81, 219
timeline, 12–15
    buttons/controls, 12
    illustrated, 8, 12
    importance of, 14
    moving around in, 13
    purpose of, 9, 12
    zooming in, 19
timeline grid, 20–21
Timeline Grid button, 12
timeline grid menu, track editor, 181
Tollett, John, 278
tonic, 36
tool tips, 7
touch sensitivity, keyboard, 115
track automation, 255–256
track controls, 9
track data area, 181
track echo effect, 241
Track Echo feature, 231
track editor, 177–198
    about, 180–182
    Advanced section (See advanced section)
    buttons/controls, 180
    displaying tracks/regions in, 183
    enhancing track timing in, 193, 194, 195
    enhancing track tuning in, 193–195
    expanding, 188
    fixing timing in, 196–197
    illustrated, 180
    and MIDI data, 200–215
    optional nature of, 177
    purpose of, 10, 24
    and Real Instrument regions, 178, 180, 181
    renaming tracks/regions in, 186–187
    showing/hiding, 183
    and Software Instrument regions, 179, 180,
        181
    switching between views in, 182, 205
    transposing regions in, 189–192
    undocumented features in, 178, 198, 208
Track Editor button, 8, 9, 183
track headers, 8, 9, 43
Track Info button, 8

Track Info window
    applying effects in, 218, 222–223
    choosing presets for display in, 224
    effects controls, 220–221
    and Manual setting, 229
    for master track, 219, 220
    purpose of, 9, 65
    for Real Instrument tracks, 65, 136
    for Software Instrument tracks, 66, 221, 243
    viewing, 66
track level meters, 132
track mixer. See also mixing
    illustrated, 8, 47
    purpose of, 9
    showing/hiding, 43, 47
    volume slider, 134, 252, 255
Track Name field, 182
tracks, 41–69
    about, 42
    adding, 51–58
    applying effects to, 221, 222–223
    bouncing, 291, 294–296
    changing characteristics of, 65
    changing instrument assigned to, 67–68
    changing stacking order of, 61
    choosing/setting volume levels for, 250–252
    choosing type of, 51
    color-coding of, 42
    copying and pasting, 59
    defined, 13
    deleting, 64
    displaying in track editor, 183
    duplicating, 59
    enabling for recording, 135
    freezing, 63
    headers for, 8, 9, 43
    illustrated, 12
    locking/unlocking, 43, 62–63, 291
    maximum number of, 69
    monitoring, 128
    muting, 45
    naming/renaming, 60, 186
    purpose of, 41
    Real Instrument (See Real Instrument tracks)
    reducing dynamic range for, 236
    selecting, 44
    setting pan position for, 254
    Software Instrument (See Software
        Instrument tracks)
    soloing, 46
    types of, 42, 48
    viewing Track Info window for, 66
transducers, 106

transport controls, 8, 10, 15
transposition, 189–192
    about, 189
    defined, 189
    and Musical Typing keyboard, 150
    of Real Instrument regions, 178, 189, 190,
        191–192
    of Software Instrument regions, 24, 189,
        191–192
    ways of using, 190
Treble Gain slider, 235
treble reduction effect, 241
tremolo effect, 241, 300
trills, 300
troubleshooting, 7, 154. See also Help file
tuning fork, 17
tutorials
    Audio Unit effects, 246
    SoundTrack Loop Utility, 100

U

Undo command, 39, 40
undocumented features, 198, 208
Universal Serial Bus, 111. See also USB
up-tempo beats, 33
USB, 111, 112, 113, 117, 118

V

velocity
    defined, 181, 201
    increasing/decreasing, 150, 182, 201, 209
    range of values for, 201
    and Symphony Orchestra Jam Pack, 299
Velocity keys, 150

vibrato, 241
virtual keyboard. See onscreen keyboard
vocal transformer effect, 241
Voices per Instrument pop-up menu, 293
volume curves, 255–259
    editing, 258–259
    enabling, 257
    illustrated, 12
    for master track, 264
    purpose of, 13, 250
    and track automation, 255, 257
Volume slider, New Track dialog, 54, 55
volume slider, track mixer, 134

W

WAV files, 100, 274, 279
waveforms, 181–182
weighted key action, 115
Williams, Robin, 278

X

Xtra instruments, 300

Y

You Have Made Changes to the Current
        Instrument Setting dialog, 229
Your Preset Will Be Hidden dialog, 224

Z

Zoom button, 11, 148
zoom slider, 8, 9, 19, 181